POLITICS IN POPULAR MOVIES

MEDIA and POWER

David L. Paletz, Series Editor
Duke University

Published in the Series

Forthcoming in the Series

POLITICS IN POPULAR MOVIES

RHETORICAL TAKES ON HORROR, WAR, THRILLER, AND SCIFI FILMS

JOHN S. NELSON

Routledge
Taylor & Francis Group

LONDON AND NEW YORK

First published 2015 by Paradigm Publishers

Published 2016 by Routledge
2 Park Square, Milton Park, Abingdon, Oxon OX14 4RN
711 Third Avenue, New York, NY 10017, USA

Routledge is an imprint of the Taylor & Francis Group, an informa business

Copyright © 2015, Taylor & Francis.

All rights reserved. No part of this book may be reprinted or reproduced or
utilised in any form or by any electronic, mechanical, or other means, now
known or hereafter invented, including photocopying and recording, or in any
information storage or retrieval system, without permission in writing from
the publishers.

Notice:
Product or corporate names may be trademarks or registered
trademarks, and are used only for identification and explanation
without intent to infringe.

Library of Congress Cataloging-in-Publication Data

Nelson, John S., 1950–
   Politics in popular movies : rhetorical takes on horror, war, thriller, and scifi films /
John S. Nelson.
      pages cm. — (Media and power series)
   Includes bibliographical references and index.
   ISBN 978-1-61205-556-5 (hardcover : alk. paper)
   1. Politics in motion pictures.   2. Motion pictures—Political aspects—United States.
I. Title.
   PN1995.9.P6N45 2014
   791.43'6581—dc23
                                                                2014012418

ISBN 13 : 978-1-61205-556-5 (hbk)
ISBN 13 : 978-1-61205-557-2 (pbk)

for Bob Boynton,
treasured colleague in lifelong learning

CONTENTS

ACKNOWLEDGMENTS

Movies can be exciting to see, and many are joys to discuss! Popular movies can be surprisingly smart about politics. Sometimes these are the portentous politics of state or war, but often they are the everyday politics of family, romance, business, church, neighborhood, school, and such. This book analyzes politics in several handfuls of well-known films from four popular forms: horror, thriller, science fiction, and war. The aims are to appreciate the individual movies and their shared forms, to understand their many politics, and to provoke some rollicking conversations. The means are loosely related "film takes" that advance some fairly ambitious arguments about recent movies and their politics.

Many of these arguments spring from viewing movies and discussing their politics with family members, especially with Connie Nelson. Several of these analyses arise from conversations with students in various college courses I have ventured on the politics of film. Thoughtful responses have greatly improved the concepts, arguments, and prose in pages to come. The same goes for many reviewer suggestions about the full manuscript. To the family, friends, students, and colleagues who have contributed such insights, let me offer thanks.

Comments on some of my initial forays into the politics in popular movies came from a group of impressive colleagues who converged in 1998 on the Vakava Finnish Graduate School in Political Science and International Relations at the University of Jyväskylä in Finland. It's been an instructive pleasure to follow the inquiries of such talented social scientists as Matti Hyvärinen, Kia Lindroos, and Kari Palonen. This book owes much to them as well.

Early inspiration came also from David Paletz, then editor of *Political Communication* and now of the Paradigm series on Media and Power in which this book appears. David has long encouraged scholars of political communication to keep an eye on film. His appreciation for politics and movies is keen, and his suggestions for my work have been incisive. I thank David for his personal help and his larger efforts. I also thank the manuscript's principal reviewer and the Paradigm staff—especially Annie Daniel and Jennifer Knerr—for their valuable advice.

My favorite venues for the scholarly discussion of politics in movies and other media have included the University of Iowa Project on Rhetoric of Inquiry; the Foundations of Political Theory Workshop on Political Myth, Rhetoric, and Symbolism; and the Summer Conference on Argumentation provided by the National Communication Association and the American Forensic Association. All promote an intense but informal exchange of experiences that I find especially invigorating, and I thank the many colleagues who have shared enlightening ideas there. For the same reason, I thank the graduate and undergraduates students who have used scores of seminars at the University of Iowa to share with me their enthusiasms for movies of many kinds. I offer the following takes on films in the hope that the politics in popular movies may continue to intrigue us all.

Chapter 1

Film Takes

Rhetorical Appreciations of Popular Politics (Featuring 2001, Blade Runner, 1984, Brazil, and The Matrix)

Movies are often about politics, sometimes when they least seem to be. . . .[1]

—Roger Ebert

Why study the politics in popular movies? This can make the movies themselves more enjoyable and enlightening. It can enhance our accounts of politics. And it can enlarge our understanding of popular cinema in our politics and lives. Plus it can be lots and lots of fun!

Movies help make the myths that we live every day.[2] They influence the looks we like, the sounds we make, the words we speak, the attitudes we take, the possibilities we imagine, and the deeds we do. Films dramatize the stories that symbolize who we are as individuals, institutions, and communities. They show whence we have come and where we might be going. There are many important politics in movie mythmaking, for politics permeate these aspects of ourselves and our lives. They are not only the momentous politics of government but especially the mundane politics of popular culture and everyday life for ordinary people.

Even when it might seem otherwise, the art of movie-making is powerfully political.[3] As Murray Edelman wrote to culminate a career in comprehending political communication, "Art is the fountainhead from which political discourse,

1

beliefs about politics, and consequent actions ultimately spring."[4] Even "the conduct, virtues, and vices associated with politics come directly from art, and only indirectly from immediate experiences." Edelman recognized how events on the big screen of cinema are "hyperreal ... typically more portentous than personal affairs."[5] We know from everyday experience that these extend to television through reruns, VCRs, DVRs, DVD and Bluray players, imitations, and spin-offs. For us, cinema and television are "screens of power."[6] They invite our political exploration.

Our primary disciplines of power are politics, and our principal disciplines of politics are rhetorics. The ancient Sophists invented rhetoric as the study and practice of oral, and especially oratorical, politics.[7] This fit the politics of speech-in-action-in-public predominant in Greece and Rome.[8] Yet media beyond oral speech induce different politics. Already in the Roman Republic, reliance on letters, writing, and reading started to produce republics of laws and legislation—words that stem from *legere, to read* in Latin.[9] Print from movable type promoted the centralization of authority in modern states and later the rationalization of rule in bureaucracies.[10] Telegraphy magnified the speed and scope of politics.[11] Radio made even the highest politics more intimate, bringing them into our homes and changing our tones of voice.[12] Television put images of politics into motion, reforming leaders and publics alike.[13] Now the Internet bypasses and erases some national boundaries while deepening others.[14] For far more than a century, the oratorical politics connected to classical rhetoric have been decentered and restyled by electronic politics.[15] And these come together with special power in cinema.

Our kinds of communications make—even *are*—our kinds of communities, each with its own kinds of politics. As our kinds of communication change, so do our rhetorics, keeping them current as studies of our politics. This is to say that all media develop in tandem with distinctive politics, and all politics pursue characteristic rhetorics. As we come to good terms with politics in electronic times, we need to articulate rhetorics of popular cinema. This is the aim of the several, related studies pursued in the pages ahead. In form, they are film takes.

What Are Film Takes?

Film takes are not movie previews to sell tickets, copies, rentals, or downloads. Nor are they film reviews of the newspaper, newsmagazine, or website sorts that focus on what you might want to watch. Instead they are film appreciations. They trace how devices, kinds, or works of cinema contribute to our communities and politics. Film takes analyze what movies do individually and conventionally to help shape our looks and sounds, characters and settings, or standards and trajectories. Chiefly film takes assess the modes of experience available in movies. Especially they assess the practices and theories of politics in popular films.

Hence the movies at the focus of a film take are more often popular cinema than high art. These films are "Hollywood" productions in the loose but telling sense. Their planning, shooting, or financing need not come from California to qualify them under that category. They might be written in Iowa, financed in China, filmed in Egypt or Peru, then screened at Sundance or Toronto. The film is "popular" if it engages the modes and means of cinema that succeed in vernacular cultures. It can do so by production, presentation, or reception. For film takes, the ambition is rhetorical analysis of movies. With special attention to audiences and politics, a film take assesses ways and means of cinematic communication, explicit and implicit. Thus a film take parses plots, characters, acting, lighting, sound, scenery, costumes, camera uses, popular genres such as horror or romance, special effects, and other elements that configure families of films or specific movies.

In filmmaking, a *take* is the unit of continuously recorded action. Directors often shoot more than one take for each scene, to tap different performances of it. Some takes prove better than others, of course, at least for specific uses in a film; yet each aspires to a distinctive validity as a telling perspective on the events they show. In analyzing a rhetoric of cinema, likewise, a film take is a perspective on devices that movies use to make meanings, persuade viewers, and create realities. Each take leaves room for others, even invites and elicits them in response. My take on a movie or a genre can augment yours. But it also can inflect, redirect, confound, or provoke your take.

"Take five!" can start the fifth performance of a scene, but it also can announce a break from the usual action: a period for rest, relaxation, entertainment. Thus a film take might not be an orthodox work of scholarship. It should be intriguing in topic, surprising in treatment, lively in style. Film takes can be article- or even book-length, but many are shorter: just enough to say something meaty and provocative. Aspirations should include illuminating the specific movies, devices, or genres at issue while piquing the reader's interest overall in how films do their mythic and political work.

A film take could inquire why vampires and zombies are converging as political figures in recent movies. It might wonder what politics emerge from the dark streets, rotating fans, and corrupt police that characterize the recent resurgence in film noir. Since movies and comics use the super powers of superheroes to tame the Will-to-Power politics of perfectionism, a film take could investigate what we can learn about current politics from superhero movies returning to prominence at the same time as noir films. A film take could ponder what is happening culturally when westerns take a detour into horror in *High Plains Drifter* (1973), *Unforgiven* (1992), *Tombstone* (1994), *Wyatt Earp* (1994), *The Quick and the Dead* (1995), *Jonah Hex* (2010), or *Cowboys & Aliens* (2011). A film take could ask why the populist politics of movie musicals depend on dancing as much as singing. A film take could examine what cinema has been doing lately with Hamlet, and why. A take could explore how movies that feature water reconfigure political power. Or a take could trace how Hollywood feminisms might be remaking romances. Film takes on innumerable topics can be intriguing, and there are diverse examples to come.

To track most current releases is an impossible project for film takes. Yet they benefit from an angle that ties to some present setting for movies or politics. Film takes are less for established classics than recent films, less for individual works of art than families of popular movies. To achieve adequate depth, though, the analysis almost always features a particular film or several. The main aim is to inform re-viewing that can heighten the appreciation of movies already seen. If a secondary effect is to motivate first-time viewing, that is an excellent bonus.

A close comparison to film takes might be to the "mythologies" from Roland Barthes.[16] In France in the 1950s, Barthes focused his skills as a scholar of signs and symbols on analyzing objects and images familiar to newspaper readers from ads, movies, news, or other aspects of their daily lives. He wrote about the iconography of military posters, the morality plays in wrestling matches, and the meaning of a movie star's face. He probed the appeals of foods, cars, and myriad consumer products. He assessed cruises, landmarks, elections, photos, and songs. In unpacking the myths of everyday life that lurk in these many components of culture, Barthes took care to learn about their imputations of power, their implications of language and movement, their intimations of justice, change, and style: in short, their politics. Film takes are "mythologies" for the movies.

Thus film takes are appreciations of movies more than criticisms, let alone "critiques," of them. This is not because film takes lack critical acumen, but because they mostly target good films to consider how cinema performs its rhetorics. As a form, the film take is not for condemning cinema as popular spectacle—or television as mass entertainment. Books to that effect have been written many times over, and we might wonder whether they have much left to teach us about either medium. (The same goes for video games.[17]) Nor is the film take a form for unleashing the university's awesome arsenal for denigrating, denying, decrying, debunking, or altogether destroying targets disliked by the analyst. The key principle for appreciations is sympathetic connoisseurship: seeking to understand how what we value might work, while doing so to share the joy and learning with others. Film takes are free to find faults, as they should where faults are to be found. But there is seldom much gain—or enjoyment—in calling our attention in detail to something for the purpose of explaining why it does not deserve our detailed attention.

Where Are Movie Politics?

There are at least two approaches to analyzing the political theory in popular culture. Some analysts start with a political topic then choose popular works overtly about it. Others select appealing works or devices of popular culture then explore their meanings for politics. The two approaches connect too much to pursue either exclusively. But for the most part, I begin with intriguing works and devices that seldom seem political on the surface. Politics that emerge from a creative focus on scenery, sound, story, characters, or even sales can be more provocative and informative than any intentional messages about parties or ideologies.

Since I study political advertising and campaigning, I might see what I can learn about them from popular movies like *The Candidate* (1972), *Power* (1986), *Bob Roberts* (1992), *Bulworth* (1998), *Primary Colors* (1998), *Man of the Year* (2006), and *Swing Vote* (2008). Because these directly address campaigning in general and advertising in particular, such films mostly can teach us what their makers learned about elections or ads from books by scholars or talks with politicians and consultants. But why not read the books and listen to the talks instead or, better, augment them with our own research on campaigning and advertising?

Furthermore some of these are good as movies go (the first five), but some are not (the last two), and none are great. Why not dwell longer in movies that are especially exciting as cinema—even when they do not focus overtly on high, official politics? Then the politics that emerge from their camera angles, color schemes, genre conventions, musics, myths, stunts, voices, and such can often prove more provocative and informative than I could have imagined in advance. The creators of any popular film are likely to be many, diverse, and focused on considerations of drama, stage craft, or box office. They seldom try directly to develop a detailed, intentional message about politics. Yet film takes reveal their works to offer more insight into the politics we live every day than any intentional message about policy or ideology is likely to provide.

Cultural studies of race, class, and gender have concentrated for decades on film politics pitched at more everyday levels.[18] Typically the targets for analysis of race or ethnicity are films that focus overtly on them, such as *Guess Who's Coming to Dinner* (1967), *Rosewood* (1997), *Crash* (2005), *Glory Road* (2005), and *The Great Debaters* (2007).[19] The same goes for movies that feature dynamics of social class, among them *Gosford Park* (2001), *Maid in Manhattan* (2002), and *The Great Gatsby* (2013); yet analysis can readily extend to movies with strong but still secondary interests in the everyday politics of class, such as *Blue Crush* (2002), *The Lookout* (2007), and *Young Adult* (2011).[20] And an even larger range of films attracts analytical attention for the everyday politics of gender and sexuality: from *Nine to Five* (1980), *Thelma and Louise* (1981), *Tootsie* (1982), and *Working Girl* (1988) to *The First Wives Club* (1996), *A Thousand Acres* (1997), *North Country* (2005), and *The Girl with the Dragon Tattoo* (2011).[21] In a way, the film takes in this book simply try to address further kinds of cultural politics in Hollywood films.

Popular cinema is as close as we come these days for people in electronic societies to a communication technology of full-bodied, virtual reality.[22] Cinema engages our senses more fully than print or even television.[23] It can even bring to life the high, distant, official politics of state and war.[24] Take the early scenes in *Saving Private Ryan* (1998), where director Steven Spielberg places cameras and microphones to put us viewers into the midst of D-day action. These scenes are filmed as though we were soldiers storming the beach, so that we can learn from experience why we must make good on the sacrifices of Allied fighters in World War II: more on this in Chapter 7. Or see, as explained in Chapter 6, how Robert Zemeckis intersperses virtual and vicarious experiences in *Contact* (1997) to show how electronic communication has changed the foundations for political community in our times. And consider the subtle interplay of virtual with vicarious and symbolical realities that Ridley Scott generates in *Black Hawk Down* (2001) to restore a sense of virtue and virtuosity to the 1993 American military action in Somalia.[25] Film takes can analyze how movies make and remake our senses of reality.

Cinema can embed us in experiences of the ordinary, everyday, democratic politics of popular culture. Arguably no other art or medium now treats these more or better. Consequently film takes can become exercises in figuring out how popular movies inflect the cultural politics of ordinary people in their everyday affairs, even beyond race, class, and gender. A movie may be "popular" from its modes of presentation or its arenas of reception. Thus a rhetorical analysis emphasizes the interactions of words and deeds with specific audiences, and a film take is no exception. It just adds typical responses to other cinematic sorts of sights and sounds. Each chapter to come is a perspective on this.

The usual targets of film takes are good films, not overtly political ones. Not even the special interest of film takes in political implications of cinematic rhetoric can override the requirement for overall quality. The aim is seldom to analyze movies about official politics. There are too few of those, and especially too few especially good as films, to justify such a focus for the full form of analysis. Instead film takes seek to explicate the politics in effective films, even when they do not seem at first glance to address politics. And film takes usually find their politics in movie uses of conventions from popular genres.

Genre began as a French word for a *general form* or *type*. Gradually it has been appropriated into English to indicate an artistic form or aesthetic type. A genre is a network of conventions. *Convention* traces to ancient Rome and its republic.[26] In Latin, *con-* means *with-* and *ven-* is to *come*, so a *convention* is a *with-coming*, a *coming-with*, often taken as an *assembly*. Especially but not exclusively in politics, conventions are the occurrences—but also the consequences—of our coming-with each other. Therefore conventions are the meanings, standards, and procedures we share. They *are* our cultures. A constitutional convention involves people coming together to *con-stitute*—literally to *with-stitch*—themselves together as a people and a polity.[27] A cultural convention involves people cultivating situations, experiences, and actions to share. In convening, we can create the definitions (settings), identities (characters), and directives (events) for our conduct to come. These are the community's conventions: the commitments that give it enduring (but flexible) form.

What happens politically can happen culturally and artistically too. Genres are places and ways we come together, but the "we" can vary. Analytical genres are produced by and for analysts and critics. Like anthropologists' accounts of other cultures, analytical genres are patterns seen by outsiders; these forms might not be recognized by participants and play no concerted role in their activities. But popular genres are generated by and for artists (or other actors) and their audiences. These are insider accounts that participants use continually and often consciously to inform their activities. Popular genres of cinema are made and modified in the interactions of filmmakers and movie viewers. We use popular genres to seek and assess movies: fantasy, horror, romantic comedy, western, coming of age, war, thriller, epic, satire, and so on.

Each popular genre has distinctive (though not unique) conventions for its characters, settings, and events. Many spy thrillers have secret agents and cunning bosses work in foreign lands or lurk in our own bureaucracies to rig elections or sabotage attacks. These conventions are the genre's figures, tropes, devices, markers, and more. Yet a genre's defining conventions are neither necessary nor sufficient conditions for an individual film to fit that genre: some spy thrillers leave their agents in the open or leave out any bosses; some romances, too, have foreign lands or bureaucracies; and so on. To identify popular movies by genre, we operate instead by the prominence and preponderance of conventions. Especially we pay attention to the ways that particular movies do (or do not) use their genre's figures to make meanings. In these popular conventions and their specific uses lie most of the politics in popular movies.

A cardinal principle of rhetorical analysis is that the analyst ought to have some sympathy for a popular genre or a particular work in order to understand it well. At any rate, I personally have little enthusiasm for performing academic criticism that merely tears things apart or stomps all over them. For one thing, sneering can be too easy, and for another, it teaches too little. So I try to develop a considerable appreciation for the virtues of a specific work or the advantages of an entire genre before I try to analyze aspects of it in print.

For a couple of decades, I have been moving into one popular genre of literature, film, and television after another. (Popular genres often stretch across many media.) My method might be all too much like Sherman marching through Georgia, but the principle is that such conventional, cultural politics can be appreciated accurately and helpfully by comparing politics implicit in the conventions of any one genre with others. For me, film takes on whole genres and individual works are the principal ambition. To introduce the form of a film take, this book experiments mainly with analysis of horror, war, thriller, and science-fiction movies. Yet each analysis draws from comparisons with many works and genres mentioned only in passing or not at all—for the meanings and thus the politics of each work and genre depend in important part on relations to the conventions and politics in several other genres as well.

Which Takes Do What?

Since this book uses rhetorical analysis to link movies and politics, it includes glossaries of key terms for analyzing movies and politics that might not be familiar to readers previously focused on one but not the other. Each chapter offers a film take that stands on its own. A third are fairly short, a third are decently long, and a third are for Goldilocks. Similarly three of the takes focus on only one or two movies each, whereas the rest address whole genres of popular films. After this initial, introductory chapter, the takes form groups of three, because they also work together to illuminate key aspects of analyzing movies for their implicit politics.

Part One analyzes three genres in turn. In each case, it demonstrates how surprising and instructive politics can emerge from the conventions of a popular genre that configures a great range of specific films. Chapter 2 defends conspiracy thrillers from critics who fault the films for simplistic accounts of politics. It explains instead how movies in this genre often use its conventions to evoke complicated systems of politics in terms clear and vivid for ordinary viewers. Chapter 3 traces how movies can use sets of conventions to construct subtexts that comprehend many kinds of politics. Horror films typically create subtexts to help us confront political evils in our everyday lives, and the analysis shows how some recent horror movies use subtexts to face current troubles in three different media of communication. As a popular genre, horror antedates cinema, and the thriller is almost as old. Chapter 4 identifies the emergence of a genre still coalescing in the twenty-first century. Answering critics along the way, this fourth take explores how the conventions of fractal films cohere in attempting to make sense of nonlinear systems that defy modern, historical modes of drama.

Part Two examines several sorts of political experiences that popular movies have become especially good at imparting. It suggests how better recognition of these kinds of experiences can change our practices and theories of politics in important ways. Again there are three genres at issue; but this time, they are horror, science fiction, and war movies. Chapter 5 compares two horror movies that push current viewers to share sensibilities mostly gone from modern civilizations. Their techniques of empathy make both movies controversial, and there is a lot to learn from the politics in their strategies of communication. Then Chapter 6 shows how a science-fiction film that focuses on communication calls into question the way to enforce communities that western civilization has been pursuing for half a millennium. With movies, television, and other electronic media in mind, it suggests a radically different philosophy for enabling people to trust each other and prosper. Turning to war movies, Chapter 7 studies how the several cinematic modes of experience help recent films make arguments about political lessons we do well to learn from specific wars.

In the last few decades of Hollywood movies, the pivotal political event in American life has been the terrorist assault against American institutions on September 11, 2001. Part Three of this book takes stock of what popular movies are making of political terrorism. This lets us put to work what the earlier sections have explored about popular genres and political experiences. Chapter 8 focuses on the collective portrait of terrorism available from films released in the couple of decades before 9/11. It considers how these movies, mostly thrillers, might have prefigured the phenomenal field for our experience of 9/11—with films providing conventional figures for shaping our senses of what happened that day and thereafter. Chapter 9 returns to horror films to argue that the major figures in the War on Terror launched by the administration of President George W. Bush have unfortunately followed the movie mythos of vampire hunting. And Chapter 10 ponders how Hollywood might configure its continuing treatments of political terrorism by working with at least four different genres for popular cinema: not only thrillers and horror movies but also noirs and dystopias.

In the end, Chapter 11 enlarges the focus to evoke further patterns of politics in popular movies. This helps us learn from recent theorists of politics how popular films feature styles of personal action. These include the politics that we ordinary people enact in our everyday lives. Through their uses of conventions for popular genres, entertaining films practice us in the moves and sensibilities for bureaucracy, capitalism, conservatism, existentialism, feminism, liberalism, populism, and many other politics. Even in the midst of exotic technologies and surroundings of science fiction, which tops my personal list of popular genres, the political styles in movies speak directly and influentially to the experiences and responses in our daily encounters.

Why Start with Science Fiction?

Among the many human sciences, the best attuned to political action is often political theory.[28] This holds for political theory as a field of learning, even in comparison to other fields of political science. That is because political theory addresses action issues of ethics, skill, style, and timing that seldom surface in more recent sciences of politics.[29] Yet this holds even more for political theory as an activity, because it often happens in the midst of political projects that range from government, economy, and technology to art, culture, and media. To do political theory is to explain how communities of many kinds could, should, and have made and unmade themselves. Political theory is what I do, where I start in studying movies, and thus where this book begins.

Teaching theories of politics, I soon learned to assign fiction and film. College students seldom have much experience with what we usually take as politics. My first thought was that literature and cinema could place students vicariously into

FILM TAKES: RHETORICAL APPRECIATIONS OF POPULAR POLITICS   11

political situations and acquaint them specifically with political characters. This works well enough, but relevant selections can seem unduly limited in number and quality. To complicate matters further, most of the novels and movies that interest me personally are not overtly political in any of the standard senses. So my second idea became that the informal politics in fiction and film could engage students where they live. These can bring out our awareness of the unofficial but pervasive politics of everyday endeavors, politics in which we all participate firsthand. Yet few of the assignments that work best are among the celebrated classics of literature, cinema, or even television—taught at times by theorists of politics the world over. Hence my third recognition has been that the conventions threaded throughout works in the popular genres of fiction, film, and television are modes of mythmaking that encompass all cultures, high and low, in doing practical theorizing on politics.

With other enthusiasts of popular culture, I am exploring territories where political theory is done for democratic populations who practice it every day. The aim is to engage theories of popular importance—and therefore political importance—and not limit ourselves to treatises for scholars who sometimes stay distant from the daily activities of ordinary people. The ambition is to glean the politics in popular genres: buddy movies, coming-of-age stories, detective dramas, martial-arts movies, and more. Here the effort is to show how takes on popular movies can tell us about making myths and doing theories of politics, especially directed to everyday life.

As a fan of science fiction, I see it as some of the best political theory going; and as parts of this book show, that holds fully for science-fiction movies.[30] Yet it seems not to occur to many academic theorists of politics to treat science fiction as political theory. Nor does it occur to many scholars of politics to view popular movies for their takes on politics. In part, this is because the politics in popular movies emerge mainly from their uses of genre conventions. Thus the political theorizing in science fiction takes popular, mythic, conventional forms. Like all popular genres, science fiction narrates and dramatizes more than it argues and analyzes, at least overtly. Similarly it symbolizes more than it says, at least literally. Unlike most scholarship, science fiction can show—even more than tell—about politics. Its evidence is sometimes scientific, sometimes humanistic, but often artistic—which is to say, experiential. In popular works of fiction, film, and television, the evidence and reasoning rely crucially on conventions. Even so, scholarly theories of politics, whether scientific or humanistic, depend on similar tropes—which is to say, familiar figures—of story, inference, and argument.[31]

Nonetheless political theorists seldom stop to think whether effective works of popular mythmaking also can be good exercises in doing political theory.

Analysts miss that there can be advantages in stories and dramas for coming to terms with the action central to politics.[32] Scholars miss that there can be insights in popular terms for making sense of everyday deeds, ideas, institutions, and conventions. Theorists miss that there can be benefits in keeping our emotions and imaginations attuned to our arguments. Popular media like literature, cinema, television, video gaming, and music operate on all these levels. The popular genres that span these media use all these resources for making our political myths, especially of everyday life. Hence we do well to appreciate the patterns of politics in epics; in cinematic capers, cons, and heists; in pirate tales and gangster stories; in disaster or western movies; in satires, noirs, and scifi flicks. But so far, political theorists have been slow to think of such works and learn with them.

The exceptions are few and prove the unreflective rule. For example, George Orwell's *1984* has long been canonized as a minor classic in the political theory of totalitarianism.[33] Yet most other literary and cinematic dystopias at the intersections of horror and science fiction get scant attention from political theorists.[34] Furthermore academic theories of environmental politics ignore the careful and creative political thinking that Kim Stanley Robinson advances in three series of science fiction.[35] Do scholarly theories of information and cybernetic societies notice the popular theorizing in cyberpunk science fiction by William Gibson, Bruce Sterling, Rudy Rucker, and Pat Cadigan?[36] Not often. Do academic theories of populism learn from the populist campaigns staged in science fiction by Sterling and Neal Stephenson?[37] Not so far. Do our political theories build on science-fiction experiments with institutions by David Brin, Marge Piercy, or Sheri Tepper?[38] Not much. Political theorists neglect science fiction as a form for doing political theory. They slight it even when the theoretical attention to politics is unmistakable; and they ignore it even when the politics are governmental, electoral, or otherwise official by contrast with the subtler, everyday varieties.

Of course, the blind spot of political theory for popular fiction and film has been much bigger than science fiction. It is unfortunate, for instance, that theories of the national-security state have not learned more from John le Carré's spy novels and the movies based on them.[39] It is odd that theories of political spectacles in electronic societies have not concentrated more on the self-accounts in cinematic spectacles such as *Anna Karenina* (2012), *The Avengers* (2012), *The Hunger Games* (2012), and *Watchmen* (2009).[40] Examples abound of novels, movies, and television series that speak eloquently to principles of justice, vengeance, punishment, and forgiveness: see *Barbarosa* (1982), *Thinner* (1996), *A Thousand Acres* (1997), *The Jack Bull* (1999), *Munich* (2005), *The Interpreter* (2005), and *The Debt* (2011)—among many others.

Consequently I began to do political theory with works of popular culture by recognizing that the standard dismissal of science fiction is a mistake for political theory as a field of inquiry. In pondering the reasons, though, I started to learn more comprehensively how popular genres can work as political theory in practice. Soon I saw that I could not grasp the full politics of any single work of science fiction without a better understanding of politics in that genre as a whole.[41] In turn, this led me to realize that I would not be able to comprehend the usual politics for science fiction or any other popular genre without gaining a decent sense of how several of these forms operate politically. I would need to compare the conventions across many genres.

Rational-choice and other formal theorists of politics take depth interviews, surveys, and thick descriptions of institutions or traditions as their behavioral information about legislators, lawmaking, and campaigning. Then they try to save the appearances, by explaining how various particulars cohere into patterns of politics that can sustain themselves in practice. The present approach is similar. To understand politics in everyday life, we can turn to the thick descriptions in novels, the dramas on television, and the virtual realities of movies. The challenge is to learn from them the political patterns and principles that configure what we do—and how we might do better. The politics we learn from popular movies are not limited in the least to the genre of science fiction. Yet like horror films and thrillers, science fiction is a genre keenly attuned to our styles of political action in everyday life.

Might Films Prefigure Our Futures?

Especially for Hollywood, dystopia has become a subgenre shared by horror and science fiction, for dystopia typically projects aspects of current societies into an imagined future to show them going disastrously bad. For an initial sense of how film takes might work, therefore, let me offer a quick take on how several science-fiction films have helped prefigure the future for us—in utopian as well as dystopian ways. And to emphasize that we are analyzing movies rather than stories, let us sideline characters and occurrences to concentrate on settings as evoked vividly and memorably by a handful of influential films. The suggestion is that these striking movies about possible futures have given us worlds with looks and sounds that we start to realize because each enters for at least a time into what we have already experienced momentarily, but firsthand, as where we are going. Chapter 8 provides a further analysis of similar prefiguration by movies on political terrorism. But unlike those films, where the primary figures for terrorism come from the characters and plots, the five scifi films might have influenced our futures more through their looks and perhaps their sounds.[42]

Stanley Kubrick's 1968 vision of *2001: A Space Odyssey* is streamlined in stark, clean, primary colors.[43] As an epic drama of evolution, it travels from a leap beyond ape to human, a human leap beyond Earth to Jupiter, and a leap beyond humanity to children of the stars. Yet across this vast reach, *2001* dramatizes our future as one where odysseys into outer space and beyond could begin as close as the regional airport down the road. If your airport is like mine, it already advertises itself as "international" in service. So why stop before "interplanetary" or "intergalactic?" At a facility strikingly like the airport less than twenty miles from my house, *2001* shows, we could soon board a space shuttle akin to an airliner, complete with microwaved meals and service by a stewardess. It would take us to a hub that orbits the Earth, rather than sitting in the suburbs of a metropolis, and we would go on from there by similarly routine means to the moon then the stars. The Earthly habitat, too, would be clean, bright, and prosperous—with electric cars and clear waters of sparkling blue. For years after *2001*, Americans like me moved with increasing confidence into that modernist world.

Then along came Ridley Scott's *Blade Runner* (1982).[44] Ordinary people are being left behind on Earth, which seems shabby and garish, while policing tries to keep increasingly superior androids from infiltrating human lives. *Blade Runner* evokes a cyberpunk future that fuses neon advertising to giant monitors. Everywhere these console and cajole the losers left earthbound on a polluted planet subdued by dreary, dripping skies and littered streets. Those venues resemble the warrens of medieval towns or recall the inscrutable bazaars of the exotic Kasbah. They teem with cultural contradictions, and they crawl with strangers who connive simply to survive another day. Looming above "the little people" on these treacherous and dirty streets are vast arcologies in Middle Eastern shapes of pyramids and ziggurats, closing themselves against the swarming insecurities of the grungy surface. Huddling on the ground are old industrial buildings and dilapidated hotels that house a populace depleted in numbers and hope. Street people show their edges with radical colors and clothes, retro tattoos, and decorations. When John Leonard, the late culture critic for CBS and the *New York Times,* wanted to epitomize how California pulls America in dystopian directions, he put onto the screen a few frames from the downer Los Angeles projected by *Blade Runner.*[45] Knowing that the turn from *2001* was unfortunate, Americans all too easily could start to see their future in degrading hues.

Next came the dream of liberation through personal computing trumpeted by Apple for the merchandising of its Macintosh model in 1984. Yet this has remained memorable less for its celebration of technological freedom than for its look of grainy, gritty blue-gray. Thus the figures of digital dystopia that *Blade Runner* promoted were degraded further for the 1984 version of George Orwell's *1984* as directed by Michael Radford.[46] Other movies, some music videos, and innumerable ads have reproduced it to permeate our grim anticipations of politics to come. As Yogi Berra put it, we could know at a glance that "The future ain't what it used to be."[47] And we could hear in a tune that it might never be that way again. The modern March of the State on Earth strangely anticipated by Hegel in the nineteenth century and projected anew by technology in the twentieth had degenerated by 1984 into a palpable sense of corporate decline and state terror.[48]

Soon, Terry Gilliam's *Brazil* (1985) joined this dystopian turn by making the art deco touches in *Blade Runner* into aesthetics of suffocating bureaucracy.[49] The movie's protagonist dreams throughout of flight and freedom, but his waking world is one of relentless spying, oversight, and manipulation. Thus the movie's streamlined curves become rounded audio receivers for one-way communication of propaganda and subjugation as well as two-way screens for surveillance. Puffy pneumatic ducts for cooling, heating, and air supply loom from every structure; and nearly everywhere they are under apparent repair because the system suffers chronic breakdowns. If our future prefigured by *Blade Runner* is cyberpunk, our future courtesy of *Brazil* is steampunk: dystopian in a different register. The carefree samba of the title song ironizes the frustration at every turn of any resistance. The sharp and jagged lines of struts and cables that cut across these swoops and flows of tubing call to mind the continual intrusions of bureaucratic order into regimented lives. The film's fable of freedom as sheer fantasy reinforces the dismal prognosis that fans of *Blade Runner* could feel already in their future bones. *Brazil* viewers might have been fewer than those for *2001* or *Blade Runner,* but they, too, knew their sad future when they saw it—and felt wistful when they heard it.

For me, at least, this twentieth-century string of prefigurations culminates in *The Matrix* in 1999, with its two sequels in 2003 possibly starting to turn around the future's degeneration.[50] Pursued by Agent Smith (Hugo Weaving) even into a 2013 ad for General Electric, Neo (Keanu Reeves) takes viewers on wild rides from a suburban dystopia to a paradoxically apocalyptic recovery of life in the postmodern city. The shared look of the *Matrix* films trumps the blue-gray of a dystopian "real" with a striking blend of goth, noir, and martial arts. The digital rain of glowing green on black already has echoed resoundingly through American advertising, sports shows, teen clothes, and current events. The politics implicit in the *Matrix* aesthetic work to distrust the bright image of the bustling and reflective city, still the symbol of the triumphant civilization of the West. Under the glittering surface, things are now dark and dystopian, to be sure. Yet effective resistance and radical departures are possible. More than that, they are cool. Let us see, these movies challenge, what we might make of all that. And so we move teen-quick, with Neo, Trinity (Carrie-Anne Moss), and Morpheus (Laurence Fishburne), past the deadly obstacle courses that can look and work like video games. The plots of these movies hint at futures more rich in adventure than progress; their looks might literally "style the way." The middle film is strikingly white and bright in much of its appearance, whereas the concluding movie offers a return to the rich palette of colors for a restored environment on Earth. Among their many other ambitions, film takes can assess the politics in such aesthetics.

Between the first *Matrix* movie and its sequels, though, terrorist attacks intruded into American life. As Hollywood knew instantly, 9/11 called into question even these emerging looks and sounds.[51] Yet such terrorist acts have not undone all previous aesthetics or politics. Old looks, myths, and sounds might collapse or linger; but either way, their fragments remain for making new ones. As Chapter 6 argues, with further assists from science fiction, the revelations of new truths through surprising experiences can be literally the reveilings that invent rhetorics and realities in tandem. Hyperbole can be too kind a word for declarations that art is dead in the wake of the Holocaust, that hope has been killed by the Gulag, or that irony is impossible after September 11, 2001.[52] To the contrary, atrocities call forth art, irony, action, invention: in a word, poesis.[53] We weave new fabrics of meaning from the remnants that we can collect—as figures for sensing our altered surroundings and selves. We forge new courses of conduct from the ruins that popular cinema shows us to foreshadow *über* crimes that shock and attempted annihilations that appall. We act also from movies that help us experience individuals and institutions that endure—as well as virtues that we still can hope to prevail.

These endeavors we conduct in important part through popular cinema. They make the film take a valid, even vital, form of inquiry for our times. Moving pictures are not just images that move but also images that move us. Political analysis that omits movies misses too much. Cinema engages our senses in different ways than speaking, writing, or printing. We need film takes to learn the implications for our realities. Please enjoy the ones to come.

PART ONE
POPULAR GENRES

CHAPTER 2

POLITICS IN CONVENTIONS

CONSPIRACY AS A CINEMATIC TROPE FOR SYSTEM (FEATURING BOB ROBERTS, FROM HELL, AND THREE KINGS)

Every metaphor is the tip of a submerged model.[1]

—Max Black

Apparently President George W. Bush once took a dim view of *Conspiracy Theory* (1997), "the weird, noirish tale of a comically paranoid taxi driver (Mel Gibson) who discovers—when the CIA crashes into his life to torture him—that 'they' really are out to get him."[2] *Newsweek* reported that Bush "didn't like it—big time. Slow start, confusing plot, just a mess."[3] Social scientists have not always agreed with Bush or any other president, but here they find some common cause. Social scientists scorn conspiracy theory—big time. Likewise they scoff at the conspiracy politics in popular films.

Yet this can lead them, like President Bush, into confusion. Theirs is the fundamentalist mistake. They literalize film conspiracies as accounts of causation. Then they condemn movies with conspiracy plots for pandering implicitly to extremist politics. These films can be colorful and popular, the knock goes; but they remain simplistic, distracting, deeply unrealistic, indeed downright dangerous for American or other audiences. The complaint is that conspiracy films fail to show how complicated, structural, and systemic politics can be. Instead they arouse the rabble. Thus many a scholar of politics and communication condemns conspiracy theories and movie conspiracies for their fantasy themes, magical thinking, scapegoating, and similar devices that dupe the insufficiently scientific or politically unsophisticated.[4] Unfortunately this misses the Hollywood use of conspiracy as a trope for system.

Conspiracies Personal and Literal versus Political and Figural

Conspiracy theories strive to expose the shadowy bosses who communicate behind the scenes to pull the world's strings. They premise that paranoia is unappreciated prophecy: we have secret enemies, and "they" have been scheming (with real success) to get us. Conspiracy movies supposedly enact paranoid fantasies of implausible ties among impossible powers who connive in private to manipulate hordes of ordinary people. Some conspiracy films mystify the actual mechanisms of exploitation and coercion, leaving viewers with "no recognizable enemy" to oppose. Some are said to horrify viewers through "faceless" conspirators so omniscient and omnipotent that resistance seems futile and people become immobile. Most conspiracy movies have "excessively personalized systemic wrongs."[5] They suppress popular awareness of power structures by fingering only a few puppeteers. Or so scholars say.[6]

An especially persuasive indictment is "Devils and Demons: The Group Mediation of Conspiracy" in *Mediated Political Realities* by Dan Nimmo and James E. Combs. This is a smart, well-argued attack on conspiracy theory as "a lurid melodrama of illegitimate and venal power exercised by a group to which [conspiracy fantasies] attribute a wide variety of negative traits." The logic of conspiracy theory is occult. As Nimmo and Combs summarize, "If the country is going to hell, then someone must be responsible; and because the visible people of power seem ordinary enough, real power must be secretly exercised by hidden powers."[7] I have often taught their book, particularly this chapter, because its anticonspiracy case is strong against the likes of literalist yet wildly fantastic films such as Oliver Stone's *JFK* (1991). To be sure, conspiracy theorists typically are literalists.[8] But the people who make most popular movies are not, at least when their mythmaking comes to political conspiracies.

Criminal conspiracies are a dime a dozen in Hollywood films. *The Heist* (2001), written and directed by David Mamet, shows a handful of criminals planning and conducting one final job. Is theirs a mission impossible? Can they trust each other? Will justice prevail? Shown not long after 9/11, the film unsettled viewers with an airplane hijacking; but otherwise its elements are unremarkable.

Like it, hundreds of popular films include conspiracies to commit crimes. If we pull for the criminals, and they succeed, we call the film a caper. The sympathetic criminals who fail induce a sense of tragedy, as in gangster-noir movies such as *Road to Perdition* (2002). There we admire and lament Michael Sullivan (Tom Hanks) as he makes an honorable death for himself from a dubious life. More often, though, we cheer the forces of law and order who foil the criminal conspiracies in a lion's share of detective films, police procedurals, space operas, spy stories, and western shoot-outs. Seldom does Hollywood give these garden-variety conspiracies among criminals implications for politics that go beyond overt themes of crime and punishment or law and order. Seldom, therefore, does the academic criticism of conspiracy theory seem relevant to the resulting films. (Neo-noir films are another matter: even though they often include criminal conspiracies and typically unreel as tales of detection, neo-noir films involve the politics of systems—and need separate analysis, as in Chapter 4.)

Two Kinds of Political Conspiracies

Political conspiracies are the issue. Please notice, though, that they come in at least two kinds. Even for academicians, republican conspiracies should be no problem for popular films. Conspiracy in a strict political sense begins, in fact, as a political device for republics. Ancient Romans named it: *with-breath* is what the word says in Latin. Conspirators politic by whisper. Rather than proclaim their complaints or plans in public, conspirators huddle off-stage, behind closed doors. Conspiracies can usurp power from public authorities, but they also can unseat tyrants. In *Gladiator,* which won the 2001 Oscar for Best Picture, the heroine and heroes literally go underground to conspire against the Roman Emperor and plan a restoration of the Republic. *The Man in the Iron Mask* (1997) brings back the Three Musketeers to act as a protorepublican order, on guard against abuses of power. They leave the court, even the city, to conspire in the countryside on replacing a tyrannical Louis with his just, virtuous, legitimate twin. Republican conspiracies in Hollywood films can offer politically informative fictions without ever entering the dubious realm of conspiracy theories: no paranoia, no puppet masters, no anonymous *they,* no occluded systems, no scapegoats. Instead they provide incipiently public contests for honor and glory. However concealed republican conspirators may stay from their target, we viewers follow them throughout the movie. We learn in detail their motives, devices, and characters. Directed by Robert Redford, *The Conspirator* (2010) is a historical example.

'Tis the other kind of political conspiracies in movies that invites academic concern. In these, the conspirators remain shrouded, disguised, or off-stage for much of the movie. Not to honor a poor film by this name (1997), but to draw a contrast with semi-public conspiracies, let us call these shadow conspiracies. Again they can target just or unjust regimes, promoting various sorts of politics; yet most of these films unfold as conspiracies by figures in power against good or ordinary people. This is the set of films that scholars excoriate as propagations of conspiracy theory. Antigovernment conspiracies range from *The Manchurian Candidate* (1962, 2004) and *Arlington Road* (1999) to *Vantage Point* (2008) and *The International* (2009). Of late, examples of government conspiracies include the *X Files*, both the television series (1993–2002) and the films (1998, 2008). *Nick of Time* (1995), *Enemy of the State* (1998), *Echelon Conspiracy* (2009), and *The Way of War* (2009) are others. Yet the shadow conspiracies most analyzed by scholars include *The Parallax View* (1974), *Three Days of the Condor* (1975), and *All the President's Men* (1976). Their timing and contents shout "Watergate," with reverberations of the Kennedy and King assassinations. Hence they turn film critics more toward history and allegory than toward the system politics implicit in the subgenre of shadow conspiracy—let alone the specific systems in each film.[9]

These are "systems" in the cybernetic sense advanced by structuralists and poststructuralists alike. Their politics are structural, seamless, interdependent, and pervasive. It is hard even to recognize systems, let alone analyze or contest them, because systems include so much and become what people accept as normal. Typically systems encompass and co-opt their possible critics. *The Parallax View* shows American government and politics suffused by violent, authoritarian dynamics that produce and feed on patriotism composed of consumerism, sexism, racism, sadism, and chauvinism. These form the film's famous barrage of images for screening assassins directed by shadowy conspirators. As a journalist trying to expose them, Joseph Frady (Warren Beatty) passes their tests only to become a fall guy for assassinating a popular candidate opposed to these fascist politics. In probing the conspiracy, the reporter exposes specific elements of America's system of politics in the second half of the twentieth century. This is how the film displays the USA *as* a "Parallax Corporation" that displaces political realities and responsibilities from their proper positions.

Conspiracies as Devices of Resistance

In Hollywood films, shadow conspiracies are less literal devices of power than narrative figures for evoking the organizations and operations of distinct systems.

The implication is that people can attend more and understand better when complicated structures appear as engaging characters and subtle interactions surface as dramatic deeds. *Bob Roberts* (1992) "documents" a hokey but successful conspiracy to elect a new U.S. Senator. At every turn, the preachy incumbent, played by Gore Vidal, explains how elements of the conspiracy symbolize structures and functions of the national-security system that the film implies to dominate America. Each campaign figure and every plot episode identifies a component or process of this specific system: structural sexism, modern racism, fatuous television, drug wars, Congressional hearings, corrupt finances, beauty contests, campaign spots, popular musics, government scandals, political satires, lone assassins. The film shows how these components mesh. The many frissons of connection and recognition to be experienced by viewers for one piece of the film after another become the *evidence* (*from-video*) for its analysis of this election-and-policy system.[10]

The discourses and epistemes displayed by Michel Foucault are systems in this sense.[11] One target of Foucault's is the Victorian culture of sexuality, discipline, science, and class. *From Hell* (2001) is a stylish film that analyzes this system. Based on a graphic novel of the same name, it traces a shadow conspiracy behind the horrible crimes of Jack the Ripper.[12] The conspiracy involves upper echelons of the police, a Royal Society of Physicians, and the secret society of Masons. Yet behind them all is Queen Victoria: as political sovereign and cultural icon. In detecting hidden identities of the criminals, convoluted motives for the crimes, and especially secret steps in the cover-ups, this movie indicts myriad details of the Victorian system.

The film's tragic protagonist (Johnny Depp) is a policeman modeled on Sherlock Holmes. He works in Whitechapel, the red-light district of London, where virtually everyone is a victim of Victorian society. He follows the tradition of placing coins for Charon, Greek boatman for the River Styx between life and death, over the closed eyes of dead victims. These sovereigns bear the Queen's image. The film ends with the detective's death from opium overdose, whereupon his partner (Robby Coltrane) closes the systemic circle by covering his eyes with her round portraits in metal—for he, too, is a victim of the Victorian system. The film begins with a declaration attributed to Jack the Ripper: "One day men will look back and say I gave birth to the twentieth century." This is the analysis shared by the film, Foucault, and more: Victorians invented the next century's system of sciences, professions, repressions, violations, wild zones, and policings.[13] *From Hell* parses these in detail.

On occasion, as this shows, Hollywood even puts criminal conspiracies to political uses. A telling example is *Three Kings* (1999). Oddly it enjoyed greater success in DVD than on the big screen, due to America's second invasion of Iraq.[14] Set at the end of the Gulf War, *Three Kings* turns a criminal conspiracy among four soldiers to steal Saddam's Kuwaiti gold into a republican conspiracy to overcome a foreign-policy system that is betraying Iraqis to retake Kuwait's oil (black gold). Each conspirator and opponent symbolizes part of what the film depicts as a dysfunctional system of U.S. foreign policy in the wake of the Cold War. We get a career climber, an image-maker, a religious fundamentalist, a middle-class businessman, a charismatic leader, a foreign terrorist, a media maven, and (most memorably) a village idiot who evokes mass publics in America.

Conspiracy has become a popularly accessible figure for analyzing particular systems. To literalize film conspiracies is to enact the fundamentalism that insidiously authoritarian or totalitarian politics effect through their systems. To debunk conspiracy films as fantasies that obscure the subtleties and structures of systems is to miss the cinematic symbolism of many—though by no means all—conspiracy thrillers. Through narrative tropes, ironically, conspiracy movies often analyze the very systems that scholars would target in place of conspiracies.

So the next time you see a conspiracy thriller, ask how its ingredients might be evoking a sinister system of economy, society, culture, or politics. Rather than scoffing at *The International* for its shady bankers and cloak-and-dagger assassinations, consider how it could be tracing ways that armaments industries, financial institutions, and foreign policies depend on each other lately. Instead of dismissing *The Net* (1995) for its cartoon characters, think through the components of its case against the systematic reliance on encryption in computing and communication. There are no guarantees that a conspiracy thriller develops the telling details needed to symbolize a specific system of interest. *Olympus Has Fallen* (2013) and *White House Down* (2013) each announce an interest in a political system, but neither even begins to enact anything systemic. *Enemy of the State* might not update the *Bob Roberts* analysis of America's national-security system for times of electronic surveillance; but then again, it tries hard enough to earn our attention to its details.

Conspiracies in republics can be devices for resisting tyrannies; conspiracies in movies can be devices for resisting the totalizing politics of systems. Popular movies often use the mythic figures of conspiracy to specify systems that otherwise elude popular attention precisely because their politics are structural and pervasive. Conspiracy is a Hollywood trope for system.

CHAPTER 3

POLITICS IN SUBTEXTS

HORROR MOVIES AS FACING POLITICAL EVILS IN EVERYDAY LIFE (FEATURING PHONE BOOTH, THE RING, AND THE MOTHMAN PROPHECIES)

The secret of horror movies is subtext—metaphors that attack like viruses and produce a fever of associations in our minds.[1]

—Terrence Rafferty

Lurking in darkness, seen seldom and then only for a moment at the edge of the frame, the Monster is coming. It comes angrily, hungrily, uncannily, ceaselessly for our stand-ins on the screen. (It comes for us!) When can they know? Where can they go? What must they do? (Run! Run!!) Early victims panic in terror as they glimpse the disfigured form. They shiver in horror at the supernatural size or speed or strength. They cower in dread of the sinister sound and strangely seductive gaze. (Don't Look Now!) The Monster comes. The night goes red!

In desperation, a few of the prey turn on the predator. They pursue the Monster to the lair, down the rabbit hole, into the abyss. They show more bravery than brains. They still don't know what they're doing, because they have yet to face the Monster. It waits. (For us!) Once in the Monster's terror-tory, the hunters soon divide in path or strategy. (*Never* do that!) And the Monster undoes them, one or more at a time, leaving the others to puzzle over disappearances or stumble over remains. The Monster wants them to realize they can never survive. (Us, too!!)

Even so, the final few have seen more of the Monster and its moves. The hunt-ers rejoin forces, compare lessons, improve plans. They must face the Monster, figure out the sources of its power and perversity, recognize the springs of its distinctive evil—in themselves—then band together in battle against it. They have the barest chance of success, but that is better than none.

Here is the core of horror in fiction and film as a primer for political action: Awaken to evils in our midst. Turn to face those shadows, revealing awful forms more human than we had imagined. Unite to track down those troubles, con-fronting them at home. Learn from defeats and divisions to resist discouragements and recognize the evils in ourselves, even as ourselves. Reunite. Look each evil fully in the face.[2] Then fight to the death to defy or destroy it . . . at least for now. As horror knows, after all, there are holes in the middle of everything; and the spawn await us everywhere.[3]

Political Subtexts

The gist of horror is facing evils in everyday life. This is to say that the genius of horror is subtext: symbolism that creeps beneath surface meanings to assault our dreams and awaken our minds. Subtext is implicit text underneath the explicit, literal text, that is, the message in the communication medium. Subtextual mean-ings are undertones produced by symbolical interplay among the contents, forms, and media of particular messages. The forms could be conventional genres like horror; the media could be familiar entertainments like cinema. Or they could be momentary improvisations like the sign for help in *Cast Away* (2000), cadged together from island resources and drift goods.

No individual symbol, no matter how dense with meanings, makes a subtext. Subtexts are networks of meaning that coalesce when many textual details provoke one another to reveal cogent and shared symbolism not apparent on the surfaces of a speech, novel, movie, ritual, or institution. When the Supreme Court says that the U.S. Constitution implies rights to privacy, it adduces a subtext of per-sonal privacy that permeates the Constitution. That is why William O. Douglas found privacy rights in the Constitution's "penumbras" of meaning. These are not specified in any provision by itself, nor implied by every article and amend-ment, yet they lurk in the logics of many Constitutional phrases considered in mutual implication. Privacy is not the only Constitutional subtext, but it emerges as systematically important for us. Its particular inflections from one case to the next help Americans face government limits and obligations.

The situation is similar in the horror resort to subtexts for confronting re-current evils of our lives. To face everyday evils is tough personally, let alone politically. They seem familiar, often friendly, aspects of what we know and do and are. As evils that implicate or even define us, they are so awful that they hurt our minds, and we work to keep their polite appearances in place. Yet we secretly dread with glimmering awareness that their mundane forms conceal the deadliest dangers to our neighbors, families, selves, and souls. These troubles can be so terrible (or simply, sinfully convenient) that we want to turn away. We do not want to recognize them as evils. And when we repress them, they grow stranger, stronger, more sinister by the day. The subtexts of horror films push us to penetrate the repressions, face the evils, and undo them.

Everyday Evils

What evils? Directed by Mike Nichols and starring Jack Nicholson, *Wolf* (1994) targets the business world to face how capitalism can make us rapacious. *Bram Stoker's Dracula* (1992), directed by Francis Ford Coppola, probes the seductive evils of cinema in terms that outdo even Jean Baudrillard, the poststructural theorist of simulation and spectacle.[4] Jonathan Demme directs *The Silence of the Lambs* (1991) toward horrors of workplace sexism, while Ridley Scott's *Hannibal* (2001) faces evils of Machiavellian politics in bureaucracies, elections, and institutions.[5] *Wolfen* (1981) confronts what happens when big-city classes develop into castes.[6] In *Se7en* (1996), David Fincher indicts our deadliest sins, especially apathy. Stanley Kubrick's version of *The Shining* (1980) displays the evils of patriarchy.[7] In *The Sweet Hereafter* (1997), Atom Egoyan taps the Pied Piper of Hamelin to trace how parents help realize their own nightmares that drugs can carry away their children. Neil Jordan's *Interview with the Vampire* (1994) turns two novels by Anne Rice into a libertarian drama of the modern state as it lives in perverse symbiosis with us humans.[8] The lists could be legion.

I say "evils" more than "troubles" because that is the language of horror. Indeed horror is *the* popular genre of evil, even Evil. It pits us mortals against Monsters; and it insists that we draw a bright line between Good and Evil, more or less absolutized. Politically it demands that we take a stand.[9] Yet those are the literal levels; and the subtexts usually are more humble, subtle, sophis-ticated. The Evil alerts us to trouble and urges us to action, while the symbol-ism slyly specifies the danger and informs our deeds. Seldom are subtextual evils the least supernatural. They are complex, mundane, even debatable. But these evils, lowercase and plural, can be insidious and difficult for us to face. Horror devices help us.

Why resort to symbols, to subtexts? Why have recourse to horror, when documentaries can expose sexism or family dramas can literalize the dangers of drugs? The more evils imperil us or emerge from us, the more difficulty we can have in facing them. We sense that extremities of dread or criticism can devastate and incapacitate us. Just to limp along, we ignore or repress some of the sins and troubles that threaten us the most. As Freud argued about dreams, subtexts can slip dreaded figures past our devices for inattention by shifting their forms.[10] This is the dynamic of *In Dreams* (1999), directed by Neil Jordan. In horror films, the evils of our times ease into the edges of our awareness under the cover of specific symbols. Experiencing these evils in disguise, we can begin coming to realistic terms with their sources, dynamics, and effects.

On the surface, horror threatens us with an enormous range of conventional characters: vampires, madmen, mummies, ghosts, poltergeists, ghouls, demons, aliens, cannibals, zombies, sirens, boogeymen, werewolves, witches, rapists, sadists, serial and mass killers, totalitarians—monsters of every kind. *The Cabin in the Woods* (2012) takes its diverse inventory of figures from only the teen-menace corner of a genre that includes many other provinces. Such generic symbols of horror are existentialist.[11] So are the politics. The stock characters, settings, and scenes of the genre evoke themes of doubt, absurdity, nihilism, perseverance, and resistance. They challenge us to take responsibilities and make meanings. In fact, some midcentury scions of existentialism wrote stories of horror as well as treatises of political theory.[12]

Thus classic characters of horror signal subtextual politics. By convention, zombie films examine mass societies. Ghost films face injustices. Vampire movies explicate the charismatic and totalitarian politics of perfectionism. Werewolves involve the politics of development and transformation. Mummies implicate disorders of tradition and authority. Yet the key devices for horror films to help us face political evils in everyday life are the telling details that differ across films to individuate their monstrosities, specify their settings, and animate their scenes.

These telling details articulate subtexts. In horror films, subtexts are more ample than a few allusions but less articulated than full-fledged allegories of the strictest kind. Few work like *Animal Farm* (1954, 1999).[13] Its literal particulars offer a dark, talking-animal fantasy about pigs who lead a barnyard revolution against human owners. Taken allegorically, almost every detail comments satirically on the Russian Revolution by linking systematically, one by one, to the revolution's main facets and figures. On the other hand, few effective horror films miss opportunities to activate several levels of symbolism at once, whereas allegories typically confine themselves to one symbolical meaning for each literal detail. Some horror subtexts are sustained; some are hit-and-run; none accounts for every important part of the movie, yet most address in considerable detail how to face everyday evils we might try to ignore. Peculiarly suited to ordinary people, horror films often put humanly apprehensible and actionable—hence political—faces on everyday evils.

Communication Examples

Recent horror films show keen interest in technologies and activities of communication. Several can clarify how horror movies communicate by subtext, while illustrating the dynamics of telling details. As the title suggests, *Phone Booth* (2003) develops its themes of communication as much in the text as the subtext. Colin Farrell plays a publicist who answers a ringing telephone on the street, only to hear—and see—that he has been targeted for death if he does not act as the caller instructs. Operating on the literal level as a thriller about terrorism, the film turns the apparatus of stationary telephones in booths versus mobile cell phones into fairly explicit figures for urban modes of distant ties and dishonest lives. The following year, *Cellular* (2004) uses the conventions of a thriller to shift a similar set of concerns into the suburbs. Each detail about how the characters communicate becomes a comment on the destruction of trust and meaning in an impersonal setting.

Yet the frisson of horror in *Phone Booth* comes instead from the main subtext: a religious wake-up call to personal repentance and rededication to making every moment moral. When we hear "the Caller" (Kiefer Sutherland) less as a human terrorist talking on a telephone and more as a Divine Voice sounding in the Soul, we enter the movie's deeper currents of meaning. As an exercise in horror, *Phone Booth* works symbolically to disrupt our complacency by calling us radically and wrenchingly to account for our everyday treatment of others. Yes, *Phone Booth* unsettles us with its literal and symbolical dimensions of surveillance, along with its disorders of communication as evils in community. But its main horror is the merciless specter of Judgment.

The Ring (2002) shows how the rumor of a videotape that, seven days later, causes the death of any watcher is turning out to be true. Remaking a Japanese movie, *The Ring* is rich in subtexts. One evokes horrors of divorce.[14] But the most insistent subtext attacks evils of overreliance on telecommunication, especially telephone and television. Its focal figure of horror, the deadly videotape, strings together images that detail a literal mystery but also symbolize everyday troubles of our attunement to TV. The indictment echoes long-standing complaints by Roderick Hart, Joshua Meyrowitz, Neil Postman, G. W. S. Trow, Raymond Williams, and many others.[15] An early panorama of the Seattle building where a mother and son struggle against the murderous dynamics of the tape shows the son along with myriad others in apartments unto compartments of everyday life where televisions run almost continually. The film's opening words are, "I hate television. It gives me headaches." A teenage girl says this just before she breaks down under the onslaught of terrible deaths among friends more engrossed than she in TV. The film bursts with details that castigate our dependence on TV: 'twould take an entire essay to analyze them all.

To symbolize our difficulty in facing everyday evils of television, *The Ring* defaces its victims before destroying them. It distorts their faces in photographic and televisual images and has its victims mark over the faces of others. The horrible embodiment of television is a demonic child. She has telepathic powers that project images at a distance onto film and that insinuate voices into the minds of others, driving them to suicide. Her father imprisons her in a loft with only a television for company; and when this does not work, her mother asphyxiates her and casts her down a well. Eventually the protagonist, an investigative journalist, finds the body; but the evil spirit survives in the tape, which the journalist copies and passes along to save first herself then her son from its deadly effect. They become desperate accomplices to the crime, the horror, of television.

The Mothman Prophecies (2001) strands a newly widowed reporter for the *Washington Post* in a West Virginia town that suffers visitations from a weird creature who cryptically evokes terrible events, like his wife's death and worse, that soon come to pass. How does the creature know these things? What can people do about them? The movie sustains a religious subtext, yet it is even more impressive as a horror story about the recent shift in news from reporting events to anticipating them. When Paddy Chayefsky wrote the script for *Network* (1976), still among the greatest films about television, he spotted an incipient trend for television news to predict happenings rather than relate or analyze them after the fact. To satirize this, he made "Sybil the Soothsayer" a regular on the evening news with Howard Beale (Peter Finch), that "Mad Prophet of the Airways." As with so many of Chayefsky's blatant exaggerations, this *Network* prophecy arguably has been exceeded by our realities in the subsequent half-century.[16] Pause to notice how much of the news is now about tomorrow's schedules and next month's possibilities rather than yesterday's occurrences.

In *The Mothman Prophecies,* the newspapers, radios, telephones, and televisions parallel our own in anticipating triumphs and troubles almost as much as they report them. The film faces the everyday evils in this development by sketching strange figures, the Mothmen, who sometimes communicate their apparent precognitions to ordinary humans. The film says that this "news" might result from a "higher" vantage point for viewing (temporally) distant events than allowed by our ordinary perspectives in everyday life. Yet we humans cannot see how to turn this mysterious information into effective action, and calamities ensue one after another.

The prophecies of the Mothmen bring daily premonitions of troubles around the world. This "news" can be true after a fashion, but inevitably the humans misinterpret its claims and hints. Worse, trying to live with the responsibilities it seems to impose can overload people and drive them insane. Seldom do they manage to avert or diminish even small aspects of disaster. More often, people compound looming troubles. The "future news" from our media may come from higher, wider, longer views than we can sustain as individuals. News perspectives might be categorically less personal, perhaps even less practical, than we can handle. Yet to show how the motives and moves of the Mothmen are not "human" in any personal and individual sense can be to suggest how the same goes for the media. Scholars of political communication know that conventions for news come from professional and institutional norms often unconnected to what ordinary people find intelligible or useful.[17] Myriad details about the Mothmen and their interactions with humanity work to inform provocative criticisms of our mediated lives. The movie brings this home to viewers through vivid figures. These horrify to attract our attention, even as they slip unsettling possibilities into our dawning awareness, so that we can recognize and analyze them.

Possibly the only popular genre of cinema with a worse reputation than horror is porn. Yet horror deserves scholarly, as well as popular, respect. A purpose of democracy has been to empower ordinary people. The social sciences and humanities teach that this requires mundane individuals to get good senses of their situations, resources, and responsibilities. The idea is that people who know themselves and how distant events could change their lives can act to direct the changes. As we learn anew that people get much of their practical instruction from popular media, we do well to appreciate how popular genres communicate their politics. Horror films helps us face the evils in everyday life by tapping subtexts to alert and inform us. The Monster has many ways and meanings; but horror lets us learn them, refine our defenses, improve ourselves, and come together in action. As Ursula Le Guin chants, particularly about horror stories near the campfire, "In the tale, in the telling, we are all one blood."[18]

CHAPTER 4

POLITICS IN INNOVATIONS

FRACTAL FILMS AS NEW RHETORICS FOR NONLINEAR POLITICS (FEATURING BABEL, CRASH, AND CLOUD ATLAS)

*To find a form that accommodates the mess,
that is the task of the artist now.*[1]

—Samuel Beckett

The splintered, jigsaw-puzzle structure of Babel *... belongs to an increasingly common, as yet unnamed genre*—Crash *is perhaps the most prominent recent example—in which drama is created by the juxtaposition of distinct stories, rather than by the progress of a single narrative arc.*[2]

—A. O. Scott

The message here is that movies are among America's most prominent sites of political mythmaking. This keeps cinema on cutting edges of rhetorical invention for American politics. Powerful cases in point are the movie rhetorics emerging for movements, styles, systems, and other arguably "chaotic," nonlinear politics. These postmodern unto postwestern politics elude many disciplines of modern states and ideologies.[3] They even escape classical templates of public deliberation and decision of the sorts that dominate dreams of deliberative democracy.[4] Hence linear narratives and civic rhetorics misconceive important political opportunities and troubles in our times. Yet movies have been developing ingenious narratives and engaging rhetorics to help us respond to dynamics of nonlinear systems prominent in current situations.

Overlooking nonlinear logics, critics slam films that many, especially younger viewers, love and learn from. Repeatedly David Denby and Anthony Lane in the *New Yorker*, A. O. Scott in the *New York Times*, and other commentators decry "The New Disorder" in film narratives.[5] It is a disease of the times, they say, devoutly—if erratically—to be condemned. They denounce all too many recent exercises in nonlinear plots for incapacitating fatalism or infantile wish-fulfillment. Rather than face actual difficulties responsibly, they suggest, nonlinear movies too easily settle for hopelessness or merely "Wishing Things Were Otherwise."[6] They also keep us at an undue distance emotionally.[7] Watching these movies is too much work for ordinary viewers, moreover, whom they leave unsure about what has happened or why. Like the continuing critical assault on conspiracy thrillers, which also concern system politics, the effect of these attacks can be to prevent viewer attention, through encouraging a contempt that sneers at nonlinear cinema as incoherent or beneath notice.

In response, let me sketch what the nonlinear innovations can be seen to address, why, and with what effects. Of course, I am especially interested in their implications for politics. In a sentence, they clarify nonlinear systems, styles, movements, and comparable politics so that we can learn to resist or pursue them, as appropriate. The aim here is to help us viewers figure out such films, so that the films can help us viewers figure out our politics. Knowing better how to view these movies, we can experience more adequately these films, their nonlinear rhetorics, consequently our nonlinear politics. The mathematics of chaos and complex, nonlinear systems feature fractional dimensions or fractals, for short; so it makes sense to talk about the families of movies with figures from chaos mathematics as fractal films.

Our challenges insistently involve nonlinear politics. Ecosystems of climate change and population collapse, racism and imperialism, totalitarian regimes and movements, globalization and nuclear proliferation, microsystems of domination or discipline, cultures of celebrity and consumption: all these seem susceptible to nonlinear principles of chaos mathematics. All seem to necessitate nonlinear narratives of butterfly effects, feedback loops, self-similarities, sensitive dependence on initial conditions, one-way thresholds, strange attractors, and related tropes that mathematicians and physicists have been articulating to get beyond linear logics in settings that exceed them. Popular cinema contributes to this political mythmaking via several networks of rhetorical conventions for apprehending and acting in nonlinear conditions. Four frequently nonlinear forms are conspiracy thrillers, neo noirs, time travels, and mosaic movies. The noirs attract fair respect from critics, but the other forms of fractal films often generate undue disdain.

Confounding Disorders?

Even critics who approve various plot experiments miss the political rhetorics of many nonlinear films. In consequence, some superb commentators disparage some superlative films. Denby applauds *Pulp Fiction* (1994), *Memento* (2001), *Eternal Sunshine of the Spotless Mind* (2004), *Crash* (2005), and *The Good Shepherd* (2006)—all noir, not so accidentally—plus several instances of *cinéma désordonné*. Otherwise he hates "the overloading, the dislocations and disruptions" of narratives in recent movies, where "the rich ambivalence of art somehow slips away as we reconstruct the way one thing connects to another."[8]

So Denby joins Scott in excoriating *Babel* (2007) and its immediate predecessor, *21 Grams* (2003). In Scott's words, "Perhaps the most common feature of movies of this kind is that they are more interested in fate than in psychology. The people in *Babel* behave irrationally—if often quite predictably—but any control they appear to have over their own lives is illusory. They suffer unequally and unfairly, paying disproportionately for their own mistakes and for the whims of chance and the laws of global capitalism."[9] Denby also dislikes "a related group of clogged-sink narratives, like *Traffic* (2000), *Syriana* (2005), and *Miami Vice* (2006), which are so heavily loaded with subplots and complicated information that the story can hardly seep through the surrounding material. *Syriana* made sense in the end, but you practically needed a database to sort out the story elements; the movie became a weird formal experiment, testing the audience's endurance and patience."[10]

The rhetorical complaint is incoherence, while the political condemnation is that this antiform incapacitates us for decent judgment and effective action. Imagine, two philosophers urge in the same vein, if we found ourselves "in the film *Mulholland Dr.* (2001), where events occur in no coherent order. We'd have to forget about making *any* kind of statement or judgment about the world because we couldn't count on the world to be consistent from one minute to the next."[11] What, though, if linear chronology were not the only coherent order? The film's writer and director, David Lynch, says that *Mulholland Dr.* is mostly a dream, a network of nonlinear psycho-logics; and so it is. As neo noir, it lambastes Hollywood as a corrupt system. Some commentators see this; others don't.[12] Critics who find no coherence in a film might pause to learn from other viewers about its possible intelligibility—about its dream dynamics, for instance—before denouncing it as incomprehensible. And critics impatient with narrative "disorder" might consider nonlinear logics before dismissing complicated films as clogged, incoherent, or incapacitating. There are more logics in story and film, let us notice, than are dreamt of in our linear philosophies.

Natural Experiments

Two "natural experiments" in nonlinear order have reinforced these inferences for me. I saw *Network* (1976) for the first time in a theater that misarranged the reels. This great movie treats television as a corrupt system enveloping us. Several midmovie reels out of linear order made the film an intriguing yet comprehensible puzzle. Staying throughout, the audience was irritated but entranced. Some complained to the theater manager. He admitted the mistake but wondered why people had not walked out. The answer is that viewers could make nonlinear sense of what they saw, so that engaging the puzzle imparted a richer sense of entanglement in television as a system. The viewers could tell that the reels had not been shown in the intended order, because the resulting "cuts" were especially abrupt and dislocating, accomplished from one frame to the next for radical disruptions out of the blue. Thus the viewers wanted to return for the film that they had paid to see. Still they stayed for the "disordered" edition because they found it intriguingly comprehensible.

Likewise I saw *Next* (2007) for the first time in a theater where the reel for ending credits did not run. *Next* is a time-travel film that repeatedly retracts its timelines. It plays insistently with ventures a few minutes at a time in directions of action not eventually taken, because they turn disastrous. It does this with a subjective camera that lets viewers share the experiences of a wildly talented man who can extend his "experiences" a few minutes into futures that would result from acts he then decides, based on those "experiences," not to take. When deeds start disasters, the hero simply cancels them and starts over in different directions; but viewers have no way to tell the false starts from continuities of actual action, until the false starts end in midevent. There are no signs of extrapolation into the future, until the film abruptly puts us back a couple of minutes into a frame that we recognize as one we experienced on the way to more recent moments. Consequently viewers learn that they cannot trust as actual the occurrences of just about any two minutes (or even more) at a time in this film. It starts disasters only to cut back to presents not yet transcended in actual action by the hero.[13]

Shadowing the film throughout is the possibility of a nuclear explosion in Los Angeles. So when the screen went abruptly blank as a happy ending unfolds, viewers could have been seeing another future not actually taken. Waiting for events to restart, we stayed in our seats, wondering if the black screen was a clever insertion or a grim conclusion consistent with the film's nonlinear exposition. This was not so, in fact, but the film might have been better for it.

We can make good, effective sense of nonlinear situations. When nothing followed for us in *Next,* members of the audience sought the manager to learn if there was a reel for closing credits that somehow did not run. As a whole, the audience could see how the abrupt ending could make sense; but it wanted to know if that was part of the meaning to be gained from the film as normally presented. This is comparable to the consternation and debate provoked by the notorious, arguably nonlinear, nonending of *The Sopranos* (1999–2007). It is not that people can make no sense of the screen going black at the climax. Instead they can and do discern several possible but somewhat incompatible meanings. Some people condemn the discontinuity as a dramatic cop-out, while others welcome the ambiguity as an existential truth.

From epistemology and aesthetics to cognitive science and cinema theory, the lesson is less that we can make sense of putative nonsense than that we often do so through nonlinear logics. These logics show supposed signs of incoherence instead to be aspects of strong systematicity, where the "connections" are intrinsic rather than extrinsic and mechanical. Discontinuity, inversion, reversal, fragmentation, juxtaposition, disproportions between action and reaction, effects at a distance, absence of linear causation, inseparability of independent and dependent variables, asymmetry of explanations and predictions, fractional dimensions, cusps and tipping points, irresolvable ambiguities: these inform sciences of uncertainty.[14]

Nonlinear Genres

The lesson is that important aspects of life are nonlinear. This is because life flows, and flows are turbulent: not incoherent but turbulent. The cinema of systematic turbulence offers rhetorics for knowing and doing in turbulent politics. What politics are turbulent? Movements crowd politics in the postmodern period, from the nineteenth century onward; yet movements are notorious for departing from the linear, creedal coherence of modern ideologies. They hold together tropally, figurally, as self-similar flows of action that we can analyze into characteristic moves or devices that sustain family resemblances.[15] Styles have been crucial for politics since their inception; but they, too, are inchoate in form and content as measured by modern, linear terms. Again their coherence is gestural rather than creedal, turbulent rather than mechanical.[16] Political cultures, genres, media, and myths establish their strange consistencies through family resemblance and self-similarity rather than linear logics.[17] Especially cultural, ecological, social, and other systems in our times display the turbulence of nonlinear politics and the coherence of tropal consistency.[18] This is evident in fractal films, and conspiracy thrillers start to show how.

Conspiracy Thrillers

As we have seen, intellectuals and scholars have long disparaged "conspiracy theories" and the related cinema as low-brow populism that refuses to face the real, sophisticated complications of governments in our world.[19] Actually conspiracy thrillers are more sophisticated and politically intelligent than critics have appreciated.[20] These treat conspiracies as tropes for systems and then show how to resist them with politics promoted by existentialists, phenomenologists, and such followers of Friedrich Nietzsche as Michel Foucault, the French philosopher of discourse, knowledge, and power.[21]

The familiar academic misunderstanding personalizes thriller conspiracies into secret collaborations among powerful individuals or institutions; but the genre often uses these as figures for larger interests and processes of impersonal, interdependent systems. To be sure, some popular movies do personalize and literalize conspiracies, but these often prove to be documentaries in the Michael Moore mode of *Fahrenheit 9/11* (2004), where the argument is that family ties among the American Bushes and their acolytes plus the Saudi royal family and the bin Ladens literally became a conspiracy against American interests before and after the terrorist attacks of September 11, 2001. Conspiracy thrillers often increase the comprehensibility of systems by personalizing them, but this does not make audiences literalize the conspiracies. As Chapter 2 explains, the genre instead develops its major characters, acts, and settings as figures for the components of specific systems that it shows harming people. Some thriller conspiracies operate pointedly as allegories for specific systems of power; others work loosely and multiplicitously as subtexts for systematicity; still others work mainly as hit-and-run allusions to entire families of systems.

But systems come in different kinds. Linear systems are machines. Operating by Humean cause-and-effect, they maintain themselves as systems by processing inputs through continuous but individualizable steps into outputs. To keep most disturbances outside, their boundaries are precise and strong. To dampen input turbulence, their internal dynamics are homeostatic, self-adjusting toward equilibrium. The systems of Newtonian physics and neoclassical economics are linear. Their mathematics are branches of calculus, and their powers are sorts of leverage.[22]

To date, most conspiracy thrillers are linear. Their chronologies are historical. Strong, clear boundaries divide the perpetrators in each conspiracy from the victims and saviors outside it. A menacing system is hard to defeat because it controls massive resources and works relentlessly to maintain itself. Put into a sinister system, victims begin befuddled by logics both complicated and concealed. Sensing ruthless logics and overwhelming resources, victims easily become fatalistic and compliant, caught within the system. Heroes stay sufficiently outside such a linear system to glimpse its logics whole, evade their machinations, and leverage the apparatus at its tipping points.[23] The heroes are not fundamentally encompassed and tainted by the linear conspiracy as a system. The defeat of corruption systematized in linear terms can be categorical and lasting. Consider *Three Days of the Condor* (1975), *All the President's Men* (1976), *The Pelican Brief* (1993), and many James Bond movies.

The most completely interdependent systems are nonlinear. They offer flows and fields more than parts and particles. Quantum physics, hydraulics, and ecologies are nonlinear. Their mathematics are chaotic, facing uncertainties; and their powers are modes of flow. Nonlinear systems can be stylized and studied as though they were linear. This is what "systems theories" in the social sciences attempted in the last century by cutting systems into arbitrary "units of analysis" divided further into independent and dependent variables for calculating inputs, throughputs, outputs, equilibrations, and such.[24] It is what conspiracy thrillers often do figurally with social systems.

Yet some movie conspiracies are nonlinear. These often include time loops, flashbacks, and flash-forwards. Their corrupt systems engulf almost everyone, including would-be heroes, leaving clarity—if it ever comes—to the virtual end of the film. In *Shooter* (2007), a mentor (Levon Helm) tells the hero (Mark Wahlberg), "The world ain't what it seems . . . . The minute you think you got it figured, you got it wrong." Then the movie and the hero demonstrate this. "What if it's a trap?" a helper (Michael Peña) later asks the hero, who replies, "Oh, it's a trap: guaranteed, every time. The question is for whom." That is how nonlinear systems seem to people who would resist their pervasive corruptions: mystifying therefore frustrating. *Shooter*'s nonlinear conspiracy is "too deep; it's not clear who can be trusted." With all the principals gathered on a mountaintop, the hero declares, "Nobody out here's innocent," including himself. Starting to discern the system's dynamics, nonetheless, the hero does act effectively—albeit in alarming ways. The film might be unduly disillusioned with government, but it is neither cynical nor fatalistic, and it is nothing like incoherent.[25]

Something similar can be said of *Vantage Point* (2008), which rewinds repeatedly to show a terrorist attack from more than a handful of perspectives enacted by different characters. The film falls short of an ambition to display perspectivism in Friedrich Nietzsche's sense, because it insists in the end on a single comprehensive truth about its conspiracy plot.[26] It accomplishes this by showing how all the initially disjoined experiences fit together into a seamless reality, and it does so to take subtextual issue with a Bush-Cheney doctrine of preemptive strikes for a global war on terrorism. Again thriller complexity turns out to be the farthest thing from incoherence, although this nonlinear drama is not exactly revealing nonlinear politics of a full-fledged kind.

Neo Noirs

Classical noirs show protagonists awakening to personal complicity in corrupt systems, struggling to resist, then succumbing. Neo noirs often show protagonists escaping, liberating others, even overthrowing systems. Systems are so conventional for neo noirs that several key characters can be named accordingly: system bosses, minions, fixers, and sleepers. Neo noir's stock characters, deeds, and scenes literally let us *figure out* situations that systematically resist actionable understanding in modern, linear terms. Noirs generally have their protagonists and viewers confront their systems from inside. That puts a premium on learning to recognize these systems and respond effectively in especially daunting conditions.

Amply fractal films are more prominent by far in neo noir than in classical noir. One way to understand this is that linear systems dominate classical noir, whereas neo noir makes more room for nonlinear systems. Presumably the mechanisms of linear systems encourage us to construe them as determinist. When defined as self-sustaining and disinclined to run down, therefore, linear systems especially suit the greater fatalism of classic noir. The long, singular plot loop conventional for classical noir is a ready symbol for the encompassing determinism that we associate with linear systems, because it traps almost all events for a movie in what is always already past for the protagonist, leaving little opportunity to twist away from his prepared fate. Neo noir shows far more interest in its protagonists overcoming awful odds to frustrate, elude, or undo focal systems—even though that still happens a little less than half the time. Cultural associations of flow and fluidity with play and flexibility lead us to regard nonlinear systems as more porous and therefore more open than linear systems. Nonlinear systems also seem more open and escapable because they are categorically less predictable than linear systems. Nonlinear "complexity" generates cusps, thresholds, phase shifts, and similar discontinuities incapable of anticipation from within the nonlinear system.

This illuminates neo noirs where protagonists in the end seem merely to "luck out" of the vicious systems that appeared only moments before to enthrall the protagonists completely. Perhaps an internally generated shift in phase has suddenly, surprisingly set them free. Then the key questions remaining are whether these lead characters will recognize the fresh start fast enough and accept its responsibilities fully enough to keep from falling back into their old traces. Examples include Rudy (Ben Affleck) in *Reindeer Games* (2000) and Laure Ash (Rebecca Romijn) in *Femme Fatale* (2002). Both seize their late, surprising opportunities decisively for fresh beginnings in largely new lives.

Neo noir includes classical-noir figures too: tough-guy detectives, spider women, frames, mean streets, chiaroscuro, times out of joint, world-weary voiceovers, and more. Accordingly noir has turned the interest of hardboiled detection in big-city undersides into cautionary tales about striving for great power, fortune, or justice. The neo-noir lesson becomes that the system will get you, if you don't watch out—and maybe even if you do. Nonlinear systems assailed by neo noirs include industrialization, patriarchy, consumer society, the drug war, technology, populism, racism, globalization, and celebrity culture. Even more adventurous are neo-noir treatments as nonlinear systems of memory and action in *Memento,* memory and personality in *Eternal Sunshine of the Spotless Mind,* gambling in *Even Money* (2006), vengeance in *Shadowboxer* (2005), even life in *21 Grams* and *Seven Pounds* (2008).

Denby's indictment of "The New Disorder" targets affinities for an ethos that combines chaos, coincidence, fatalism, and wish-fulfillment.[27] He insists that "Experience can't be random and also structured like a cage."[28] But noir is existentialist enough to know better.[29] Experience of social systems can *feel* simultaneously random and structured, even imprisoning like a cage. As phenomenologists teach, moreover, experience just *is* the feeling, the seeming; so experience can *be* random yet also structured like a cage. This can be exactly the character of experience for someone awakening to complicity in a corrupt system. The awakening heralds an incipient yet unpredictable change of phase for a nonlinear system that suddenly is generating new resistance from within.

Classical noirs are congenitally fateful, if not always fatalistic; but Denby and other critics of "The New Disorder" have long known and prized classical noirs. For conventional practices such as cinema and aesthetics, familiarity can *be* form. Genres just *are* recognizable families of conventions, figures, or tropes. The strong family resemblances of neo noirs to classical noirs probably explain why recent critics of "disorder" have appreciated the coherence of neo noirs far more than their nonlinear cousins among time travels, mosaic movies, even conspiracy thrillers. Yet rhetorics and politics are conventional too.[30] Rhetorical familiarity with nonlinear systems from nonlinear films can enable viewers to participate more effectively in our nonlinear politics.[31] Whatever the reasons, at some three hundred in English over the last three decades, neo noirs have proliferated at a rate similar to classical noirs. Plainly audiences find neo noirs engaging rather than incoherent.

Time Travels

Few kinds of films get faulted for incoherence more than time travels. Generally they intend intellectual challenges through initially perplexing, sometimes downright paradoxical, leaps beyond linear modes of time and space.[32] The first three *Terminator* films (1984, 1991, 2003) combine neo noir and time travel, but in doses small enough to escape complaints of incoherence. Still they are *tour-de-force* treatments of technological societies as nonlinear systems. Leaping beyond timelines straight or looping, time travels become at least incipiently fractal films by virtue of their defining devices.

Even in movie form, time travels need not confuse even the most casual or unfamiliar of viewers. Time travels tied to Victorian societies or technologies feature romantic simplification of the era's mechanical tropes for temporal tours and shuttles. Thus few viewers take issue with the coherence or comprehensibility of such time-travel romances as *Somewhere in Time* (1980) or *Kate and Leopold* (2001).

When the narrative complications spike, however, critical complaints begin. Dismissed as clumsy and incoherent, *Timecop* (1994) constructs a nonlinear narrative for a thriller that features a personalized conspiracy to elect a corrupt U.S. president.[33] It clearly indicts the American system of campaign finance and government policymaking as a perverse system so effectively encompassing that it must elicit a hyperhero of the martial arts (Jean-Claude Van Damme) to resist it with even minimal success. I have yet to meet an ordinary viewer who reports any trouble following the film. People familiar with the tropes of time travels are not alienated by its *linear* disorder; they are engaged by it.

Reviled in several quarters as silly, inconsistent, or incoherent, *Frequency* (2000) uses time-travel for a psychoanalytic take on the family politics of escaping repression as a self-maintaining system.[34] As in *Timecop, Frequency* uses time-travel tropes that *can* be literalized into "inconsistencies" in linear logics. Yet these devices are specifically for turning away from linear continuities, so that we viewers can apprehend the nonlinear aspects of family secrecy and miscommunication. To insist that time travels respect linear, historical logics is to resist any respect for their distinctive figures, which announce themselves from the outset as nonliteral, nonlinear, and unhistorical.

Timeline (2003) uses time travels to show how the middle ages in Western Europe were not so much the times of civilizational darkness and stasis that modern prejudice has premised as they were early steps toward modern inventions and institutions.[35] *Lake House* (2006) reaches with devices of time travel beyond Victorian (se)verities to provide a more quirky, postmodern appreciation of romance.[36] Both these films suffer misplaced carping about temporal paradoxes, cinematic clutter, and fantastic silliness. But go with their fractal tropes, rather than fighting to literalize and realign them, and both view much better. To literalize everything in linear terms for time-travel tales has little use but to display them as contradictory or otherwise incoherent. It is to miss altogether how, and thus what, they mean.

Denby blasts *Déjà Vu* (2006), a time-travel noir, as unduly "complicated … haunting and childish" wish-fulfillment.[37] Denby misses altogether its cinematic treatment of the Bush "War on Terror" as a nonlinear system, so he fails even to consider its figural arguments for altering America's recent courses of political action. Lane likewise observes that "the chronology is all chewed up" in *Premonition* (2007), but he ignores how the film experiments with inventive responses to systematically overdetermined events.[38] Overall the situation becomes so bad for time travels that reviews damning them for incoherence must be ignored in favor of seeing the movies for yourself. Whatever the specific weaknesses of such movies, too few critics seem to follow the nonlinear tropes of time-travel films to leave the resulting reviews reliable.

Mosaic Movies

But the biggest bugaboos have become dramas "created by the juxtaposition of distinct stories, rather than by the progress of a single narrative arc." Critics acknowledge the artistry in this but distrust the resulting "disorder" as showman-ship for its own sake. I call this "yet unnamed genre" mosaic movies, because their narratives often remind me of photomosaics. They come in pieces that, seen individu-ally in no obvious order, display independent patterns and integrity. As we manage to see them in relationship to each other, though, a larger pattern and integrity emerges for the whole. Before the big picture coalesces, we experience enormous complexity and sometimes consternation in trying to keep the disparate pieces in mind and fit them aptly together. When the overarching system snaps into focus, however, we do not lose our detailed sense of the complexities and processes. Instead we see a resemblance or similar connection of each composite unit to the full film.

This connects to the principle of self-similarity from chaos theory, where similar patterns emerge as orders of magnitude change, say, for a coast mapped with ever greater precision. As turbulent flows, nonlinear systems cohere in important part by forming largely but loosely the same figures throughout and across various levels or viewpoints. Accordingly the depths and further dimen-sions of mosaic movies ramify fractally into visions more than stereoscopic. *Crash* does this for racism as a nonlinear system.[39] *Magnolia* (1999) does it for nonhistorical aspects of fathers and forgiveness, *Babel* for nonlinear dynamics of globalization, *Love Actually* (2003) for the systematic turbulence of . . . love, *American Gun* (2005) for the intertwined targets in its title, *Syriana* for the insidious system of oil politics, and *The Lookout* (2007) for celebrity as a nonlinear force in postmodern communities.[40]

Mosaic movies are akin to epics. The vast lores of Arthur and Robin Hood do not come as linear narratives. Their stories share characters, deeds, and settings—but raggedly and without linear chronology.[41] The Bible shares this kind of coherence. Epics come in episodes, and these resemble scenes and story skeins in mosaic mov-ies. Each episode is an emblem of the hero and the community. Elements of the Arthuriad are what the 1984 film calls *Places in the Heart*, rather than stages in the history of England. What Thomas Malory and T. H. White do for the Arthur stories is refine them toward the novel modern taste for linearity.[42] Similarly *Love Actually* is a postmodern epic of love: each episode is a distinct facet of the love which is their union. And *The Dead Girl* (2006) is, oxymoronically, a small epic on the oppression and possible liberation of women: each episode is an emblem of women caught in kinds of girlhood, dying from abuses, and struggling to be "free."

Films can pursue several narrative skeins of roughly coequal importance and eventual interdependence, yet they can refrain from trying to take advantage of any turbulence within or between their multiple storylines. To suppress incipi-ent chaos, these movies keep each individual drama from disconcerting leaps in space or time, while taking care to show early and often how all the component dramas go together. Then there is little sense of a formerly diffuse, fragmented, or otherwise confounding film snapping later into focus. Seldom do these films show much interest in tracing—let alone resisting or escaping—nonlinear systems.

A ready example is *Lions for Lambs* (2007). With only a few brief flashbacks, it proceeds largely in real time, using clocks to show insistently how it is keeping its three dramatic arenas in sync.[43] To build suspense as the clocks run out on soldiers (and perhaps countries) in mortal peril, the film's components explain clearly how they link. There is little interest here in oblique hints, and a resulting complaint is that the film lacks subtlety. Unsurprisingly the concern is not a social system, linear or nonlinear, but a political challenge and a personal choice. The call is not to individual resistance or escape but to personal and generational engagement. *Lions for Lambs* is regimented and streamlined. It is not ragged, rambling, spacious, sprawling, or encompassing like an epic. Nor is it long disjointed like a mosaic movie. It marches through a linear argument—rather than exploring a complex system in the manner of *Magnolia, Love Actually,* or *Babel.*

Babel is neither incoherent, fatalistic, nor otherwise perverse. Rather it is a postmodern epic of global displacement. The film presents four networks of characters from Japan, Mexico, Morocco, and the United States. Jumping abruptly among them, it gradually uses a tour, a hunting rifle, news, a wedding, a police investigation, and many other oblique links to show how their routines, troubles, and joys echo and turn on each other. So *Babel* evokes how we can recognize our lives as nonlinear mosaics of unanticipated connections and consequences, precisely in order to reclaim our capacities for action.

Contrary to the charge of naïve wish-fulfillment, *Babel* displays permanent damages. Yet contrary to the worry about fatalism, it follows most of its characters to the point of some hopeful, promising initiative. I side, plainly, with the people who would name *Babel* one of the best films of 2006. It is telling that *Babel*'s naysayers often concede that the film has many cinematic merits, even as they lament what they lambaste as overdone contrivance, overall incoherence, and overactive artistry. The plea here is to recognize how there can be systematic method in the linear madness of fractal films.

Fractal Films

Whatever the overall quality of *Babel* as popular cinema or political mythmaking, its specific devices of cinematic mythmaking feature tropes that are chaotic, turbulent, nonlinear—in a word, fractal. No doubt there can be many ways to advance such an argument; but for the moment, let us sketch just one quick account in terms of figures familiar from chaos theory for complex systems. The figures are narratival, yet they are simultaneously visual and aural too.

Gaps and leaps disrupt the irregular phases of flows, so that their momentary states do not trace continuously in lines, straight or curving. Prominent tropes of turbulence accordingly include discontinuities. Fractal films jumble their settings by leaping arbitrarily among them, or so it seems. *Babel* cuts without explanation among scenes that eventually depict an emerging global disorder. Turbulent storytelling also involves wrenching shifts among characters rather than the smoother modulations familiar from linear storytelling. The early parts of fractal films such as *Babel* pose for viewers their greatest challenges of character recognition and connection, before recurrences of characters become numerous enough to help us identify and link them with decent confidence. Of course, fractal films leap quasi-historical timelines and jettison chronologies to generate discontinuous plots. *Babel* episodes insistently violate the linear chronologies of historical timelines. They show us putative consequences well before what we might later come to regard as their causes, while they let temporal coincidences and juxtapositions replace linear conceptions of causation for the most part. Strong, sensitive, systemic interdependence among the various elements is the point.

Complaints from critics establish that these discontinuities of setting, character, and plot appear prominently in *Babel,* although still other fractal films such as *Syriana* can be even harder to "follow." For the social sciences, especially, chaos theory for nonlinear systems is called (and comprehended as) "complexity theory." This can help explain the kinship of *Syriana* and other "clogged-sink narratives" with more "chaotically" developed narratives that make linear leaps or leave linear gaps—in times as well as in spaces (or settings) and in character networks. Since *Syriana*'s writer and director, Stephen Gaghan, talks of cutting out at least a couple of narrative skeins and complicating sets of characters as he edited the initial footage into a theatrical version of his film, we might wonder how much the evident discontinuities tend to escalate as fractal films move beyond three or four sets of characters and events into six or seven. Yet Gaghan did something similarly nonlinear in writing *Traffic,* which won him an Oscar for Best Adapted Screenplay. Likewise *Crash,* crafted by Paul Haggis, goes into such fractal fluidity with Best-Picture lucidity. Perhaps it accomplishes this in part through care to keep all the action in just one city, Los Angeles, whereas *Babel* and *Syriana* hop around the globe. Nonetheless *Crash* shows viewers how the many different neighborhoods of L.A. link in geography, socioeconomic class, and daily business done within the turbulence of racism as a semiconscious cultural system—rather than a singular act or creed. On the other hand, particularly as the primary home for noir, Los Angeles is notorious as "nineteen suburbs in search of a city."[44] So the smooth intelligibility of *Crash* might have other sources too.

Especially celebrated figures from complex, discontinuous systems are butterfly effects. These involve disproportionate consequences at a distance (without mechanical contact). The chaotic canard is that meteorology is nonlinear, so that a butterfly flapping its wings in Brazil can induce a tornado in Texas. The jump in magnitudes can go the other way as well, of course, with superintegrated systems dampening huge happenings into seemingly insignificant results right next door. Notice, too, the self-similarity of figures: both the butterfly flapping its wings and the tornado spinning its destruction are tropes of wind turbulence, notwithstanding their vast differences in magnitude. Thus the figural logic of self-similarity dominates *The Butterfly Effect,* a time-travel noir from 2004, and its sequels (2006, 2009).

Likely butterfly effects appear throughout *Babel.* Thus a Japanese woman's suicide might prompt a Japanese man's hunting trip (or vice versa). It results in a gift gun left in Morocco that falls into the hands of children, inducing a semi-accidental bus ambush of Americans, even as this international incident helps through coincidence to strand American children overnight in a desert where they—unlike the Moroccan boys—are not at all at home, thereby inducing the deportation from America of a Mexican woman (Adriana Barraza), at more or less the same time that the deaf daughter (Rinko Kikuchi) of the Japanese man (Kôji Yakusho) and woman might start to find places for herself in adult life. "Consequences" extend outward but also backward, downward, upward, and otherwise. They spread erratically, jumping intermediate moments, places, and people in *Babel.* They violate and disorder the linear, modern, historical causality familiar to us from earlier, nonfractal films. Nevertheless they do cohere as sensitive-dependence in a complex system of erratic, spotty globalization construed as interdependence through-and-through.

Babel takes globalization to displace, dislocate us. As a chaotic system, its globalization coheres importantly through self-similarities. Recurring figures of dislocation and alienation fill the film. The Japanese man has been in Morocco hunting—rather than at home, where he could be helping his daughter (or, earlier, his wife?). The American couple played by Kate Blanchett and Brad Pitt are touring Morocco rather than caring in person for their children, but then they seem to leave much of this care to the displaced Mexican nanny. In *Babel*, people get stuck out of place: the American couple becomes stranded in the Moroccan village, the Japanese girl is a fish out of water in late-teen traps of self-humiliating sexuality. The gift gun meanders into the hands of Moroccan boys not ready for the responsibility that must discipline its power. The unplanned absence of the adult Americans keeps the Mexican nanny from her son's wedding until she drags the American children with her, eventually abandoning them on foot in a desert where she leaves them desperately alone to seek help. The Japanese girl throws herself sexually and pathetically at men not fit for her, then gets ready to throw herself from the high-rise balcony of her family's apartment home. These motifs of displacement give effective meanings to the film; they make it cohere for us viewers.

Feedback loops arise at least momentarily in some of the whirls and eddies that make flows turbulent. Until the end, the Japanese girl flounders in a negative feedback loop of self-exertion unto self-humiliation as she throws her body around an increasingly globalized Tokyo. Just about everything she does to escape travails makes them causally but also coincidentally worse. The American family suffers from a similar loop of negative feedback. Noir films often configure their conventional plot loops in comparably negative, fateful-unto-fatalistic modes. Chaotically, however, positive feedback loops can form too. That is how neo noirs sometimes provide for surprisingly successful resistance, even escape or liberation, in the end. *Babel* is not big on positive feedback loops, but it at least lets us hope in the end that one is starting for the Japanese girl. *Looper* (2012) "literalizes" and "linearizes" its feedback loops into time travels; yet its swirls and eddies, too, are both tragic and hopeful.

Entry and departure points for feedback loops are the cusps that chaos theory traces at the strangely elusive boundaries of phases. Learning to induce phase changes, we turn cusps into tipping points: in figural effect, turning turbulence into leverage. *Babel* displays cusps and phase changes: the Japanese girl seems to turn more than momentarily away from suicide, the Mexican nanny cannot return to work in the United States, and the Moroccan boys must leave home for a long and potentially consequential time. *Babel* does not encourage much sense that people are leveraging their situations effectively in the manner of modern action, where plans plot lines of conduct and where disciplines move people reliably and continuously along those tracks. That is why Denby and Scott see *Babel* as fatalistic. Yet *Babel* does not disable action altogether; it disrupts the pieties and pat expectations of linear politics in favor of trying to fathom the complexities of action within nonlinear systems. With erratic but crucial help from Moroccans, the Americans recover enough to return home to children somehow (from undue, arbitrary contrivance by the light of linear standards) recovered from the Mexican desert. Dynamics of sheer coincidence or, more likely, complex systematicity return the Japanese father home in time to help his daughter draw herself back from the brink. All the action in *Babel* is not fated to misfire, prove futile, or turn into magical wish-fulfillment. Yet the sensitive interdependence, the sheer systematicity, of globalization according to *Babel* yields a film full of linear coincidence rather than causality.

Additional tropes of chaos can be sought fruitfully in fractal films. Arguably there are cinematic equivalents of undertows, overflows, strange attractors, even the strange networks that Deleuze and Guattari term "rhizomes" and the strange actors they name "nomads," who live without settled homes in nonmodern conditions.[45] These would need ample definitions if we were to search *Babel* or any other film for them. Let us risk supposing, though, that we have now surveyed enough nonlinear figures to evidence how *Babel* might cohere chaotically. Then we can return in the end to the critics' question of whether the penchant of fractal films for over-the-top effects and hyperactive aesthetics tend to leave them deficient as political cinema.

Hyperactive Aesthetics?

Critics of "The New Disorder" complain that "Some of the directors may be just playing with us or, perhaps, acting out their boredom with that Hollywood script-conference menace of the conventional 'story arc.'" Still the recognition is that "others may be trying to jolt us into a new understanding of art, or even a new understanding of life."[46] Yes, I would say, and the new understandings are largely nonlinear. That is why mosaic movies, time travels, neo noirs, and even conspiracy thrillers can provide effective rhetorics for political action in times postmodern unto postwestern.

The critics complain that newly disordering movies are rife with confusion and arbitrary contrivance rather than meaningful art. They allege four bad consequences. Nonlinear cinema supposedly produces undue reliance on a chaos that induces incoherence and consternation for viewers. It purportedly relies on improbable coincidence that serves directorial caprice and the perverse manipulation of viewers. It apparently induces fatalism that promotes cynicism and despair by viewers. And it tends to replace concerted action with merest wish-fulfillment that favors fantasy (over reality) and irresponsibility (over duty).

From the perspectives of critics, the new disorder in popular movies arises from a family of deficiencies that incapacitate viewers for knowledge, judgment, and action. The indictment has it that fractal films, as I suggest we call them, suffer from aesthetic hyperactivity. They are "full of sound and fury, signifying nothing." Their "blooming, buzzing confusion" cultivates viewer incomprehension unto incomprehensibility. In turn, this promotes a pervasive laziness at once intellectual, moral, and political. Unable to motivate action, these chaotic films induce a disposition toward passivity. And even when there is some capacity for inspiration, these films lack the connections literal, coherent, and specific enough to direct action in any particular and potentially effective fashion. The aesthetic hyperactivity is evident in fractal narratives, visuals, and soundtracks.

Hyperstories

Movies are not just dramas or stories communicated by celluloid or, increasingly, digital media. Nonetheless most popular films do enact narratives.[47] Documentaries and war movies, at least of late, tend to make arguments—but still not to the exclusion of storytelling. Thus the hyperactive aesthetics of many fractal films encompass their narratives. The cinematic tales that fail linear tests of consistency still use narrative figures to cohere fractally.

Denby's "clogged-sink narratives," where the flows of cinematic stories become partly occluded and strikingly turbulent, operate through a seeming overabundance of distinct stories that resolve somewhat in the end into a whole that can range from epic to oneiric to ragged. Stephen Gaghan's scripts for *Traffic* and *Syriana* aspire in unmistakable ways to trace America's drug war and oil politics, respectively, as nonlinear systems that entrap countries throughout the world. The intricate showers of distinct stories let similar flows in the different (sub)plots for a fractal film configure a coherent narrative overall as much by repeating turns of events for largely separate levels and characters as by showing a few strategic intersections among them.

For narratives that seem to overflow with distinct stories that overlap only a little, the possibility remains of reconstruction into a host of largely separate but individually continuous "storylines." We can, in other words, reassemble what we see and hear into linear terms—even if it means representing a fractally unified film as though it were four or five or more separable (but linear) movies. Apparently the Wachowskis and Tom Tykwer more or less reversed this process in turning David Mitchell's *Cloud Atlas* into a fractal film (2012).[48]

Other fractal films defy ready reconstruction in linear terms by juxtaposing fragments of stories that purposely puzzle viewers, mislead literalists, and frustrate efforts at linear interpretations. Again the fragments cohere by echoing or ironizing each other in plots, as well as by sharing visual icons, ideational themes, musical motifs, and further figures repeated on various levels of exposition and experience throughout the individual film. The dreams and hallucinations of *Mullholland Dr.* propagate such a hyperactive narrative. The perspectivism of *Slipstream* (2007) also strives to apprehend Hollywood through hypernarrative, but without the noir aesthetics so entrancing to David Lynch. The four "previews" and two "feature-length films" that comprise *Grindhouse* (2007) also offer a similarly overloaded and turbulent narrative for that cleverly chaotic movie mainly from Robert Rodriguez and Quentin Tarantino.[49]

Fractal films that feature time travels or what we could call psycho-logics use abrupt leaps in time, space, and character to foil linear chronologies. These films confuse viewers who insist on trying to make linear sense of them, but they engage and inform viewers who explore their chaotic flows of figures to appreciate nonlinear meanings in them. *Jacob's Ladder* (1990) taps drug-induced hallucinations and speculative psychodynamics of dying to indict perverse logics of the national-security state. *Conspiracy Theory* (1997) does something similar as a neo-noir conspiracy thriller. *Dark City* (1998) turns lucid dreaming into reality reconstruction in a jagged noir-scifi narrative of existentialist liberation. *Memento* turns time every which way but loose in a noir experiment that shows disabling short-term memory as a route to Nietzschean politics of the *Übermensch*. *Vanilla Sky* (2000) uses lucid dreaming and psychodynamics of dying to engage postmodern issues of personal identity. *The Number 23* (2007) has obsessive, literarily induced visions do something comparable, also through noir. Taking advantage of similarities between time travels and psychotic symptoms such as hallucination and hearing voices, *The Jacket* (2005) addresses mortal remorse from recent war. Inviting viewers to mistake psychodynamics of dying for time travels, *Donnie Darko* (2001) explores existentialist concerns of guilt and regret. *Stay* (2005) does much the same with fragmentary, turbulent psycho-narratives from dying. *Eternal Sunshine of the Spotless Mind* invokes the selective elimination of memories to plumb related existentialist motifs of (be)longing. Dreaming and photomosaics enable a neo-noir *Femme Fatale* to scramble toward personal escape from systematic troubles of celebrity cultures. All these narratives jump repeatedly, even relentlessly to confound linear patterning. Moreover all offer the viewing pleasures of an exciting provocation to intense attention, along with an enjoyable instruction through informing and exercising our (sometimes nascent) nonlinear sensibilities.

A common complaint is the reliance of fractal narratives on what linear logics reckon as mere coincidences. For critics, the risk (and often the result) is a risible sense of implausibility. From linear perspectives, these coincidences are plot lapses, discontinuities, turbulences. There are postmodern novels that treat figures of chance, luck, coincidence, contrivance, randomness, and such as echoing tropes that define the strange consistencies of nonlinear lives.[50] To cram a film full of mere coincidences of linear kinds is a similar device for narratives in fractal films.[51] From sheer coincidences, they evoke subtle systematicities. The loose trilogy of films written by Guillermo Arriaga and directed by Alejandro González Iñárritu enrage some commentators and entrance others with this fractal form in *Amores perros* (2000), *21 Grams,* and *Babel. The Burning Plain* (2008) from Arriaga is similar. In a comedic and satirical epic like *Love Actually,* where the tone is far lighter and less "realistic" in historical senses, the proliferation of linear coincidences offends fewer viewers but works in similar ways.

The seemingly incomplete contrivance of loose "ends" that elude the usual linear duties of neatly tied endings can be a comparable device for fractal narratives in films. Unconnected fragments of narrative dangle alone, lacking linear causes or consequences in some fractal films. For the critics, this is failed art: poor form rather than different form. Unresolved skeins of plot leave viewers hanging for no good reason or lose viewers in confusion and frustration. For the critics, that is bad politics: careless or high-handed narrative rather than nonhistorical drama that fails to clarify, motivate, and direct action. But instead it can spur un(pre)scripted innovation. And for some of us, fractal films such as *Donnie Darko, Stay, The Sweet Hereafter* (1997), and *eXistenZ* (1999) deploy loose ends as nonlinear configurations that belie these criticisms. The same might be said for merely imposed, pointedly arbitrary "resolutions" that fail to persuade and thus resolve their films in plausibly linear terms.[52] Examples might include *Déjà Vu, A Scanner Darkly* (2006), and *Suspect Zero* (2004).

Other narrative devices in fractal films function in similarly disordering fashion. At the level of characters, blatantly arbitrary or absent motives stymie linear viewers with persons who seem simply jerked around: puppeteered in unexplained and incomprehensible ways. Even as a conspiracy thriller, David Cronenberg's *Videodrome* (1983) gets accused of this; as something of a psycho noir, so does *The Number 23.* Yet such apparently arbitrary puppeteering is virtually a convention of movies about sinister systems that initially include unaware protagonists in the systematic corruption. For related reasons, some commentators dislike protagonists too ambivalent and ambiguous for viewers to identify with them.

But this strikes me as an effective strategy in such fractal films as *Exotica* (1994), *Swordfish* (2001), *Where the Truth Lies* (2005), and *The Prestige* (2006).

Hypersights

At a cinematic intersection of stories and sights is the frenetic pace achieved with rapid cuts, narrative elisions, hand-cranked cameras, and other devices familiar in many fractal films. Not all fractal films pursue a jagged, breathless sense of speed. But when they do, critics worry that this enervates, even stuns, viewers rather than energizing, informing, or entertaining them. Four late films directed by Tony Scott all provoke complaints that their hyperkinetic styles are superficial, self-indulgent, a little silly, and mostly overwrought. Each is a neo noir that I and at least some other viewers see by contrast as powerfully intelligent and artistic. *Spy Game* (2001) indicts covert U.S. action from the Vietnam War onward as a perfidious system. *Man on Fire* (2004) shows eerily self-similar violence now spreading systematically into everyday lives in Central and South America. *Domino* (2005) offers a feminist examination of hyperviolence emerging likewise into everyday lives in North America. And *Déjà Vu* takes on the "War on Terror"—conceived as a self-sustaining yet self-defeating system in need of nonlinear correction or, failing that, peculiar combinations of collaboration and resistance.

These films generate sneers for their experiments with captions that move, dissolve, weep, shift or juxtapose fonts, meld into their scenes, and so on.[53] They join neo noirs like *Fallen* (1997) in supervening the black-and-white cinematographies of chiaroscuro in classical noir with antirealistic, superstylized colors and visual textures. The complaint is that these turn images cartoonish. The same gets said of erratically flowing shifts of speed or timing for the actions in films that feature hand-cranked cameras or their vague equivalents courtesy of digital editing. Yet Disney, Pixar, and anime films show on occasion that there can be great, engaging beauty and further meaning in cartoon action. Well, maybe *some* beauty, critics acknowledge; but strictly *surface* beauty that mesmerizes viewers and conceals emptiness, lack of depth, passivity, and similar sins. If nothing else, fractal films from Tony Scott and Robert Rodriguez bother some critics with a visual busyness that crowds the screen and threatens to overwhelm viewers, disabling their capacities for reflection and action, if not always comprehension.

Especially for fractal films, the critical concern has been that hyperkinetic cameras and cuts replace real significance with sheer rush. Many thrillers these days seek hyper modes of action, and this sometimes prompts their critical condemnation as superficial entertainments. Yet the widespread appreciation for recent films from Paul Greengrass makes clear that there can be trenchant significance in hyperkinetic movies. None of these—*The Bourne Supremacy* (2004), *United 93* (2006), *The Bourne Ultimatum* (2007), or *The Green Zone* (2010)—strikes me as a fractal film, although Greengrass relies a lot on flashbacks in the Bourne films. They indicate even so that hyperactive visuals need not discombobulate or alienate viewers. When commentators allege that fractal films proliferate fast, jazzy, attention-grabbing cuts for their own sake and that these distract viewers, we know from largely linear thrillers—let alone fractal films—that 'tain't necessarily so. The same goes for exotic cameras that supposedly unsettle or hyperstimulate viewers by estranging angles of vision, erratic movements, fantastic distortions, and hosts of computer graphics.

As with visual icons that help coordinate some fractal films through recurrent figures, such as *The Number 23* in the film of that name, the argument is that other visual dynamics of linear incoherence can cohere for us fractally. Big egos are not hard to find in Hollywood and other precincts of popular cinema. So it is not surprising that some critics see fractal visuals as devolving into overstylized looks that feed the egos of filmmakers rather than the experiences of viewers. This can happen, of course. But big imaginations are prominent also in filmmaking; and the visuals that resist linear, literal parsing sometimes make insightful political sense when apprehended as nonlinear figures.

Hypersounds

Much the same can be said of the aural devices familiar in fractal films. To some, myself included on occasion, the soundtracks in fractal films can seem overwrought. The worry is that they pummel then numb listeners. (But scores by Philip Glass repeatedly do this for nonfractal films too.) A different take on these experiences is that they favor postmodern immersion in tribal beats and operatic swells that help carry audiences into virtual worlds of chaotic cinema that otherwise might stay off-putting. Such music helps *The Tree of Life* (2011) achieve much of its power as a mosaic and epic movie. *Magnolia* gets faulted for musical contrivances that reach way beyond what we have ordinarily accepted from popular films, even though we might do better to recognize a growing number of—chaotic?—crossings or eradications of boundaries formerly respected between "musicals" and "dramas." When focal characters in their different settings break simultaneously into the same song, one that laments their sad lots and surrenders their former hopes so truly and completely that it somehow transcends fatalism, we can decry the cinematic moment as a preposterous, over-the-top, ham-handed abandonment of canons for dramatic credibility.[54] And that can make good linear sense. Fractally, by contrast, we may embrace the musical moment as sublime epiphany, taking us over a dramatic cusp into a different phase of human endeavor and experience from ultramodern follies. For this is how I hear it.

Related complaints are that fractal films offer over-busy soundtracks that distract by shifting tones too often and arbitrarily: Tony Scott's recent movies elicit that response from friends of mine who struggle with their scores, even though I admire them immensely. Maybe my ears are just more attuned than theirs to music by Harry Gregson-Williams. An oldster like me might be especially ready to recognize in the near-cacophony of soundtracks for popular teen flicks that film music also could be getting more disordering and overwhelming for emerging generations. Might this induce a greater receptivity to fractal films? Or might it work the other way around? The chaotic answer, of course, is "both."

There are dialogic concomitants. Fractal films sometimes favor overdelivered dialogue that irritates listeners with declarations too formal in language and in voicing for everyday lives these days. Think of the Shakespearean language in *Deadwood* (2004–2006). Or compare the epic formality of pronouncements (and even bodily movements) throughout the David Lynch version of *Dune* (1984): the talk and the gestures are stiff, posed, didactic, declamatory, and the like. *Grindhouse* goes there for a few passages, presumably in part to satirize conventions of dialogue from its subgenres of horror. Fractal films show even more interest so far in the overlapping delivery of dialogue made notorious and poetic by Robert Altman's movies. For linear, modern listeners, it is cacophony; for nonlinear, postmodern ears, it can be music. Films from Quentin Tarantino and Robert Rodriguez do not favor this as much as clever speeches, but they insistently include moments of it. Likewise fractal films from Tony Scott, Paul Thomas Anderson, and Michael Mann, at least in *Miami Vice* (2006), make good use of wild yet clever aural match-cuts that skirt epic formalism on one side and postmodern chaos on another.

Quick Codas

Because they often leave loose ends, fractal films also like to complicate their conclusions with quick codas. The action is done; yet the film then ends with another scene or two, typically from later times and larger perspectives. Thus these stand somewhat apart from the film's body and twist it a tad. A striking example is the coda for *Places in the Heart*. The camera pans pews in the community church. Gradually it shows all the film's notable characters abiding together, those still living along with those dead by the end of the action. Hence it can shift our sense of the whole film from linear history to nonlinear epic. What we had experienced as a chronology of events turns in the concluding perspective to moments and emblems of the community: the title's "places in the heart." The coda for *Cloud Atlas* tries in a somewhat similar way to link the film's narratives and clarify its nonlinear logics. Then the closing credits do much the same with the movie's focal actors and characters.

The *Swordfish* coda shows its ambiguous system boss escaping by boat to become a rogue avenger of terrorism similar to his own terrorism in the film, and this can reshape our conceptions of what has occurred. After the action, *Domino* uses a concluding legend to let us know that Domino Harvey, the historical inspiration for its title character, died young as the film finished production. Working like a quick coda, this fractal addition can adjust meanings throughout the film. *Sin City* (2005) introduces as well as concludes its other fractals by bracketing them with somewhat emblematic scenes of "The Man," a contract killer who serves as fixer for its corrupt system; and this, too, functions as a quick coda to focus or even twist the film's significance.

Let us follow suit. In coda, more than routine conclusion, it is worth remarking (off to the side of our main scenes for analysis and argument) that the candidates for fractal films come overwhelmingly at this point from the twenty-first century. Only a few models or provocations—more than actual anticipations, perhaps tellingly—come earlier. And most of those date from the 1990s. Directed by Adrian Lyne, *Jacob's Ladder* appeared in 1990. In 1994, Atom Egoyan did *Exotica*, and Quentin Tarantino released *Pulp Fiction*. Egoyan followed in 1997 with *The Sweet Hereafter*, joined that year by David Lynch's *Lost Highway*. Then Alex Proyas added *Dark City* in 1998. All the other "fully" fractal films identified in these pages arrive from 2000 onward.

Popular genres seldom limit themselves to a single medium. Comparably chaotic tropes and pleasures proliferate lately in martial video games, musical scratching, video mash-ups, the vignettes colliding in fan blogs, and the pictures or videos collaging in photo blogs. Such media join cinema in taking advantage of digital electronics in general and, increasingly, the Internet in particular to craft nonlinear, chaotic forms. Along with fractal films, they find forms that can accommodate the "mess" emerging in our simultaneously, chaotically late-modern, postmodern, and postwestern lives. Let these fractal forms do no less for our persistently emerging politics of systems, movements, styles, and more.

PART TWO
POLITICAL EXPERIENCES

CHAPTER 5

EMOTION AND EMPATHY

FROM SINS AND PAINS TO BODIES AND DEEDS IN HORROR MOVIES (FEATURING THE PASSION OF THE CHRIST AND SE7EN)

This is the most violent film I have ever seen.[1]

—Roger Ebert

There are many ways of putting Jesus at risk and making us feel his suffering.[2]

—David Denby

Notwithstanding some astounding success for Michael Moore's *Fahrenheit 9/11,* the cinematic phenomenon of 2004 remains *The Passion of the Christ.*[3] Mel Gibson's reactionary view of the trial, torture, crucifixion, and resurrection of Jesus generated acclaim and controversy worldwide.[4] It is the anomalous blockbuster that resounds with religious as well as political implications. *Newsweek* criticized it in detail over five different issues.[5] The principal reviewer of films for the *New Yorker* took the rare step of condemning it with careful respect not once but twice.[6] The movie made a mint for Gibson.[7] It challenged the Hollywood aversion to religion as a theme for cinema.[8] And it sparked again the smoldering discontent with graphic violence in popular movies.

The veteran reviewer for *Newsweek,* David Ansen, complained that "*The Passion* plays like the Gospel according to the Marquis de Sade."[9] Roger Ebert reported that

"*The Passion of the Christ* is 126 minutes long, and" he guessed "that at least 100 of those minutes, maybe more, are concerned specifically and graphically with the details of the torture and death of Jesus." He warned that "you must be prepared for whippings, flayings, beatings, the crunch of bones, the agony of screams, the cruelty of the sadistic centurions, the rivulets of blood that crisscross every inch of Jesus' body." This, wrote Ebert, "works powerfully for those who can endure it."[10] As another reviewer added in the film's defense, "Gibson's premise is simple: the brutality is needed to remind mankind of the nature of Christ's sacrifice. Under that principle, anything is fair game." Yet "even when he is manipulative," argued this last reviewer, "Gibson pulls all the right strings on his audience."[11]

Well, we needn't go that far. Nearly inevitable, the backlash had begun by that year's September release of the DVD.[12] Even from a first viewing, the film's music by John Debney has struck me as moving at some moments—but more often as heavy-handed and intrusive. At times, it becomes nearly as overbearing as the notoriously distracting score that composer Philip Glass (and director Stephen Daldry) inflicted on *The Hours* (2002). Gibson's reliance on Aramaic, Latin, and subtitles is more peculiar than persuasive or poetic.[13] As cinema, the Gibson movie gains in some ways but loses in others from the sheer familiarity of its story. In places, such as the early action at the Garden of Gethsemane, the *mise-en-scène* is murky or unimaginative. ("At first," observes critic David Denby, "the movie looks like a graveyard horror flick."[14]) To take issue with these or other features of the film can be more than to pick at nits.

On the whole, though, *The Passion of the Christ* may be welcomed as an intriguing effort to help humankind experience the significance of its own sin. It would short-circuit human insensibilities. It would awaken us to the suffering we inflict on others or even ourselves. And along the way, it would teach us again how movies spur empathy to move us into political action.

Christianity teaches that Jesus takes upon Himself the harrowing pain of human evils—high and low, large and small, relentless and literally excruciating. The Gibson film would help us feel this superhuman sacrifice, empathize with this terrible pain. It would do so in the service of ethical action to minimize sin and mitigate suffering. Sense the awful harm of our sin, and sin less: that is the strategy evident in Gibson's film. For all the furor about feeding anti-Semitism and patriarchy that publicized the film so effectively, it bears better comparison to other recent movies that tap graphic violence to mobilize a personal sense of moral responsibility for our everyday conduct.[15] By this take, *The Passion of the Christ* benefits from assessment alongside *Se7en* (1996), directed by David Fincher.

The Sensing of Sin

By genre, of course, *The Passion of the Christ* is a passion play. This is a medieval form that dramatizes the arrest, trial, torment, crucifixion, burial, and resurrection of Jesus. Its generic ambition is to help us sinners know the sacrifice of Jesus in dying for our sins. Christianity emphasizes the human suffering of Jesus as a man, taking upon Himself the evils of the world. Gibson's film seeks this personal knowledge of divine sacrifice through an individual experience of physical pain, hellish bodily torment. To help us humans sense this body in pain, it gives us skin torn to tatters; palms flattened and pierced by spikes; muscles twisted, slashed, and mangled; blood that runs and pools onto unyielding stones. It closes on the forehead ripped by the crown of thorns. It dwells on the face spewed with gobs of spit. It shows the chest pummeled and stung by jagged rocks. It turns insistently toward the back flayed then crushed and raked by the unbearable cross. It watches the legs bludgeoned and twitching, the feet scraped and deformed. The film has us see this nearly unbelievable brutality, not in glimpses, but in sustained shots of gore. It has us hear the related hate and torment in cascading cries of abuse, agony, and lament. Whatever the fidelity to history or Gospel, the Gibson film shows an unspeakable violation of dignity, morality, and mentality—yet most insistently of body.[16]

The aspiration to empathy, in *feeling with or as others,* differs from sympathy as *feeling for others.*[17] The Christian teaching is not merely that Jesus sympathizes with humans in their fallen state of sin and suffering. It is rather that Jesus is one with God *and* humanity. In dying, Jesus takes upon Himself our sins: to know us at our worst and to forgive us when we repent of evils. In those last hours, leading to and beyond the cross, Jesus feels our harm as His pain. The passion play celebrates this sacrifice as incomprehensible yet also, somehow, communicates it.

Across the absolute abyss between God and us as human, all too human, the passion play strives to make the sacrifice of Jesus—as the necessary suffering of each and every sin—not just memorable for us but tangible, tastable, actionable. To do this, the Gibson film displays a body under fierce, unremitting assault. One way to think of this, explains Denby, is that it calls on our continuing capacity to conflate cinema with reality:

> A train chugs into a station, and the audience screams in terror and ducks under the seats. It is 1895, everyone's favorite moment in film history—the time of naïveté when the cinema was born. The audience that turned up for the Lumière brothers' pioneering exhibition, in Paris, was not yet comfortable with

the idea of illusion. The image onscreen was not just a picture of something real; it was reality itself. That idea hasn't quite faded: to some degree, many of us still believe that the cinema has a scandalously intimate connection with life. After all, movies are a photographical medium in which figures tread across the screen in what appears to be real time; the dominating impression that *this is real* is a large part of the primitive power of the art form. If the notion weren't still alive, the culturally advanced wouldn't be at such pains to assert the contrary—that the cinema is always some form of illusion, that "realism" is itself no more than a single style among many. One of the startling things about the response to Mel Gibson's *The Passion of the Christ* is the way the movie burns through this kind of sophistication and reaffirms, for better and for worse, the primordial sway of the image: the people who love the movie, bound by belief, give themselves over to the ecstasy of the real. There it is onscreen: every blow, every step up to Golgotha, right there in front of us. It happened.[18]

"*The Passion*," Denby writes, "is junk, but at least it's not trivial, cynical junk in the usual style of postmodernist pop—the gleeful rooting around in the scrap heap of discarded illusion, Kill Bill-ism for nonbelievers. No, *The Passion* is medievalist junk, a literal, blood-and-bone rendering of agony and death, and, for the audience coming to it with the right emotional wiring, seeing is believing."[19]

It is odd to treat the middle ages as signally literal-minded, but it is not odd to see the approach of *The Passion* as a bodily equivalent. The politics of bodily display are fully figural. As Robert Hariman shows, they incline toward the courtly and thus, we might say by extension, toward the medieval.[20] In promising comprehensive corporal punishment, Marcellus Wallace, the gang boss played flamboyantly by Ving Rhames in *Pulp Fiction* (1994), declares memorably that "I'm gonna git Medieval on your ass." To violate the Christ's whole holy body— part by visible part, with every corporeal element given symbolical significance, taken apart and so defiled most definably for us—suits politically the Christian appreciation of Jesus as the King of Kings.

To suggest bodily lessons for each terrible step on this tortuous path is to court the same politics of medievalism pursued by *Se7en*. The name evokes the seven deadly sins at the dark heart of medieval Christianity. The film may have been the single most influential movie of the 1990s when it comes to political aesthetics. Aspects of *Se7en*'s plot, with cryptically connected acts moving step by step to larger, possibly astonishing lessons, seem to have been appropriated by films as various as *8 MM* (2000), *Fallen* (1998), *15 Minutes* (2001), *Pay It Forward* (2000), even *Unbreakable* (2000). Yet the features of *Se7en*'s look and sound have been imitated even more widely and effectively: scratchy frames of jumpy, flickering film in seeming deterioration from earlier technology somehow mismatched to current equipment; the graphic grunge of shut-ins consigned to stink and clutter their closed places with various forms of animal, vegetable, mineral, and moral filth; the aural grunge of chants, by nine inch nails in the case of *Se7en*, replete with an electronic repertoire of sounds such as the scratching that slides needles over the grooves in phonograph records; especially the images of light overwhelmed by darkness, with dim beams from flashlights probing bleak houses or blacker closets. In this way, *The Passion*'s beginning murk in the Garden of Gethsemane echoes the nearly impenetrable gloom of *Se7en*'s opening, where flashlight beams try with little success to illuminate dark interiors.

In *Se7en*, these devices rev, twist, and adapt elements from earlier aesthetics of horror for latter-day sophistics of neo noir. Likewise they seek to update and aggravate medieval sensibilities of sin to fit them for atrocities mundane in our postmodern settings. The project in *Se7en*, as in *The Passion*, is to provoke in postmodern viewers something akin to a medieval recognition of mortal sin in everyday deeds. Unless we feel the violence in every fiber, how can we repent and resist it? In postmodern apathy, *Se7en* insists, we currently tolerate, even cultivate, practices for which medieval Christians knew we humans deserve to die—and suffer eternal damnation. The challenge is to help us jaded, worldly viewers sense how daily gluttony, greed, anger, and all the rest are now destroying our souls. *Se7en*'s strategy is to give us momentary glimpses of bodies, one appalling part after another, in startling extremes of distortion and torment. To make the sin as bodily and visibly violent as possible on the big screen is to venture postmodern recuperation of a medieval device. *Se7en* is high-concept horror and noir with graphics to match. Returning in much the same spirit of gloomy rampage to its own medieval genre, *The Passion* is a similar descent into horror.

For most viewers, *Se7en* manages suspense and surprise denied to *The Passion*. *Se7en* is a tale of more or less hardboiled detection. Day by day, it relates the week-long investigation of a series of ongoing tortures and murders. When the horrors start coming to light, William Somerset, played by Morgan Freeman, is seven days away from retirement from the homicide squad. He works with his heir-apparent. David Mills (Brad Pitt) is an experienced detective but new to the big city. He has brought his wife Tracy (Gweneth Paltrow) and their dogs to an apartment that turns out to be rattled intermittently by commuter trains. Everything and everybody gets shaken to the core.

The murders form a pattern that comes to encompass Somerset and especially Mills. The pattern is constructed by the perpetrator to provide a wake-up call to the inhabitants of the whole society, and it seems clear that the film intends the same for its viewers. Apathy is the antithesis of empathy; and the denizens of *Se7en*'s city are mired in an apathy—an absence of feeling and passion—so profound that they accept as commonplace or perhaps appropriate the whole roster of sins that medieval Christians could recognize as deadly torment to the soul, let alone the body.[21] Each atrocity in the movie turns a mortal sin back onto an egregious sinner of that kind. But aren't we all? The sins are gluttony, greed, sloth, pride, lust, envy, and wrath. The perpetrator—known only as "John Doe" and enacted with chilling plausibility by Kevin Spacey—leaves clues that function in noir fashion as wake-up calls. They are to alert the police to his overall pattern and the public to the larger lessons it is supposed to provoke.

Mills and Somerset pull out all the stops. They enact most major tropes for noir and many for horror as well. They play hardball by bullying witnesses and cutting legal corners. They tape interrogations. They face reflections. They peer through blinds and frames. They track the beast to his lair, but he eludes them and turns the tables on them. From the very first murder, Somerset foreshadows the film's fateful, fatal conclusion. He even provides a dose of world-weary voiceover. For all Somerset's sagacity, though, the ruthless cunning of John Doe looms greater. He is the perfectionist monster especially available in vampire films, and he runs rings around the two detectives. In the end, Doe makes them into primary audiences for his jeremiad. Worse, they become the principal props for his desert prophecy of damnation. If the civilization does not somehow turn back from its awful acceptance of sin, it will deserve and reproduce the demonstration that John Doe has provided. Or so *Se7en* would sermonize.

Somerset calls Mills a "champion." This little David is the lone knight of justice from hardboiled detection, but he has become the addled knight of justice who tilts at windmills. William keeps trying to tell him that he misconceives the foes, because they are us. In a key scene, the two talk in a bar; and the issue for Mills is whether Somerset still cares enough to contest injustice. Mills is right that Somerset does. But Somerset insists that this is not enough; Mills must wake up to the apathy that corrupts current cities—as consumer societies where people favor cheeseburgers over aiding each other.

Instead Mills targets Doe, who folds Mills into his machinations. When Doe explains his crime spree, in a car on route to the climax, Mills never quite gets it. Doe is doing for society, he says, what Somerset has been trying to do for the naïve Mills: impress on him how people have accepted pervasive, deadly sin as a fact of everyday life. Possibly the worst of the Doe murders is the torture of the slothful man, and sloth is the medieval Christian word for the apathy we all show daily by accepting all seven mortal sins into our latter-day routines. Does

Doe want us as mad as hell, too angry to take it anymore? Not exactly. When his awful climax finally brings home to Mills the systematic sinfulness that surrounds him, we learn that wrath, too, is a cardinal sin.

For all its conventions of noir and horror, *Se7en* maintains a Biblical frame inflected for medieval effect. For the first six days, the city in the film experiences the deluge. The detection proceeds in continual rain. This symbolizes by pathetic strategy that the big city is undergoing a time of terrible troubles.[22] Perhaps it is also suffering the flood that can wash away most of its sin and corruption, at least for a little while. Meanwhile the city is being soaked in blood, gore, and torture by the crimes of John Doe. By Sunday, the culminating day, the rain stops. There is still water standing on the streets, but no more pummels down. The sun shines brightly for the climatic drive by Somerset, Mills, and Doe from the drenched city to a dry prairie or desert that stretches beyond it. There the countryside displays no sand dunes, but the grass is parched and intermittent at most. And there, framed by electrical towers, John Doe delivers the punch line to his prophecy. He is a desert father declaring a plague or foreseeing a purge for the city gone bad.

On his way out of the city, Doe hints at his cryptic plan: bodily symbolism so gruesome that it engages people and makes them ponder his apocalyptic demonstrations of daily sin. Then they will heed his shocking signs and work to repent. Or they will sink irredeemably further into apathy and their sinful sickness unto ultimate death. The routines of civil sophistication leave us numb to the gravity of sin in ourselves and others. To revive morality, we need to feel mortality. We need to know it in our bones. As sinners in the paws of an apathetic life, we must see our everyday peril far more vividly and sense it far more bodily than before. This is the medieval and postmodern exercise in empathy provided cinematically by *Se7en*. That we may likewise feel anew and acutely the gravity of our own sin, *The Passion* turns from the bodily distention and destruction of our neighbors to the bodily violation and resurrection of our Savior.

The Body in Pain

The Passion's enterprise is for us to know our sin and the sacrifice of Jesus by somehow sensing His pain on the path to Golgotha. In *Resisting Representation*, Elaine Scarry extends her work on *The Body in Pain* by analyzing physical suffering as "obdurate sensation" that humans can communicate only in part and with great difficulty.[23] This might seem to make bodily pain or damage unpromising as a trope for symbolizing the awful harm in sin or the incomprehensible sacrifice of Jesus in taking all human harm into Himself, so that it does not instantly destroy the world. We can take Scarry to argue, however, that pharmaceutical companies face a somewhat similar challenge in persuading doctors to prescribe ample amounts of medication to treat pains in their patients.

To market pain medicine effectively to the sufferers themselves, Scarry shows with ads for magazines and television, the companies need only suggest that the medicines alleviate their target pains in swift and sustained ways. This leads, for example, to before-and-after pictures of pain victims: frowning, rubbing, or saying that some part of the body hurts in the first sequence then smiling to announce that the pain has disappeared by the second. Because they experience the pains for themselves, people viewing these appeals need not be persuaded that the suffering is real and urgent, merely that it can be treated effectively by the advertised medicine.

But the physicians called to prescribe some medicines are another matter. Like the rest of us, doctors are supposed to face epistemological troubles in sensing reliably and thus responding adequately to any experience as intrinsically internal and personal as pain. As pharmaceutical companies know, moreover, doctors are especially susceptible to insensitivity for bodily pain on the part of their patients. In order to prosper in their profession, doctors can and often do harden themselves to the suffering of patients. Intentionally or not, typical doctors can inure themselves somewhat to patient feelings and expressions of pain.

Arguably there are several routes to this seminecessary disability.[24] The sensitivity and response of physicians to patient pains decline as doctor experiences of patients in pain become grindingly familiar. Doctors desensitize themselves because they cannot afford psychologically to feel along, empathetically, with their patients. Or doctors may have trouble feeling along with their patients because the doctors have not experienced for themselves many of the same kinds of pain. At a "deeper" level, the modern epistemologist maintains, doctors must face such limits on feeling because they cannot get inside another's suffering. Moreover doctors cannot even read a patient's suffering in many cases from bodily signs, which can be subtle or simply absent. As a result, research by pharmaceutical companies suggests, too many doctors do not empathize or even sympathize adequately with patients in pain. Hence doctors do not prescribe alleviating medicines or other treatments in accordance with the best-practice instructions approved by the medical profession.

This is why medical schools often require training on pain and its treatment, yet epistemic barriers for pain remain between doctors and patients. In consequence, patients suffer more than need be, because doctors underutilize existing resources for ameliorating pain. At any rate, they do not buy as many prescription pain medications as the pharmaceutical companies want to sell. For reasons good as well as bad, presumably, physicians sometimes practice the anti-empathy encompassed in what Robert Jay Lifton has called "psychic numbing."[25]

Likewise for reasons bad as well as good, the drug industry spends hundreds of millions of dollars to elect politicians and lobby officials on patent, insurance, and healthcare provisions. It seeks profits, and this also leads pharmacy companies to spend hundreds of millions of dollars on ads and other devices to promote use unto overuse of specific drugs. So the point is not that strategies of emotional appeal need be noble, but that they struggle in some cases to be effective, and we can learn from similarities in the rhetorics of pathos for *Se7en, The Passion of the Christ,* and ads to sell pain relievers, especially to physicians.

A telling challenge for pharmaceutical companies is to make patient pains clear, legible, or otherwise adequately apprehensible to doctors. Then the doctors can comprehend the needs of their patients for prescription of the pharmaceuticals sold to redress pains. When pharmaceutical companies sell their wares over the counter to consumers, without the intermediation of doctors and prescriptions, ads can devote much more time, space, and creative talent to depicting patient relief (from pains). So these ads show patients active, festive, visibly feeling good. The ads also provide testimonials from people about how dramatically better the medicines have helped them feel. Sometimes the pharmaceutical advertising pursues this path for prescription drugs as well, urging each prospective patient to "ask your doctor about" help from the drug at issue. But when the pharmaceutical companies target the doctors directly, Scarry notices, the persuasive strategy shifts to vivid depictions of pain by discoloring, distending, and otherwise distorting body parts.

Ads for physicians seldom depict whole people as individuals in pain. Instead they twist arms, shatter legs, peel joints, diagram nerves, wither organs, inflate vessels, open skulls, pound hands, pierce feet, shred skin, and so on. In these ads, the hypertrophy of muscles in pain looks like a gallery of close-ups from supervillain photos. As in the Gibson movie, the ads portray individual sites of affliction as physically transformed by torments that induce horrendous pains taken to arise at these sites. To doctors, the ads might show whole faces grimacing in pain; but the ads favor foreheads in flames or kidneys exploding. At times, the ads display entire bodies contorted in pain; but they feature elbows stabbed by knives, temples pounded by hammers, throats purple with infection, or toes swollen seemingly beyond the point of bursting. The logics and aesthetics are those of magical realism, where fantastic events and radical exaggerations convey disorders so deep and potentially devastating that they elude ordinary modes of human communication and comprehension.[26]

Gibson's film implies the plausible principle that even the most devout of Christians can be like the desensitized doctors. How can people imagine, how can they *feel* the terrible evil, the horrible pain of human sin? Gibson's answer—in the form of *The Passion*—is similar to the one that Scarry ascribes to pharmaceutical companies. To display awful bodily wounds in lingering, graphic, sickening detail might work for many viewers. The hope is that a religious experience of graphic injuries to Jesus can spring from overwhelming observational impact of the images.

The dynamic is closely akin to gross-out horror. America's master of that move has been Stephen King.[27] Verbally or visually, he crafts images meant to overwhelm our everyday senses of reality. These horrifying sights and sounds would overpower our ordinary capacities of calm, measured, critical assessment. We flinch and twitch out of the way. We yelp and groan in reply. We feel sick at heart, unsettled in mind. What we see and hear (or think in response) edges into awe. For a moment, at least, it is beyond ugly, beyond beautiful; beyond good and bad; beyond true or false. It is simultaneously subliminal and superliminal, thus sublime.[28] It is at once awful and awesome. It provokes revulsion, wonder, and possibly repentance.

Observes Ansen, "There is real power in Gibson's filmmaking: he knows how to work an audience over." But Ansen's critical concern is that "The dark, queasy strength of the images—artfully shot by Caleb Deschanel—and their duration (the scene in which the Roman soldiers tie Jesus down and torture him goes on endlessly) tends to overwhelm the ostensible message."[29] What this worry misses is that Gibson's movie does not operate mainly in the communicational mode of some articulated "message," ostensible or otherwise. *The Passion* means to overwhelm, by providing experiences of sin that it takes us to resist with most of the modern skills of intellect and articulation available to us.[30] Hyperreality does engage some people, and presumably many in our electronic times, whose apathy or other resistance to attending and feeling along with their neighbors can reach the disturbing levels evoked in films such as *Se7en*.[31]

The resistance to facing our sins can be especially strong, and there is no guarantee of cinematic success through *The Passion*'s devices or any others. Viewers vary. "From a purely dramatic point of view," says Ansen of *The Passion*, "the relentless gore is self-defeating."[32] No doubt that is true for some viewers, whereas others can open themselves to vivid senses of sin only when overwhelmed by hyperreal sights and sounds on the order of *The Passion*. And what works for one or two or three screenings might dull and numb some viewers by a fourth or fifth.

Yet for many, not even acutely realistic pictures are persuasive, let alone empathetic. Abuse photos from the Abu Ghraib prison had poured from televisions and newspapers for days when a survey showed that only a third of Americans would agree that torture had occurred there on the U.S. watch. It is telling that the same survey recorded that four-fifths and more of Americans defined "torture" to include some of the acts dramatically visible in these pictures.[33] Empathy, persuasion, or even the most minimal recognition can be excruciatingly hard to effect at times, especially for (other) bodies in pain.

To witness damage to another's body need not be much the same as feeling damage to your own. The degrees of similarity, kinds of association, and modes of feeling can depend on empathy. Like *Se7en*, Gibson's *Passion* relies on strikingly realistic images and horrendously realistic sounds to give viewers a sense of suffering sins that they usually resist experiencing. The sights and sounds feature bodily tortures. The physical or nervous pains of the body might not be much the same as the moral or mental pains of the soul. Still this is the connection that Gibson pursues. Aesthetically it is a familiar move in western civilization, possibly effective for many Christians and others. The same goes for the further resonances between physical and spiritual pain. To mobilize our emotions as viewers, Gibson's film packs its pictures with gore as graphic bodily passion.[34]

The torment extends to the soundtrack. It vocalizes pain in bodily, inarticulate sounds. It also turns the voices toward sounds purged of meanings that are not emotional. The Jews speak in Aramaic, and the Romans in Latin, so the audience hears passions rather than words. (It sees subtitles for the words in its own language.) The aural dynamics of Gibson's *Passion* are more or less operatic. As Stanley Cavell says, the words sung in opera become "passionate speech."[35] Attention shifts from logos to pathos. The film's effort is to make our virtual experience of Jesus suffering *our* sins (and not just *for* our sins) as full-bodied as cinema permits. Like *Se7en*, *The Passion* aims for empathy.

The Movement to Act

Empathy, like sympathy, can move us into ethical action. David Hume, Adam Smith, and other figures of the Scottish Enlightenment held that humans have a faculty of sympathy to inform good judgments of value.[36] The argument is that human reason requires a decent sense of any situation to judge it accurately, and sympathy is the capacity of imagination that can bring the situations of others adequately before the calm and measuring eye of rationality. Then Gibson's *Passion* and Fincher's *Se7en* recognize that sympathy is seldom enough for decent judgment of conditions beyond our ken: beyond the scope of what the Scottish Enlightenment called our common sense, especially when we resist looking into the face of what we dread as strange and terrifying.[37]

These films also anticipate the lapse of ethical action through what ancient Greeks called *akrasia* (weakness of will) and other accounts of acting against our better, rational judgment.[38] Such commonplace difficulties get radicalized by the dread and other resistance in settings faced by *Se7en* and *The Passion,* even when overwhelming images can correct for ordinary incapacities of judgment. Again in these extreme circumstances, the reasonable expectation is that sympathy is not enough to induce appropriate action. Again the need is for empathy. Chapter 7 returns to all three modes of cinematic experience evoked in this chapter, for it traces how recent war movies use such experiences as evidence to advance arguments. But here, the emphasis is on how *The Passion* and *Se7en* use vicarious but also symbolical and virtual experiences to stoke empathy that can move us into ethical action, particularly when sympathy is not apt or sufficient.

To inform judgment and energize will in settings beyond our usual horizons, Gibson's *Passion* joins Fincher's *Se7en* in pursuing the fuller-bodied experiences that can induce empathy. Thus the two share a cinematic strategy. Both move viewers through the vicarious experiences where key characters show us how to respond to screen worlds. These are sort of experiences familiar from many discussions of cinema and literature. Both films also move viewers through symbolical experiences. Those engage viewers in the exploration of associative networks of mythic connections evoked by especially striking emblems, icons, tunes, and the like. To assault us with the stench of a slothful man, whose body still lives but in a condition of advanced decay, *Se7en* shows him to us only after marching its detectives through a symbolical forest of Christmas-tree air fresheners that hang from the ceiling of the tortured man's apartment. Similarly *The Passion* focuses so grimly and relentlessly on the crude and heavy cross borne by Jesus that it seems bound to inflect viewer senses of the Christian crucifix. But more than that, both films rely strongly on the distinctive resources of virtual experiences that use subjective cameras and surround sounds to put viewers themselves into the midst of the action.[39]

In these and several other films in recent decades, much of the action is violence. It violates and harms. Or to borrow a more telling word from Anthony Burgess in *A Clockwork Orange* (1971), what we encounter in *Se7en* and *The Passion of the Christ* is "ultraviolence," which damages people way past any modern, instrumental justification for the act itself.[40] Yet in *The Passion* and *Se7en,* there is a moral and political justification not for doing but for *showing* each act of ultraviolence. The justification is that only artful, powerful, in-our-face acts of ultraviolence provide a decent likelihood of overcoming our resistance to empathizing with the victim—and thus experiencing enough of the harm to comprehend a horrendous violation that we might have urgent moral and political reasons to stop, repair, prevent, or take other responsibility for. Simply to declare the ultraviolence in such movies excessive, let alone gratuitous, is to miss this.

The complaints against extremes of graphic violence in cinema are many and troubling. Ultraviolence desensitizes viewers to violence, leaving them less able to sense its harm and pain. It promotes mindless imitation: monkey see, monkey do. It distorts motives and impacts. It caricatures victims and villains. It provides perverse parts to play and foolish lines to say: "Bring 'em on!" and "Make my day!" It cultivates prurient enjoyment of awful harm. It sensationalizes film deeds and characters to the point of devaluing everyday events and human individuals. The criticisms vary in their circumstances of relevance and in their merits. Therefore the debates over them seem enduring, but none are frivolous.[41]

Yet there is a paradox. Exactly where complaints against movie violence are warranted, they can justify some ultraviolence in cinema. For the complaints specify how movie violence can exacerbate other developments that diffuse or confuse our awareness of terrible violence. Especially the criticisms show how movie violence can aggravate other dynamics that defuse our senses of opportunity and responsibility for doing good things against violence and its harms.[42] Sensationalized, routinized, pervasive, caricatured, and other worrisome versions of cinematic violence virtually require some movie evocations of ultraviolence that are potent enough to reach through the resulting barriers to personal experience, to decent feeling, to empathy or sympathy.

The ultraviolence might come straight at us viewers or virtually surround us, as in movies of war and terror directed by Steven Spielberg: *Saving Private Ryan* (1998), *Munich* (2005), and *War Horse* (2011). The ultraviolence might arrive symbolized and stylized like a graphic novel, as in *Sin City* (2005) and *The Spirit* (2008). The ultraviolence might pummel us through thriller devices, as with *A History of Violence* (2005), *Eastern Promises* (2007), and *Drive* (2011). Or it might ironize itself through the deft writing and martial-arts directing of Quentin Tarantino in *Pulp Fiction* (1994), *Kill Bill* (2003–2004), *Inglourious Basterds* (2009), and *Django Unchained* (2012). One way or another, some ultraviolence in movies can enable empathy when that is what we need for ethical and political action. *The Passion of the Christ* and *Se7en* show how.

CHAPTER 6

CHARACTER AND COMMUNITY

FROM CONTRACTS TO CONTACTS IN SCIENCE-FICTION FILMS (FEATURING CONTACT AND CLOSE ENCOUNTERS OF THE THIRD KIND)

Truth cannot be held by one person alone but is in its essence a shared reality. It is entered into through dialogue, and effective dialogue must be ironic and inconclusive.[1]

—Glenn Tinder

The stress on truth as the touchstone for argument is surprisingly modern. To people who know only modern science and epistemology, there would seem no credible alternative nor a need for one. Yet people who know inquiries and arguments beyond modern civilization appreciate how much the attempt to turn to truth alone distinguishes societies since the Renaissance and the Reformation. And people who know the politics within actual sciences, no matter how modern, have reason to wonder at the exclusive privileging of truth as evidenced by modern technologies and criticized by modern logics.[2] From its inceptions, western civilization has known that the persuasive dynamics of argument in politics reach past truth in the narrow modern sense to credibility, plausibility, cultural figures, and personal experiences that elude the disciplines of modern evidence.

With a little help from Hannah Arendt, Thomas Hobbes, and Robert Zemeckis, let us consider the implications of electronic media, and especially cinema, for how arguments now might proceed without truth in its modern senses. In our postmodern times, arguments in politics and sciences may turn away from modern fact and logic toward the virtual realities achievable by cybernetics coupled to advanced technologies of video and audio. Thus the argument at hand is that electronic politics often operate like virtual-reality sciences. They argue through political mythmaking that persuades less in the modes of modern truth than in the media of postmodern revelation. A major implication is that we respect popular cinema as a premier medium for virtual realities and making political myths from the twentieth century onward. And a clear case in point is *Contact* (1997), a science-fiction film directed by Robert Zemeckis.

From Manipulation to Myths?

The twentieth century's premier theorist of truth and politics may have been Hannah Arendt. She took the *"Existenz Philosophie"* of Martin Heidegger, her mentor, and made it politically sophisticated.[3] After fleeing as a Jew to the United States to escape German Nazis like Heidegger, Arendt turned his hostility to western metaphysics into a postmodern revival of the republican-rhetorical tradition of politics.[4] This should make her especially interesting to people who care about the quality of political argument.

The goal was to purge politics of the metaphysical preoccupations that denigrate rhetoric and destroy action. To do so, Arendt summoned a "public space of appearance."[5] There political argument proceeds without what Arendt could regard as "truth." Through the misfortune of following the modernism of Immanuel Kant in the matter, Arendt contended that both kinds of western truth—the analytic and the synthetic—coerce agreement. Accordingly western truth must preempt the freedom needed for public persuasion and political action.[6] Yet Arendt also traced the genius of political action to public speech. Only political rhetoric can provide the refinement and invention that enable humans to avoid raw force and devastating violence on the one side, as well as compulsions of fact or logic on the other side, while creating virtuous power.[7]

The quest for public argument without western truth led Arendt to terrible errors and provocative insights. Unconstrained by necessities of truth, Arendt maintained, lying is political action.[8] Nonetheless lying corrodes the conditions of truth that Arendt conceded to be required for viable politics. Citizens must face hard facts to analyze soundly the challenges for public action.[9] In our times, the systematic lying of totalitarian ideology and propaganda plus the public relations and advertising in liberal societies are destroying the public spaces of appearance required for politics.[10] Yet the truth-seeking and truth-telling that could combat lying are supposed by Arendt to stay coercive and antipolitical. Public action retains no way to save itself from lying. So Arendt suggested that a practice of argument-without-truth is the mark of true politics, but she portrayed such public argument and action as self-destructive.

Elsewhere I have explained how the modernist conceptions of truth that Arendt borrowed from Kant are inadequate, especially for political action and argument. I also have considered how ideas of analytic and synthetic truth trouble Arendt's theories and twentieth-century politics.[11] Here I accentuate the positive, though, to explore how Arendt's writings can hint at nonmetaphysical truths for our politics in the twenty-first century. These tie strongly to rhetorical ethos, pathos, mythos, and tropos; and they augment the logological bias of western truth with commonsense criteria for doing truth and beauty as well as performing goodness in politics.

From Truth to Tropes?

The tale begins with Heidegger's inspiration, Friedrich Nietzsche. In the second half of the nineteenth century, Nietzsche turned from the West's analytical and referential truth to rhetorical tropes.[12] Beginning in philology but proceeding beyond philosophy, Nietzsche took himself to learn from western civilization in order to leave it behind. For ancient Greeks, he knew, truth was the absence or removal of coverings that hide the beings beneath. Truth was *a-letheia,* dispelling the forgetfulness of reality. For western civilization, truth-seeking and truth-telling penetrate veils of illusion to display the realities behind. Truth un-covers. Truth dis-covers what appearances cloak. As Nietzsche knew, but westerners tend to forget, to reveal realities is to reveil them. Truths are always already rhetorical and symbolical. Truth-telling cannot prevent, diminish, or undo myths. Instead truth-telling retropalizes and remythifies.[13]

The modern West regards truth as an impersonal re-presentation between words (logic) or between words and the world (fact). Yet *truth* is from the Old English root for (good) faith. It restores talkers and doers to the picture, holding words and worlds together in responsible ways. It invokes their qualities of character, of ethos in the ancient sense. Pluralized, truths become different characters, poetic figures, telling tropes.[14] Saint Paul wrote that "faith is the evidence of things unseen," but modernity treats "unseen evidence" as a contradiction in terms. Sciences evidence and communicate truth. Religions use revelation where available and faith where not.

Returning people to rhetorized truths, we speak of their opinions, perspectives, and persuasions. Arendt emphasized judgment, performance, and storytelling instead of method, experiment, and model-building.[15] Fortunately her account of judgment draws from Kant's aesthetics, not his epistemologies.[16] It stresses feelings, styles, and sensibilities that tap the republican-rhetorical tradition of the *sensus communis* to appreciate common sense as the shared understandings that are postmodern culture. This updates ancient ideas of cultivated pathos as sources for prudence and responsibility.[17]

Public storytelling complements the resources of ethos and pathos with mythos.[18] Nietzsche termed this "monumental history."[19] It reveils actions so we learn from experience. After modern times, it stands to supplement religion as the retying that enables people to share meanings through living cultures day by day, enacting repeatedly their rites and rituals. Modern cultures replace traditions with novelties. People do not return eternally through the same traces. Their experiences slide toward uniqueness. They cannot know another's revelation through insistently retracing its path, let alone listening to some speech. Instead they must communicate, re-presenting meanings across the abyss between individuals. By contrast, political mythmaking attempts a postmodern reveiling to eliminate gaps. It drapes meanings among us to (re)configure our lives. When Arendt and others made the mythos of totalitarianism, they transformed settings for politics in the twentieth century.[20] So political mythmaking revives revelation in postmodern politics—but in self-conscious, critical forms.

From Revelation to Communications?

Modern sciences and politics contrast truth to revelation. Has the West retreated from The Truth as formal logic or as empirical fact? Hardly. For moderns, truth is testable and communicable; revelation is unique and solitary. Truth is scientific or political, immanently and eminently useful for settling arguments. Revelation is religious and transcendental. As political theorist Thomas Hobbes complained when confronting the English Civil War of the seventeenth century, revelation exacerbates arguments into conflicts and feuds rather than resolving them.[21] You cannot know my revelation or vice versa, so we need another path to peace and prosperity. For our late-modern unto postmodern times, revelation degenerates into supernatural disclosure. By the root from Old French, however, revelation makes visible or divulges by discourse. Divulging by discourse encourages post-modern rhetorics of in-form-ation.[22] These move into, circulate within, and form from the inside out. Making visible provokes modern epistemics of evid-ence that come out of seeing. Hence in our electronic times, postmodern epistemics come in important part out of movies and videos.[23]

Hobbes had historical reasons to regard revelation as inadequate for grounding political argument. In the aftermath of the middle ages, ways of life pluralized; and religions pitted people against one another politically. Hobbes would have been happy enough to have resources of myth for making peaceful communities. His story of individuals turning from strife in a State of Nature to contracting rationally for communities and sovereigns always made more political than philosophical sense. It requires trustworthy promises, yet Hobbes insisted that only sovereign enforcement of compliance could make oaths reliable among in-dividuals. Hence Hobbes's solution to problems of anarchic war-of-all-against-all requires the prior existence of the modern governments that it is meant to create. Hobbes made the myth of rational individuals contracting to create sovereign governments; and he emphasized that the contracts are imaginary, hypothetical devices—rather than real, historical events. With words alone, this was the best that moderns like Hobbes could do.

With representation rather than revelation, this also was the most that moderns could imagine, both epistemically and politically. Modern theorists like Hobbes took revelations at best to be deep realities made directly, personally, immedi-ately present. Such revelations are not re-presented, not merely communicated; they are experienced completely and intimately. They convince totally rather than persuade perspectivally. In the best western tradition, modern revelations unveil (not reveil). Their pure realities not only transform, they transubstantiate and indisputably—but merely individual by individual, one of us at a time. To configure communities, consequently, even modern revelations require com-munication across societies.[24] And this provokes characteristic tropes of modern politics: individuality, right, interest, rationality, representation, deterrence, contract, sovereignty, rule, maximization, and more.

From Rule to Principles?

Modern governments rule. They make rules; then they enforce compliance through individual incentives of reward and especially punishment. Fear is the primary device of modern states, which try to turn from revenge or retribution to deterrence. The modern maxim is don't get mad, don't get even, but get ahead.[25] Yet compliance depends on rational calculation of individual interest, so compliance must be in everybody's interest—or disobedience and disorder might arise, indeed might reign. Modern states make citizens an offer they cannot refuse: comply or die, politically speaking. To paraphrase Hobbes, complete compliance requires a common power to keep us all in awe. This monopoly on the legitimate means of violence, as Max Weber termed it, is sovereignty: formally absolute authority for the state. Contract is how individuals create sovereignty, and representation is how they keep it responsive to their interests.

Arendt despised sovereignty as oxymoronic and antipolitical, so she replaced it with publicity. Arendt rejected rule, force, and motive as coercive; so she celebrated the free aspirations and inspirations of principles.[26] Arendt shared modern fears of revenge and feuding, but distrusted deterrence and reliance on instrumental rationality, so she promoted forgiveness.[27] Arendt traced the lapse of religion, tradition, and authority as western grounds for politics, yet scorned the calculation and enforcement of contracts, so she mythified foundations.[28] Political foundations generate the repertoire of archetypal characters, settings, occurrences, and criteria that authorize public argument and narrative.[29] They shape the common sense of style that informs political judgment and action.[30]

Arendt's foundations stem in modern conditions from revolutionary councils. These are small, intense publics of mutual participation in times of political urgency and personal peril. In antiquity, Arendtian foundations are legendary acts of heroes lost in the mists of history, except for the ensuing publics that monumentalize these deeds and keep their memories vital. Foundations ancient and modern involve something akin to sharing revelatory experiences to form a community. Their self-conscious mythmaking for public participation can exceed communication to create the shared styles and figures for political community. This just is the common sense crucial for politics according to Arendt. Thus foundations provide or provoke the tropes and principles for productive argument in public.

Yet as Bruno Bettelheim (Arendt's colleague at the University of Chicago) observed, such contributions in our times have come to be complemented by motion pictures.[31] Film and television have become our prime mythmakers for politics. Moving pictures enable us to share experiences on the order of revelations. They can do so powerfully enough to generate or sustain communities. In our postmodern times, movies supplement the paradoxical logics of modern individuals supposedly contracting into self-abnegating communities out of self-interested rationalities. With the nineteenth-century English poet Percy Shelley, our political myths imply poets to be the prime legislators of our worlds; and with Octavio Paz, they find much of our poetry in motion pictures.[32]

Filmmakers summon postmodern powers of argumentation greater than merely modern communication and representation. They also reach beyond words into sights and sounds. Movies approach virtual realities. They share experience with a persuasive intensity and detail more like traditional revelation than modern representation. Television and computers, too, exceed the political reach of modern communication.

The time has come to reconceive, refigure, remythify argument and action for politics that are less and less modern in form or content. Contract and representation are no longer our primary ambitions or experiences. Electronic media are moving our politics beyond contract toward virtual contacts. Let our concepts keep pace with our practices.

From Evidence to Experiences?

And let our theories catch up with our moving pictures in revealing and probing their postmodern possibilities for political argument. Take the recent film *Contact*. Based on Carl Sagan's novel and directed by Robert Zemeckis, it is an inspired sequel of sorts to his Academy-Award-winning *Forrest Gump* (1994).[33] Elinor Arroway (Jodie Foster) uses radio telescopes to search the stars for extraterrestrial intelligence. Her slogan at the Wide Array in New Mexico declares that "Astronomy is looking up." As in many movies, definition and enactment are one. The slogan, like the film, explores how seeing—as the source of modern evidence—is becoming augmented and transformed by electronic media.

Ellie comes across a stellar signal. She does her scientific and political best to turn it into a vehicle for making contact with alien beings. She encounters telling hindrance and help from late-modern states and religions. Eventually she wormholes to the stars for a virtual-reality session with another species. Then she returns to Earth to learn that her trip has left no conventional, modern evidence of itself. As a late-modern scientist, she concedes publicly that a silly conspiracy story, concocted by her chief inquisitor to explain away her incredible experiences, might be as plausible an argument as the truths she prosaically tells. Yet Arroway loves a New Age spiritualist (Matthew McConaughey), and she learns from him a postmodern lesson about the dependence of proof on faith. With the aid of several sorts of moving pictures, she shares her experiences persuasively with the whole society. She persuades people through television in much the same way that this mythic film by Zemeckis persuades us through its virtual contacts—with Arroway and what she encounters.

Contact approaches postmodern revelation differently than Steven Spielberg's *Close Encounters of the Third Kind* (1977). Each Spielberg figure called to an alien landing on Earth is given a personal, private obsession. It is a merely modern revelation of a vision to come, although most of these people learn through the mass media how to act on it. Each has the revelation, but few can share it effectively with others. The *Contact* challenge of truth met by Ellie and the movies is to provide others virtual contact with previously individual visions.

The daunting task of truth has been the territory of religions then sciences. The film insists with Arroway's lover that religions as well as sciences pursue truth, and both must realize that this is the pursuit of meaning. Arroway tells the aliens that other people need to see what she has, and this is largely what the movie accomplishes for us viewers. But often the modes of postmodern argument are roundabout in reveiling our realities. Thus Arroway's video camera in the film records only static, we learn, even though there are eighteen hours of it to stand for what she experienced in vivid detail.

From Communication to Revelations?

In his lively but sneering mode, the *New Yorker* film critic Anthony Lane inadvertently testifies to the importance in *Contact* of this postmodern problematic of political argument. With nary a note to acknowledge the film's turn from religion to science in grounding our politics, Lane scorns Ellie Arroway's attempt to communicate her experience of the wormhole excursion to the stars and her conversation with aliens.

> By the time of Ellie's return, I was dreading what would come next. She becomes a Cassandra, poor thing, with only Palmer Joss having the courage to believe her story, but even worse is the awful manner in which she is compelled to tell it. "I was given a vision of the universe that tells us how tiny and insignificant and [rare and] precious we are," she explains at an official hearing. "In all our searching, the only thing that's made the emptiness bearable is each other." How a movie that began with the promise of such excitement can fritter itself away into these plaintive consolations, I have no idea. It's a kind of dumbing up, a desperately ill-advised ascent into musings that don't have the nerve to be openly religious; *Contact* is the antithesis of a picture like *Close Encounters of the Third Kind,* which resolved itself into an array of luminous images that

hinted at all manner of annunciation but wisely stayed free of any attempt to put such awe into words.[34]

But Arroway isn't religious, even at the investigation hearing. Does Lane think that the trip should have converted her to open spirituality? It does not, nor should it. The Zemeckis film, like the Sagan book, argues that faith and meaning are not proprietary elements or requirements of religion alone. The film takes pains to show how science and everyday experience necessarily involve faith and sometimes flounder on the need to communicate personal experiences equivalent to revelations. Yet it also shows how postmodern politics can make virtual contact with others.

How could Lane miss the film's pointed, poignant irony of Arroway's inability to muster more than mundane words in this situation? In the midst of her space experience, Ellie exclaims that "They should have sent a poet!" She knows that her facility with words is categorically insufficient. The film is wise to insist that words are bound to sound empty and platitudinous in such a situation. Mere words cannot stand up to the criticism of Arroway's own science, let alone to the cynicism of high-brow criticism. The film makes clear that Ellie herself knows this even as she speaks. Yet the powers of moving pictures and stereo sounds deliver Arroway's discovery, selection, preparation, launch, and appeal.

Lane complains that Arroway's character in *Contact* displays the same facial expressions—but lacks the professional intelligence and true grit—of Clarice Starling (also played by Jodie Foster) in *The Silence of the Lambs* (1991). "Ellie, by contrast, never seems like a pro at all. The Ripley of *Alien* (1979) would shake her off like moondust and leave her for dead."[35] The film, however, presents Ellie as a modern scientist, not as an FBI agent or action-adventure hero. Within her actual role, Arroway shows plenty of *The Right Stuff* (1979) that Lane implies her to lack.[36]

Lane laments that the one decent irony in the film is when aliens play back Adolf Hitler's televised figure in their first communication to Earth: "this represents the final moment at which [Zemeckis's] movie makes contact with the forces of irony. From here on, naïveté rules."[37] But this is the trouble of merely communicating a revelation or perhaps any other experience beyond the utterly mundane. It is why Hobbes could hold that revelation cannot ground modern politics. After the fantastic effort has seemed to fail, words cannot hope to rescue it. Yet words plus sounds and pictures might, as our politics now know.

Lane misses the communicative, politically revelatory power of the movies themselves. He writes that only Arroway's lover has the courage to believe her story. Within its own world, however, the movie surely shows otherwise, from masses to elites. The applause that I heard after several screenings of *Contact* implies the contrary about our world too. As Arroway emerges from the final hearing, she meets with popular acclaim; and the politicians support her further inquiries with an ample grant.

We have the simulation unto virtual reality of the alien encounter itself, available to us on film. Yet the public in the film does not. Why do those people believe Arroway's account? They have the televised reality of her ethos. Arroway's character on television is primarily what persuades people. They see and hear her under the supreme pressure of a temptation to pretend to a religious faith that she does not embrace, in order to take the trip to the stars that she has craved since childhood. People have seen Arroway stand firm for the truth as she knows it. People have experienced through television how she can be trusted to know what is happening and—in the best tradition of modern science—tell only what she knows through her experience, without self-serving invention or momentarily emotional embellishment. Can she be absolutely certain that she was not hoaxed? How could anyone in the wake of modern skepticism be certain in such circumstances? By conceding the possibility of a hoax, while denying it an endorsement, Arroway enhances her credibility in the second televised hearings. From these virtual experiences of Arroway's character, her viewers in the film come to trust her account of journeying to the stars for a virtual encounter with the aliens.

Credibility is the modern, diminished version of character as "ethos" in the ancient Greek sense. Ethos is the performance of the speaker manifested over repeated encounters with the audience in a public gathering. It involves the audience sense of who the speaker is. Thus this "character" is not an internal dynamic or structure of psyche, as modern people have been inclined to treat it more or less since Shakespeare.[38] Instead ethos is external, behavioral, reputational. Indeed the other main face or definition of classical ethos is the standing of the speaker—with the audience.

The Greek and Roman notion of people in a "public space of appearance"—such as the assembly in the agora or the tribunes in the forum—is amphitheatrical.[39] Theirs are words and deeds presented and apprehended in the round, with members of the audience and speakers frequently exchanging roles. Even when the speaking is one-sidedly oratorical, rather than meeting the tests of dialectical interaction urged by Plato's Socrates, the orator for this hour becomes a listener in the next—as one of the previous audients takes the speaker's place. Consequently the participants develop characters or standings with one another.

As the performance and appreciation of such public or political character, ethos is intrinsically relational. It encompasses, mobilizes, and makes judgments about how each participant speaks and acts in relationship to others. Accordingly ethics are our practices, assessments, and prescriptions of interpersonal relationships.

Antiquity appreciated ethos as character in the sense that the Romans articulated as virtues and vices. In the middle ages, ethos as standing sometimes became assimilated to the offices that speakers hold or perform. Hence it edged over into authority. With modern civilization, there was a drastic constriction of ethos to credibility. The next chapter explains a postmodern meaning of ethos that moves outward instead. It is less an invention than a recognition on my part, because it is so ensconced in the culture that we find it in dictionaries and ordinary, everyday talk. I have in mind the sense of ethos as tone, mood, or ambience. I do not want to collapse all these shades of postmodern ethos into one undifferentiated lump; differences among them can be important. Here, though, let us focus on ethos as character.

Arroway's ethos is the telling evidence. First it achieves vivid, credible reality for viewers in the televised hearings for selecting the astronauts. Then it culminates in her poised, quietly passionate, but still not the least poetic appearance before the second televised investigation into her mysterious trip. From the hundreds of millions of Chinese who believed that the American landing on the Moon was merely staged as a propaganda film, we know that eighteen hours of audio and video need not be compelling evidence of Arroway's wormhole journey to the stars. The film is its own demonstration of how special effects could fake the missing evidence for anybody outside the project—and perhaps for many people inside as well. No modern evidence need be decisive, infallible, or indefeasible.

Yet we need not and must not fly to contrary errors of solipsism or cynicism. Evidence and argument are about probability, not certainty. Experience and revelation are about sharing senses of realities, not insuring truths of propositions. The contestability of evidence, argument, experience, revelation, communication, science, and every other device of learning by humans is not cause for corrosive doubt or epistemic despair. Instead it is encouragement to face existence in many, diverse ways. Arroway's testimony enables television viewers to sense her experience vicariously, through her own accounts and reactions. But it lets televiewers encounter her character personally, virtually, and convincingly. Thus technologies of virtual reality help us experience things in ways otherwise unavailable to us. Telescopes and electron microscopes do this; so do virtual-reality helmets and gloves. What they permit is not indirect observation so much as personal interaction by means beyond the ordinary. The *virtual* in *virtual reality* should not be taken to suggest *almost, deficient,* or *defective.* The technologies of virtual reality instead amplify and multiply our modes of genuine, personal experience.[40]

From Contract to Contacts?

In our times, films join television, Internet, and video games as the most widely practiced technologies of virtual experience. When *Contact* offers reaction shots of Ellie Arroway on her trip to the stars, the movie could be said to let viewers experience it vicariously, through her experience. When *Contact* provides views and sounds of the trip to people in the theater, the film becomes a virtual experience of her wormhole excursion. The subjective camera in *Bob Roberts* (1992) gives a virtual experience of documentary coverage for a U.S. Senate campaign. The "Arkansas" dystopia spot from the George H. W. Bush campaign in 1992 presents viewers a virtual experience of the character of Bill Clinton as governor; it enables watchers to experience Clinton's political character by extraordinary means.[41] Thus the character of Arroway, especially her ethos as Ellie the scientist, is primarily what warrants her claims about the stellar trip to people in her day. Within the film, her character becomes accessible to people by means of television. For viewers of the film, Arroway's ethos is amplified far beyond the hearings; and it becomes complemented by virtual (as well as vicarious) experiences of her trip. These mythic modes of experience are political revelations in common, empowering us all to share in the awe of Ellie's excellent adventure.

To drive this home, Zemeckis turned away from early plans to have Linda Hunt play the female president envisioned by the Sagan novel. Instead he used the reelection of President Clinton and recontextualized clips from Clinton's press conference to announce the discovery of fossilized life from Mars. These situate the film within the political world of its viewers. This device, too, highlights the film's case for the revelatory politics practiced every day for us by the moving pictures and lifelike sounds of film, television, and other electronic media.[42] At the time of *Contact*'s release, this device of recontextualizing video clips of presidents had recently helped *Forrest Gump* situate viewers within the world of that film's events. There, too, some undiscerning reviewers seem mostly to have missed the virtual politics practiced by the film. But again the audiences who shared its viewing with me plainly appreciated the device for precisely its virtual-reality potential. Of course, people who do not spend their careers writing critically of television, Hollywood, or politicians might be more open to the resulting revelations. These postmodern people also might be less obsessed with looking for the fine print. After all, contracts are no longer required to regulate every aspect of modern lives unable to share experiences vividly and convincingly across distances among individuals.

Contact explores the postmodern politics beyond modern contract and communication. It appreciates that electronic media enable us to share something like revelations; and it emphasizes that these never transpire without veils of symbol, trope, and myth. We should follow its lead in learning how emerging politics take advantage of powers of persuasion more accessible and powerful than those available for modern individuals and sovereigns.[43] As Arendt, Hobbes, and Spock might agree, that's how we postmoderns might live long and prosper.

CHAPTER 7

ATMOSPHERE AND ARGUMENT

FROM VICARIOUS TO VIRTUAL EXPERIENCE IN WAR MOVIES (FEATURING APOCALYPSE NOW, PLATOON, SAVING PRIVATE RYAN, AND THE THIN RED LINE)

The past is another country, and to bring it to some sort of dramatic life takes a capacity for which there is no English word. It was not until the eighteenth century that a German, J. G. Herder, coined Einfühlen—the act of feeling one's way into the past not by holding up a mirror but by stepping through the mirror into the alien world.[1]

—Gore Vidal

We have been learning how films provide political experiences. They do so for various reasons: to sympathize or criticize, to inspire actions or invent alternatives, to think through ideas or argue contentions. In doing so, they deploy myriad devices of sight and sound. These become powerful, popular conventions for informing and amusing us. Since movies and other electronic media shape our ideas and dispositions, especially for everyday life, we do well to appreciate their rhetorics.

We also have been exploring how the rhetorician who begins with cinematic modes of experience becomes something of a phenomenologist, parsing the appearances available to viewers. Since experiences offered by films come in many modes, they make a feast for the political phenomenologist. Among the most familiar are the closely related dynamics of depiction, demonstration, and illustration. Yet the insistent interaction between literature and cinema has focused accounts to date on vicarious experience. This encourages analysts to trace how viewers experience situations on screen through identification with a lead character. The character's impressions, decisions, and reactions become our guides to response as viewers.

To restrict ourselves to these sorts of cinematic connections, prominent and potent though they are, is to treat movies too much like novels or other stories. As we have already started to see, it is to miss some of the cinema's experiential modes of greatest political and rhetorical importance. With special reference to war movies, let us explore two others. And to appreciate aspects of their rhetorics and politics, let us emphasize the more distinctively cinematic of the two.

Because I had never particularly appreciated war films, I had not addressed them until recently. But I wanted to participate in a conference panel where the other people all wanted to analyze rhetorical aspects of war. Hence I gritted my teeth and got on with it, devoting every opportunity for several months to watching popular films of war. By this time, I had developed a decent feeling for how to let the movies themselves help me watch and analyze them. Still no great enthusiast for war films, I nonetheless did find myself engaged and instructed most of the time. Attention to the political rhetoric of war movies converges on three insistent interests in these pages. It links the phenomenology of persuasion in electronic media, the complementing of classical and modern rhetoric by several postmodern inventions, and the appreciation of everyday politics in conventions of popular genres. What follows here is a report on a study I started one summer and have continued for many years since.

Wars

War movies conventionally are character studies. The idea is that war puts people into the most extreme conditions of life and death. War tests us existentially. Thus war films often resemble the ship-of-fools genre, where odd concatenations of characters face exigencies that bring out the worst and the best in them. Relentless obstacles require surmounting, if we are to survive and move the troops from one place to another. But mainly in war, we must conquer our darker drives. We also must come to constructive terms with realist injunctions to fight wars all-out, no holds barred, with community gain what matters most and personal survival a distant fourth after honor and glory. In films about military training and combat, such realism spars relentlessly with personal and communal codes of honor that insist on higher values and conduct in even the most dire situations.

As I have been explaining, movies are the closest the twentieth century came to popular versions of virtual reality in electronic communication. Late in the twentieth century, war films became keenly interested in the dynamics of popular argument and resources of cultural memory available through the virtual-reality dimensions of movies. As a genre, war films often make specific claims about the wars or characters they feature; and they sometimes advance their claims in important part through mood. This is a postmodern version of ethos—as the atmospherics that characterize people, events, and situations. It moves beyond the classical mode of ethos—as the standing of speakers with their audiences. In cinema and electronic media of other kinds, arguments by mood let us viewers experience for ourselves the situations on the screen. This enables us to assess the plausibility of claims about their settings and events.[2]

So let us examine the ethos arguments in several recent, instant classics of the war genre. Like most war films, these work hard rhetorically to shape our cultural memories of the conflicts they evoke. Their sights and sounds of war seek to leave viewers with summary impressions: general judgments about merits or mistakes of the wars they target. Sometimes the theses of these films address the wars themselves less than the politics in their wake. Yet each film argues its thesis by mood as well as character, and we do well to trace the specific claims and devices of argument to analyze their political aesthetics of persuasion.

Contentions

After the Vietnam War, the popular genre of war films became far more interested in making arguments than did any other movie genre I have analyzed. To be sure, the injunction against making or taking any movie to be an argument is famous in Hollywood: "If you want to send a message, use Western Union." The implication is that it is hopelessly reductive—and bad filmmaking to boot—to treat any entertainment from Hollywood as primarily a proposition, let alone a set of reasons in support of a proposition. And in fact, popular movies show little frontal interest in such argumentation. The few exceptions—such as the romance *Playing By Heart* (1998), which argues pointedly that human love cannot be explained adequately in words—might be taken to prove the rule. Yet scores and scores of recent war movies are mostly and primarily engaged in making arguments.

The generic argument of war movies has long been that War Is Hell with Heroism. Even in war, the craven and treacherous somehow can find their match in the courageous and heroic. This can happen even though conditions of terror, futility, corruption, and death conspire to make the destination dubious, the path impossible, the leader lost, the citizen-soldier cynical or insane. Yet the specific qualities of individual wars can be strikingly different, providing diverse experiences and competing morals for future conduct. So it would be surprising if most war movies were to settle for one small complement of characters in every scene, and it would be amazing if all war movies were to reduce all their scenes to a single setting of War as Hell that continues unrelieved for reel after reel. Instead we should expect at least some war films to make more individuated arguments.

Indeed war movies from roughly the end of the Vietnam War until at least the American invasion of Iraq became character studies of individual wars. These recent war films advance arguments about the distinctive overall characters of their target wars. Such an exercise is familiar from books: World War II was the last good war. World War I ended the optimism of the western civilization. The Gulf War became an arcade game for generals, pilots, and viewers. The Korean Conflict was always already the forgotten war. The Revolutionary War founded America, and the Civil War refounded it. The Vietnam War cost America its innocence and possibly its soul.[3] The Balkan Wars pit a new world order of imposed peace against recurrent demons of chaos, tribalism, genocide, imperialism, intolerance, terror, and totalitarianism. The post-9/11 invasions of Iraq and Afghanistan were misbegotten and counterproductive. Even the exceptional books that stay focused on war in a larger sense turn arguments toward theses about what ethics and styles are appropriate for war, whether women or feminized men can conduct war successfully, and so on.

This kind of argumentative impulse is no less prominent in recent war films. It is why some commentators dismiss some of these movies as preachy and manipulative. But it would be better to say, at least of the best in recent war movies, that they exercise the republican-rhetorical drive to publicize "the lessons of history."[4] These celluloid and digitized lessons parallel the republican-rhetorical project of monumentalizing history in heroic statues, national memorials, battleground parks, and museums for wars safely past. Each of these endeavors strives to construct the "common sense" for its focal war: the "conventional wisdom" about what was at stake and what happened as a result that can give the particular war its defining character and political implications.[5]

Most of these movies acknowledge explicitly that War Is Hell. Most insist overtly on some heroism. Some even embed their distinctive claims about their particular wars within this larger argument. The genre regards it as a lesson too important not to be taught in film after film. Thus many recent war movies provide their individual arguments as specifications of War Is Hell with Heroism.

Each movie tours a somewhat different circle of Hell, letting the full Inferno unfold film by film into a generic sense of War as Hell on Earth. As Captain Willard (Martin Sheen) observes in Michael Herr's words for narrating Francis Ford Coppola's *Apocalypse Now*, "I was going to the worst place in the world, and I didn't even know it yet." In the voiceover letters that articulate the argument of Oliver Stone's *Platoon*, Chris Taylor (Charlie Sheen) explains, "Somebody once wrote, 'Hell is the impossibility of reason.' That's what this place feels like, Hell." The realist in Terrence Malick's remake of *The Thin Red Line* is Sergeant Welsh (Sean Penn). He tells the dreamer, Private Witt (Jim Caviezel), "We're living in a world that's blowing itself to hell as fast as everybody can arrange." Even *Saving Private Ryan* evokes this trope obliquely but emphatically when Steven Spielberg has General George C. Marshall (Harve Presnell) order the rescue of the remaining Private Ryan: "The boy's alive. We are gonna send somebody to find him, and we are gonna get him the hell out of there." The war over there *is* "the hell," of course, and the rescue team must go through that hell and inflict a fair amount of its own to remove Ryan from the theater of operations.

Each of these war films, like many others, argues a central thesis. A few war movies argue two or even three somewhat related theses. The thesis of a war film is not the only message of that movie, and it need not be the most important feature of the film, but it is good for comparing claims and devices of argument across war films. The focal contentions of recent war films are decently diverse, as Table 7.1, Arguments of War Movies, can suggest.

The ambition is not to try to support the identification of each thesis with detailed analysis of each movie's action, dialogue, setting, soundtrack, and cinematography. That would take a book by itself. Let me settle instead for specifying that these theses emerge from attention to such elements in each film; then I can leave the films to readers to see for themselves. For now, the emphasis is rather on how war films advance electronic arguments through ethos—especially the postmodern ethos effected by cinematic techniques of virtual reality.

Ethoi

In war, popular movies show, some people, institutions, and traditions are lost; some are found; some corrupted, some redeemed; and many change in other

Table 7.1 Arguments of War Movies

War Film (Year of Release)	Focal Thesis for the Film's Main Argument
Company of Heroes (2013)	We're boots on the ground; we lose good men every day, but we just keep marching until they tell us to stop ... do the right thing.
Ironclad (2011)	Only the weak believe that what they do in battle is who they are as men.
Green Zone (2010)	Don't be naïve; just do your job. It's not for you to decide what happens here. The reasons we go to war always matter.
The Hurt Locker (2009)	War is a drug.
The Messenger (2009)	Is this a war, or what?
Miracle at St. Anna (2008)	Safety is the greatest risk of all, 'cause safety leaves no room for miracles, and miracles are the only sure thing in life.
Stop-Loss (2008)	Unless you fall in beside us, it all falls apart.
300 (2007)	[If the enemy blots the sun,] Then we will fight in the shade.
Home of the Brave (2006)	It's a hard job being a soldier. . . . [But] These are my guys; and I need them just as much as they need me.
Letters from Iwo Jima (2006)	Do what is right because it is right.
The Great Raid (2005)	Saving them was a way of setting things right. . . . they had been left behind, but never forgotten.
Cold Mountain (2004)	War makes some things pointless.
Troy (2004)	War is young men dying and old men talking; ignore the politics. Soldiers obey; don't waste your life following some fool's orders.
Gods and Generals (2003)	Our highest duty is to defend our home, because every state has a primal claim to the fealty of its citizens.
Master and Commander (2003)	In the Royal Navy, you must choose the lesser of two evils.
Tears of the Sun (2003)	The only thing necessary for the triumph of evil is for good men to do nothing.
Hart's War (2002)	Colored men expect to have to jump through a few hoops in this man's army.

(continued)

ways. As a popular genre, war films feature arguments from *ethos*, the ancient Greek sense of *character*. As explained in earlier chapters, such ethos is not only a configuration of what the Romans eventually called virtues and vices, but also a classical mode of persuasion in political arguments. Later this classical sense of *character* constricted into modern *credibility*. Yet recent movies on war show how electronic media can shift ethos arguments into a further, postmodern mode.

Classical arguments from ethos accredit or attack claims due to the virtues and vices of the characters who make them. This happens often in electronic

Table 7.I *Continued*

War Film (Year of Release)	Focal Thesis for the Film's Main Argument
We Were Soldiers (2002)	Win the battle, lose the war: soldiers fight for each other.
Windtalkers (2002)	Friendship means not always following orders.
Black Hawk Down (2001)	Leave no man behind.
Pearl Harbor (2001)	The smart enemy attacks you where you feel safe. Victory goes to those who believe the hardest—and longest.
The Patriot (2000)	When the war comes home, the home goes to war.
Rules of Engagement (2000)	Rules of engagement may not be just in war.
Tigerland (2000)	The Army makes all men one, but you never know which one.
Three Kings (1999)	The Gulf War was conducted by America for black gold—not to liberate Kuwait, depose Saddam, or help ordinary humans.
The Thin Red Line (1998)	War is a world of endless, crazy contention; yet we can and must imagine other worlds.
Saving Private Ryan (1998)	We are obliged to make good on the heroic sacrifice of American soldiers in the Second World War.
Savior (1997)	Intervention in the Balkans offers a radically imperfect but real redemption for America.
G.I. Jane (1996)	War is women's work too.
Jacob's Ladder (1990)	The Vietnam War was a battle for the soul, that America might miraculously survive.
Casualties of War (1989)	The extremity of war means we must act with more justice not less.
Platoon (1986)	War is hell, with the Vietnam War pitting the best against the worst of America.
Heartbreak Ridge (1986)	The feminized warrior can still win.
War Games (1983)	The only way to win is not to play (fight).
Apocalypse Now (1979)	The Vietnam War pushed beyond American morality, insanity, language, and judgment into the heart of darkness.
The Thin Red Line (1964)	War effaces the thin red line between reason and insanity.

argumentation by radio, television, film, and computers. Television spots for talking heads and popular films with superstars depend centrally on classical ethos when they make arguments. They ask people to take the words of others whose character(istic)s might make them not only credible but admirable and authoritative. For us, these find a complement in the reliance of electronic media on ethos arguments that persuade instead by helping people experience more or less for themselves the character(istic)s of the situations at stake.

The argument here is that recent war films have turned for a sustained time to virtual-reality devices that argue from *ethos* in its postmodern sense of *mood, tone, atmosphere,* or *ambience*—especially as *the spirit of the situation*. As noted, this postmodern meaning of ethos has made its way into dictionaries and ordinary talk. By kinds and dynamics, postmodern ethoi amplify the persuasive resources of rhetoric, particularly in electronic media.[6]

Of late, war films often deploy a particular characterization of the war's setting as a principal character—sometimes *the* principal character—in articulating the movie's thesis about the war at issue. The setting becomes a pervasive environment for viewers to experience. This is their experience of the war. It furnishes the warrant and often also the backing for the film's thesis.[7]

In earlier war films, a prominent tendency is to collect a diverse set of soldiers in some endeavor that mandates effective cooperation for success, even survival. *The Dirty Dozen* (1967) is a familiar example set in the Second World War. But movies in other genres occasionally work this way as well: *Stagecoach* (1939), the well-known western with John Wayne, is a famous case in point.[8] So it is clear that a ship-of-fools formula can surface in various popular movies. War films in this mode trace how their peculiar combinations of warriors interact. The focus is on how individuals in these circumstances manifest or change their characters. The propositions of these older war films receive support from their character studies. Therefore theirs are precisely arguments by ethos in the classical sense, concerned with characters as networks of virtues and vices. Each in his own way, the title figures in *The Dirty Dozen* show exactly how War Is Hell with Heroism.[9]

Yet war films released in the aftermath of the Vietnam War often target the virtues and vices of their settings to explore the distinctive characters of different wars. To appreciate the arguments of war films in the several decades at issue is to analyze their rhetorics. This is to trace how they persuade viewers to accept their claims. Often they encourage viewers to experience the wars in question vicariously through focal characters in the films. At times, though, they offer viewers virtual experience of the wars by mimicking first-person access to the sights and sounds that distinguish the particular conditions of combat.

If the Greek tie between classical and postmodern ethos lies in the connection between *character* and *characteristics,* the Roman link is the republican-rhetorical sense of *spirit.* This is the permeating, animating principle of each person, event, or setting. Thus the Latin word is a major node in the network of republican politics and rhetorical practices. *Respiration* is crucial to life and speech, *perspiration* to work, *inspiration* to invention, and *aspiration* to attainment. *Spires* mark our churches and hopes, *spirals* our genetic structures and republican ideas of time. The breathing-together of *conspiracy* is a recurrent trope of republican politics and Hollywood films. *Expiration* means that time is done and we have "given up the ghost." This connotation of *spirit* as what enlivens, moves, and individuates us led the Romans to translate Plato's three parts of the soul as desire, reason, and spirit.[10] That last becomes synonymous with the personal senses of honor and self which most make people who they are as distinct individuals. Hence *ethos* has been understood as pervasive, motivating, individuating *spirit* almost from the start.

As the French-republican *esprit de corps* suggests, such *ethos* as *spirit* can be communal, institutional, or situational. Organizations, events, even settings have characters. These speak to our relations and evaluations for such collective and interactive things. The popular genre of science fiction long ago began to make settings such as other planets into principal characters in their narratives.[11] Thus *Solaris* (2002) is the main protagonist in Stanlislaw Lem's novel of that name, the character of *Dune* (1984) as a planet is the overarching concern of Frank Herbert's initial trilogy, and the spirit of Mars animates the award-winning novels by Kim Stanley Robinson.[12] The military source of *esprit de corps,* often considered the key to victory in war, makes it inevitable that some films would argue their claims about wars through characterizing their settings and evoking their moods.[13] Thus they persuade by letting viewers experience the ethos of a particular war as the spirit that inheres in its situations.

Most electronic media use music to advance whatever arguments they might make. As David Ansen writes, "We're rarely conscious of it, but what really frightens us in movies is often not what we see but what we hear. Not the guy with the knife but the man at the dials, splicing in an electronic 'boo!'"[14] It is no surprise that war films share in this. Typically the war experiences flow from ethos as character through spirit to mood.[15] The main argument by mood in the 1964 version of *The Thin Red Line* is the insanity within war; and it is made as much by the clangorous score for the battle scenes as by any cinematic devices of acting, dialogue, or plot. Almost all war movies I have seen make significant attempts to argue by mood, because nearly all use their music in this way. Sound in general and music in particular are crucial devices for creating mood. Therefore sound and music are mainstays for argument by ethos, especially in war films. We know relatively little about how to analyze music argumentatively. If we are to appreciate movies and television programs as media of public address, however, we must develop a vocabulary for musical rhetoric.

To emphasize the distinctive character of a particular war might be to take account of special combatants, purposes, weapons, tactics, or terrains. Yet war films are learning from the likes of science fiction that a fine way to evoke all these characteristics is to build them into visual and aural settings that the films treat as akin to characters in their own right. For the time being, let us concentrate on several devices of voice and cinematography that contrast vicarious, virtual, and symbolic experiences.

Experiences

Scholars of political rhetoric and communication emphasize an apparatus for analysis that traces to ancient Greece and Rome. For example, the Aristotelian schemes of forensic, epideictic, and deliberative rhetoric are prominent in analysis by students of public address. If we were to analyze each species of rhetoric phenomenologically, we would specify how various individuals experience each kind of argumentation. We might even contrast experiences by speakers with experiences by audiences for each classical mode of persuasion.

To some extent, of course, this already has been done—not so much systematically as casually in the process of analyzing individual performances or texts. The analysis might not have been labeled "phenomenology," but its attention to the dynamics of experience might be apparent nonetheless. The barest beginnings for such an appreciation of Aristotle's species of rhetoric can be evoked by Table 7.2.

The chart starts with Aristotle's tripartite contrast. Forensic rhetoric argues cases about events already past, so that we may judge them accurately and allocate responsibilities accordingly. For Aristotle, at least, this corresponds to the beginning of a story. Epideictic rhetoric praises or blames people in the present. These comments help move us through current circumstances, making this for Aristotle akin to negotiating the middle stages of a story. Deliberative rhetoric discusses or debates future actions. The decisions that issue from deliberations concert and commit the participants to action, at least beginning to end the story. The chart's last line reflects work by Stanley Cavell that suggests how Aristotle's three species already might be augmented or transcended in telling ways by kinds of rhetoric that become prominent in the postmodern times from the nineteenth century onward, but that story is for another time.[16] For present purposes, we do

Table 7.2 Three Species of Rhetoric

Species of Rhetoric	Forensic		Epideictic		Deliberative	
time periods	past events		present people		future actions	
operation types	end beginnings		negotiate middles		begin ends	
outcome kinds	making cases		making comments		making decisions	
activity modes	argue	judge	praise	blame	discuss	debate
transcendence sites	arrange	impress	epiphany	lament	converse	play

better to reach beyond Aristotle's rhetoric to a contrast of vicarious, virtual, and symbolic experiences. Analyzing political advertisements on television encourages us to notice these three dynamics of argument in popular movies as well.[17]

The encouragement of vicarious experience is to identify with a focal character and that figure's responses to the settings and happenings evoked by a program or movie. This enables us to experience the situations and events through the experiences of the featured character. A major dynamic in novels and other late-modern stories, vicarious experience stitches readers and viewers into a mediated world when and where it is apprehended by the point-of-view characters in that world. The vantages of these characters provide, shape, even dominate the experiences of readers and viewers.

Virtual experience, by contrast, mobilizes a host of rhetorical devices to enable and encourage viewers to experience a media world as though—or, at times, almost as though—the viewers are themselves one or more characters in that world. The viewers become virtual actors or at least observers *within* the invented world. Even if viewers are not given a single, continual vantage point amid the (other) characters who encounter the situations and enact the events in the imagined world, the viewers are stitched into it so that they experience its sights and sounds as though present in that world.[18] Thus ad-makers sometimes use TV to give viewers virtual experiences of events or people distant from viewers—or otherwise impossible for them to experience in what we often regard as "ordinary ways."[19] Even so, virtual experience is exceptional these days on television and film, which more often feature vicarious experience.

To keep the distinction between vicarious and virtual experience from becoming an all-encompassing dichotomy, we do well to recognize at least one other mode of experience that operates on the same levels. Symbolical experience is neither vicarious nor virtual, at least in principle.[20] Condensive symbols invite readers or viewers into probing mythic networks of associations. These typically evoke larger patterns of plot or character within a story or film. The war films under analysis cultivate symbolical as well as vicarious and virtual experiences.

Devices

Vicarious experience dominates argumentation so far in films, including war movies. When films offer virtual experience, they typically provide little touches in the midst of vicarious experience. Yet a few movies rely more emphatically on virtual experience, sustaining virtual presentations for minutes at a time. The same can be said of symbolical experience, where films seek to persuade viewers through drawing them into the contemplation of icons, sounds, and other condensive symbols. These provoke extensive networks of mythic connections capable of supporting the propositions promoted by their films. There are many reasons for the virtual and symbolical moves to flicker in and out of prominence while vicarious experiences sustain themselves for many minutes, even whole movies. Some of the various devices themselves, identified in Table 7.3, suggest why this may be so.

This is a beginning grid developed in pondering the persuasive devices in many war movies, always keeping in mind other popular genres as well. Certainly virtual and symbolical, as well as vicarious, experiences appear in all sorts of cinema, television, radio, computer gaming, and other electronic media of communication.

Vicarious experience relies a lot on *framing*. (I hesitate to invoke this overused word with so many, sometimes incompatible meanings for it these days in the academic field of political communication. The trouble is that it fits my needs exactly, and I cannot think of a decent alternative. Maybe I can encourage other scholars to quit using *framing* to evoke background, context, priming, and such—all things named already in better ways. But I had better not hold my breath to see if that happens; so let me proceed with this older, possibly less replaceable sense of *framing*.) Vicarious presentation implies or takes advantage of something like a picture frame around the moving images on the screen. This distances us as viewers from what we can see and hear on the cinematic—configured as theatrical—stage.

Table 7.3 Three Experiential Modes in Movies

Experiential Mode	Vicarious	Virtual	Symbolical
typical movie use	predominant, pure	intermittent, mixed	momentary, paused
focusing strategy	theatrical	perspectival	figural
screen configuration	conventional frame	surround or tunnel	intensive focus
camera angles	faces and fronts	backs and sides	artistic or self-aware
conventional	personal portraits	close-ups and	pseudo-stills and
perspectives	and natural vistas	midrange shots	slow or stop-motion
access principle	point-of-view	points-of-view	omniscient network
identifying marker	zoom into eyes	alternate among foci	pause and hold focus
stitching strategy	identification with	immersion in shifting	exploration of
for experiences	individual characters	moods	diverse connections
distinctive aural and	singular voiceover,	multiple voiceovers,	action, object, and
visual devices	dominant viewpoint	multiple flashbacks	sound matches
principles devices	humans	settings	icons
and elements for	characteristics	deliveries	slogans
characterizing	explanations	tones and rhythms	themes

As a result, we viewers are not part of the action; and this can be accomplished by any number of more specific devices. Shots of long or panoramic vistas are obvious examples. As on a theatrical stage, with its framing curtains or walls, the screen can be framed by curtains or the darkness beyond the edges of the images. With theatrical framing, the actors mostly face to the front to deliver their lines in the direction of the audience. The scenery and the action are configured to be seen from the same angle. Use of vicarious experience in films also features mostly frontal shots, faces turned to the camera that functions as the viewers' eyes. Frontal shots enable viewers who are meant to identify with a focal character to see the other characters turned as though to face that character, even as they also follow how that character's face registers responses to what others do and say.

Virtual experience depends on putting viewers somehow onto the stage, into the midst of the action, but for theater in the round. Hence its devices diminish, displace, or eliminate framing. They undo the usual distance between screens and viewers. Instead of vistas that suggest strong separations between foreground and background, medium shots and close-ups can offer virtual experiences of the characters and objects in films. Instead of frontal shots that turn actors relentlessly toward a removed audience that otherwise might lose their words or miss their facial expressions, films designed to impart virtual experiences turn the actors every which way but loose. In *The Thin Red Line* as directed by Terrence Malick, the camera keeps us in the tall island grasses for long periods; and it locates us on the side or to the rear of (other) soldiers on the move.[21] This is how we viewers would be placed in the middle of the action. Similar shots are sustained at times in storming the D-day beaches as evoked by Steven Spielberg's direction of *Saving Private Ryan*.[22] Such perspectival shots are indispensable to cinema in a virtual-reality mode.

Virtual experience through cinema also relies on insistent shifting of foci. The Malick version of *The Thin Red Line* provides reveries from a handful of figures, rather than flashbacks from one or two characters who serve as our vicarious sources of experience. Augmenting the visual foci are voiceovers from many characters. *Saving Private Ryan* makes us viewers into members of the Ryan family, following their father (Harrison Young) to the site of Captain Miller's grave and giving him room to help them experience in imagination what others suffered and sacrificed that they might live in political freedom. Spielberg and Malick both use the trope of closing slowly on a character's face—as though entering through the eyes into the head—before showing what that figure experienced, remembers, or imagines. So we film viewers know to expect a replay of that character's experience and personality. In this respect, the bracketing scenes in the Spielberg film focus on Ryan long after the war, and the body of the film features Captain Miller (Tom Hanks). We are to share their senses of the Normandy Invasion. The Malick movie provides a multiplicity of perspectives, giving us a sense of personally moving around in the Guadalcanal operation.

As remarked before, however, we need to avoid assuming some simple dichotomy between vicarious and virtual experiences. As a matter of principle, we do well to inform analysis with several categories. The Spielberg and Malick movies offer ample shares of symbolical experience. These connect with iconographic persuasion in social movements such as environmentalism and feminism.[23] As a popular genre, the fable seems most suited to sustaining symbolical experience for whole films: witness *The Fountain* (2006), *The Happening* (2008), *The Box* (2009), *Life of Pi* (2012), and many films directed by M. Night Shyamalan. Of course, *Life of Pi* has the further advantage for symbolical experience of being presented in 3D, which immerses us in its world of symbols. *Avatar* (2009), by contrast, uses 3D to immerse us in an alien world of characters, settings, and events that mostly give us vicarious and virtual experiences. (As generated by James Cameron, *Avatar* includes a battle; but it is not genred overall as a war movie.)

Symbolical experience is prominent in other genres too. Many movies seem at various moments to display what insists on recognition as a symbol of some larger pattern significant for appreciating the events. Typically viewers are invited to ponder the symbol before the rest of the action resumes. For example, *The Thin Red Line* ends with a condensive symbol, one that opens into many layers of meaning; and *Saving Private Ryan* offers a condensive symbol at a time of transition into battle. The argument at hand is that symbolical experience involves a different phenomenology and, for the most part, depends on distinctive cinematic devices.

In war movies, especially, symbolical experience conventionally sustains a focus on a single, telling object. The invitation to viewers is that they dwell on the mythic resonance of that object, pausing with the film to consider how the self-announced symbol serves as an emblem of something larger than itself in the film or, often, an emblem of the film as a whole. The symbol calls attention to itself as such by standing apart from the predominant flow of the movie. It appears to the side of other potential foci, and generally the rest of the action pauses or otherwise shifts rhythm so that viewers may entertain meanings for the symbol. Sometimes the symbol engenders or even is itself a change in the rhythm of occurrence. The camera usually closes slowly on the icon or holds it in a markedly sustained focus. If the symbol is aural, separating and sustaining it or calling it to the forefront of attention through dampening the acuity of engagement with visual developments also enables the symbol to stand out. (Theme songs and musical quotations can work this way as well.) The visual effect often is slowed or frozen motion: either the symbol does not move at all, or the camera slows it to heighten the contrast with the other objects and rhythms of the film.

Such symbols lure us into their networks of associations. Songs remind us with their lyrics, periods, or rhythms of some information that enriches the film. Images provoke us via their colors, components, or contrasts to call on connections and recognize patterns that we might not appreciate otherwise as pertinent to the movie. In cinema, matches of actions or objects or sounds insist that we notice how each reaches into others with meanings that can complicate and interpret a film. Cinematic symbols move our experience from one item to another by morphing, merging, matching, and more. Often these figures suggest how the whole film can be analyzed mythically. As condensive symbols, they are nodes in networks that bring together vast realms of previous experience by viewers. They encourage viewers to notice how seemingly separate elements converge and initially disparate pieces cohere. Thus we experience these symbols as the making of connections not provided literally, logically, or even superficially.

To probe these dynamics of cinematic experience in greater detail, let us augment the comparison already underway for the remarkable war movies from 1998 with a couple of their equally distinguished predecessors. *Saving Private Ryan* and *The Thin Red Line* argue primarily through postmodern moves of ethos. By contrast, *Apocalypse Now* and *Platoon* advance their theses fundamentally through classical appeals to character. All four show how war films after the Vietnam War have been conventionally inclined to argue political claims through diverse evocations of ethos in its several modes.

Saving Private Ryan and *The Thin Red Line* argue from our virtual experiences of their wartime situations to their conclusions about the Second World War. As Spielberg says of *Saving Private Ryan,* "I'm asking the audience—and it's a lot to ask of an audience—to have a physical experience, so that they can somewhat have the experience of what those guys actually went through."[24] Even most other war films argue more from our identifications with their characters. Then we share vicariously the judgments of the figures on the screen, or we distrust them; but we sense their wars mainly through the responses of these characters rather than by interacting more independently with the situations they face, as evoked by the movie's sights and sounds. Thus our war experiences in *Apocalypse Now* and *Platoon* are not virtual but vicarious.[25] We respond principally to the characters' screen reactions to their screen situations, all separated from us by various devices of framing. When the later, 1998 films generate virtual experiences of WWII, they work to counteract framing effects and mobilize different devices to situate us within the events evoked. Some of their devices are aural and vocal; others are visual.

The two films from 1998 tap first-person camera techniques and THX technologies of sound to let viewers virtually experience the combat. Closely related World War II predecessors such as *The Longest Day* (1962) and the 1964 version of *The Thin Red Line* frame actions for viewers. This keeps viewers out of the action, which they must experience through actors on the screen more than a sense of surrounding sights and sounds. The Coppola and Stone films argue from ethos, but mainly in its classical mode by framing colorful and sympathetic characters to follow. There are few efforts to locate viewers within the scenes. The Spielberg and Malick movies provide long moments of largely unframed events, putting viewers into the midst of film figures in action. Thus they manifest their characters of combat less through virtues and vices enacted on screen than through moods and other characteristics of battle experienced by viewers in the theater.

Voices

Voiceovers often function as framing devices to keep screen events distant from movie viewers. These reinforce the argumentative reliance on ethos as character because they give us the sounds of thinking, writing, or narrating by a focal character. In principle, intimate access to somebody's thinking might pull viewers into a movie. But the emphasis on a single, point-of-view-and-voice figure can draw us into that character first and foremost. Then we experience events vicariously, through the voicing figure. Add a world-weary tone to the voice, and the power to distance viewers becomes so great that the voiceover is a cherished convention of alienation in film noir.[26]

Martin Sheen's voiceover in *Apocalypse Now* borrows from these noir aesthetics for the ordinary American, decently curious and honorable, who somehow has been dragged or lured way over his head into the slime of a misbegotten war gone further awry. The sound of his voice plus the wonderful music—from the Doors to Wagner—does enable the film to argue in part by mood. Yet *Apocalypse Now* shares the war genre's affinity for spectacle, which typically offers actions far away and safely framed from a particular point of view. The vistas often are long, and we viewers float like bombers above much of the ant-like action. These two framing devices plus Captain Willard's growing sense of horror and grotesque climax in action keep us viewers at bay: away from immersion in the scenes. Instead the film argues its thesis about the Vietnam War principally through our identification with Willard's degenerating character. We journey *as* him (more than *with* him) into the heart of darkness that is Colonel Kurtz (Marlon Brando) and the American debacle in Vietnam.

In mythic homage, *Platoon* casts Martin's son as its American protagonist in Vietnam. Its argument is made primarily by Charlie Sheen's voiceover letters to his grandmother. Again they frame the action, taking us out of it for extended times. His voice is less old and defeated than young, confused, and depleted. Still it attunes us to his experiences of the Vietnam War. *Platoon* provides less spectacle and fewer long vistas to remove viewers from participation in the action. Yet it insistently offers frontal shots of the key actors on screen, framing them in theatrical fashion as a stage of action separate from the arena reserved to the audience. We pull with Sheen's character for the virtuous American (Willem Dafoe), and we may even empathize when Sheen terminates the vicious American (Tom Berenger), but we are not sensing their situations primarily for ourselves. Again the argument is importantly from ethos, but again it is carried mainly by our identification with Sheen's protagonist. *Platoon*'s music learns from *Apocalypse Now* about ironical uses of contemporary music, yet the score seldom engages us enough to shape our moods toward some specific inference about the war.

The Thin Red Line provides a quick but telling contrast. Malick turns the thoughts of many characters into voiceovers that complement music and cinematography with recurrent reveries. This lets viewers participate in the many worlds of imagination that help configure the film and demonstrate its argument. We are not confined to the singular voice often vital for vicarious experience. We experience more for ourselves the worlds promoted by Malick.

Even the treatment of the title theme is instructive. In the novel and both films of this name, "the thin red line" is the wavering, evanescing boundary in war between normality and madness, sanity and insanity, heroism and idiocy, self-sacrifice and self-destruction, or capable prudence and despicable, careerist politics. So the first film is all tumult and noise when it argues the crazy character of war; whereas the second version provides a far greater range of emotions, music, and characters for feeling our way into the invasive antireality of war.[27]

Visuals

An early scene in *Apocalypse Now* provides a point-of-view shot that closes slowly on window blinds then parts them to peer onto a Saigon street. In the middle of this sequence, we see Martin Sheen's Captain Willard as the figure sustaining this gaze. So the film stitches our sense of the situation into Willard's, as enacted by Sheen. Through Willard, we experience the tedium, anticipation, terror, and disillusionment that characterized the Vietnam War for Americans in the mode of director Francis Ford Coppola.

We hear what Willard hears as he and we look through the blinds: helicopters. The film is famous for its iconic, spinning blades, its chopper sounds, its spiraling camera, and especially its stunned yet perceptive voiceover by Sheen. These characterize the Vietnam War by immersing viewers in the war's prevalent moods. The voiceover, soundtrack, and camerawork route our sense of the situation through Sheen's performance of Willard. We see as he sees; we hear as he hears; we think as he thinks. Hence *Apocalypse Now* provides an overwhelmingly vicarious experience of the war to support its thesis that the Vietnam War pushed beyond American morality, insanity, language, and judgment into the heart of darkness. *Platoon,* constructed in considerable homage by Oliver Stone to the Coppola film before it, repeats and occasionally twists many of these moves.

The challenge for film directors and editors is to achieve an effective consistency in moving among cinematic modes of experience. Malick's movie also combines frontal shots to outline a situation, at times omnisciently but other times vicariously, with perspectival shots to stitch viewers into that situation. Down in the tall grass, we cannot see long distances. Only as we soldiers reach the edges of the grass can the camera look largely unimpeded up the hill toward the machine gun emplacements that wait to mow us down as the enemy. We see the soldiers frontally, coming toward us. But then the leader passes us, looks back at his men, whom we see frontally from his or perhaps even our perspective. When he continues up the hill, he stays mostly hidden by the grass, but we keep him in partial sight as we move up from behind and to the side. The sense of danger is close to claustrophobic: we would like to see more and better, but we feel the need to stay down and keep on the move so that no machine gunner or sniper higher on the hill can draw a bead on our bobbing helmets.

War films used to bulge with panoramic vistas that could cultivate the viewers' senses of spectacle. Recent war films sometimes favor a spectacular restraint consistent with putting viewers into particular places within the battles depicted. They downplay all-encompassing vistas and panoramic frames for spectacles presented frontally. Instead many recent war films use perspectival shots at medium and close range plus the situating and identifying shots needed to blend vicarious and virtual experiences of specific wars.

Malick's version of *The Thin Red Line* offers profound beauty, but it is mostly intimate and seldom spectacular. *Saving Private Ryan* is mainly gritty and grue-some, yet also typically American in its sentimentality.[28] It is easily the more conventional war movie of the two.[29] Yet the attempt to let us almost literally taste the D-day invasion is renowned by veterans for its virtual reality.[30] Just as telling are the similar visual techniques that structure the bracketing scenes in the cemetery. Viewers have the perspective of family members. We follow Ryan down the path and toward the grave of Captain Miller. The film argues that we are the family, the further generations, that Miller and his men sacrificed their lives to make possible—by saving Private Ryan. It offers Ryan's grief and gratitude less as entry into experiences of the Second World War, though it does that, than as evidence of the good and obligation created by Allied warriors. Then it stitches together virtual, vicarious, and other modes of experience that enable us to sense the sacrifice and feel the obligation it confers.[31]

Both Spielberg and Malick call also on the poetry of films, with dynamics of symbolical experience, to intensify our sensations of the Second World War. One symbolical moment in the Spielberg film comes in the telling transition between a march and a battle. Drops of rain drum on a leaf. Then the sound of accelerating rain becomes heard as bursts of gunfire when Miller's men ap-proach a devastated village. Assaulted at once by nature and war, these fairly ordinary fellows stay on the road to rescue Private Ryan and the generations to come, accomplishing an extraordinary transmutation of the vicious into the virtuous by fighting for our futures. Our obligations as citizens follow in important part from their heroism, however much it might be obscured by intervening waters or years. If we will experience what the warriors faced and who they were, as well as how they acted, we can know for ourselves whom to be and what to do.

Malick's movie ends in a comparable way. The reveries throughout feature visions of sailing, swimming, sinking, and rising toward light. These culminate in an ending image of a coconut washed ashore and sprouting on the beach. This condensive symbol resolves the film's contentions of earth, air, fire, and even water—where Malick's protagonist, Private Witt, has just died sacrificing himself for the other soldiers. Experiencing the symbol of the sizable seed put-ting out roots and leaves on the boundaries of land, sea, and sky, we recapitulate the film's transit of the liminal territory leading into life, death, and thought. We sense the hope needed and deserved after participating in the movie's cruel, crazy, nevertheless redemptive events.

Versions

Differences between the two film versions of *The Thin Red Line* tell volumes about the contrast between enactments and experiences, vicarious and virtual realities. Directed by Andrew Marton, the earlier film typically keeps the camera close to the ground or, when the soldiers wade through a swamp, the surface of the water. Yet its camera captures the action mostly from the front, with men moving toward the eyes of the viewers. Moreover it seeks theatrical presentations of bodily movements and inclusive frames for particular events. When we do empathize, it is with and through its protagonist, Private Doll (Keir Dullea).

As noted, the later film puts the camera where viewers must continually crane to see what is happening. Their vantages are behind or to the side of the main motions of the men. The obstructions to sight and sound are many, and the screen seldom encompasses more than the small part of ongoing events that the camera turns and squirms to bring into piecemeal apprehension. We viewers are in the midst of the action, participating. We are not kept outside some frame, witnessing the enactments of others. The camera does not give us long vistas or hover cleanly above water surfaces; in reverie and in action, it swims beneath to display light above and around us. The manner is beautifully reminiscent of the light glinting from above a jungle canopy to suffuse the tropical surroundings toward the beginning and the end of the Malick movie. (*Platoon* offers only one brief canopy shot, toward the start; Spielberg does take his camera briefly below water during the landing sequences, so that we may sense virtually for ourselves the underwater ballet of bullets, bleeding, and death.)

The 1998 version of *The Thin Red Line* could be said to argue that war is a world of endless, crazy contention, yet we can and must imagine other worlds. Thus Malick's movie pointedly addresses many modes of experience and imagination. It gives us many domains of experience and imagination to negotiate along with its many viewpoint characters. As played by Sean Penn, Sergeant Welsh is the hardboiled realist. He lacks the edgy sense of humor in the 1964 performance by Jack Warden. But the character's honorable insistence on war as a hell that effaces needed boundaries between the sane and the insane makes Welsh's hard-headed insistence on realism as survivalism as well as his brand of responsibility for the soldiers under his command much the same in both enactments. Several other soldiers act and even argue against such realism. As in the 1964 film, Private Doll (Dash Mihok in 1998) performs a stringent and fanatical survivalism that metamorphoses into a heroically reckless idealism as he strives to impose his own standards on the chaotic conditions of war.

Yet the 1998 film de-emphasizes the 1964 polarity between Welsh and Doll. It focuses instead on contrasting Welsh with Private Witt, who is more a daydreamer than an idealist. It portrays how potent and eventually heroic Witt's imaginings can be, even though Witt never asserts them with anything like Doll's relentlessness or force. Mainly, though, it concentrates on augmenting the focal contrast with many other modes of experience and imagination. We viewers also partake of the careerist realism that characterizes Lieutenant Colonel Tall (Nick Nolte) as it veers from humiliation and desperation to outrage and insanity but then to cunning and possibly even sympathy. We share the humanism of Captain Staros (Elias Koteas)—as developed from the cautious prudence of Captain Stone (James Philbrook) in the 1964 version. We drink deeply of the perspectives embodied by Corporal Fife (Adrien Brody), Private Bell (Ben Chaplin), and Sergeant Keck (Woody Harrelson). We even taste briefly the sensibilities of Privates Tills (Tim Blake Nelson) and Matti (Larry Romano), Sergeants Storm (John C. Reilly) and McCron (John Savage), Captains Gaff (John Cusack) and Bosch (George Clooney), Second Lieutenant Whyte (Jared Leto), and Brigadier General Quintard (John Travolta). These names provide recurrent opportunities for symbolical experiences, but the film's center of experiential gravity emerges from moving among its many vicarious and especially virtual realities.

Wars, the film maintains, are worlds made by modes of ambition and imagination. In a way, the 1998 thesis of *The Thin Red Line* is closely akin to the 1996 argument of Francis A. Beer and Robert Hariman for *Post-Realism* as *The Rhetorical Turn in International Relations* now needed to escape a monomaniacal hold of *Realpolitick* on reasoning for war and diplomacy.[32] The claim is not that realism is wrong or even outdated. It is rather that realism requires other ways of thinking, talking, and acting in order to address war or any other politics adequately. The twentieth-century disposition to privilege realism as the only stance or style worth taking for war or other politics needs to yield to perspectives that encompass more modes of experience and imagination. The old disposition is one that popular genres of cinema, including films of war, are eminently equipped to help us overcome. Once you have experienced Guadalcanal from the perspectives of so many different fighters, the realism of Sergeant Welsh still seems important; yet even his realism is starting to learn the necessity and legitimacy of additional principles and styles.

Arguments

The argument, accordingly, is that *Saving Private Ryan, The Thin Red Line, Platoon, Apocalypse Now,* and many other war films are themselves arguments. As a genre, at least of late, war films argue claims about wars. These are not the kinds of arguments that political scientists or even rhetoricians are used to acknowledging. They occur in electronic media rather than written texts or oral speeches. Yet the classical apparatus of rhetoric meant for oral speeches then adapted to written texts also can serve surprisingly well to appreciate cinematic arguments and electronic politics in general.

Therefore we should continue to adapt and expand the resources of rhetoric, making them even more fit for the analysis and invention of postmodern, electronic performances. As war films suggest, we can encompass the current, electronic reach of argument from ethos by expanding the rhetoric of spirit. Let us augment earlier concerns of character and standing, authority and office, as well as credibility and expertise with postmodern dynamics of mood, tone, ambience, or atmosphere. Let us practice them all as legitimate kinds of argument. And let us perform them all—academically, cinematically, and politically—as effective modes of experience.

In *Saving Private Ryan,* the bracketing scenes establish unmistakably that the film is an argument about the debt we owe Captain Miller and the myriad other soldiers who sacrificed themselves in winning the Second World War. We, like Private James Ryan, are obliged to live our lives so as to make good on their suffering and sacrifice. How are we viewers to know that this claim on us is right? The film stitches us into experiences of the European war that make lucid and personal to each of us the spirit, price, and implications of that sacrifice. We, like Private Ryan, owe our lives and futures to the likes of Captain Miller. We, even more like the members of Ryan's family, must stretch our sensibilities to encompass what Miller, Ryan, his mother, and millions of other people went through to provide the freedom for us to acquit our obligation. If you have been through something like their experiences, the film shows, you know how and why you are indebted to them.

After locating us as members of the family whose future has depended on the sacrifices of Captain Miller, Private Ryan, and the Allied soldiers who won the Second World War, the Spielberg film offers its famous evocation of the D-day landings. It has moved us into Ryan's arena of knowledge (rather than personal experience) by closing pointedly on his teary eyes, staring into space at the gravesite. Once within the invasion scenes, the camera moves almost seamlessly among omniscient, vicarious, virtual, perspectival, symbolical, and other cinematic modes of experience. To help us feel the suffering, killing, courage, cunning, cowardice, and varied fortunes of the soldiers, *Saving Private Ryan* completes the camerawork with amazing soundtracks that keep us in the middle of the assault for long, desperate minutes at a time. To draw us further into the action, Spielberg darkens the edges of the screen at times to transform any residual framing effects into the tunnel vision of one concentrating intensely and focusing narrowly because life depends on it.

This experiential tunneling comes and goes, as it does for soldiers or others in the midst of manic bursts of activity. The motion slows and speeds in erratic but intelligible ways, especially as we focus vicariously on Miller's struggle to overcome the numbing barrage in order to concert himself and his command to effective action. At the same instants, we are getting a private's virtual view of the captain's confusion and resolution while sensing the dire conditions vicariously through the captain's responses.

Please notice the implication that vicarious and virtual experiences are not exclusively cinematic. They are amply apparent in the everyday flows of experience that we naïvely label "direct" or "personal," without stopping to analyze phenomenologically. On the battlefield, military trainers know, privates do look at times to captains for experiences of the situations that they share: this, far more than simple command, helps enable them to maintain military discipline. It helps effect the coordination and facilitate the cooperation crucial for success. The same turns out to be true of symbolical and still other modes of experience. Not only do military training and leadership take advantage of them all, but everyday lives manifest these modes of experience in hosts of situations too readily classified as experienced "individually" or "simply."

If we remember this, we should be able to avoid any dubious dichotomies between ordinary, real, or personal modes of experience on one side and cinematic modes of experience on another side. Thus the politics of cinematic experiences are parts of the real and important politics of people's lives. Cinematic politics need not—and should not—be regarded as especially artificial, categorically fraudulent, necessarily manipulative, or patently immaterial. Myths, symbols, and movies are actual and potent components of the politics we experience both officially and informally. Therefore it is high time that we respect films as significant arenas of political action. In making political arguments about our events, settings, and characters from the mundane to the world-historical, popular movies can shape our political sensibilities—even when the films do not focus on politics but leave them to the subtexts and other symbols. And in making political myths that we live virtually, vicariously, and symbolically, popular movies can become potent modes of political action.

PART THREE
CINEMATIC TERRORS

CHAPTER **8**

MOVIES PREFIGURE POLITICS

HOW THRILLERS ANTICIPATED TERRORIST ATTACKS ON AMERICA
(FEATURING THE SIEGE, THE PEACEMAKER, AND PATRIOT GAMES)

The most powerful influence on the arts in the West is—the cinema.[1]

—Kenneth Tynan

Works of art do not represent "reality,"... art creates realities and worlds.[2]

—Murray Edelman

Therefore cinema, especially popular cinema, can powerfully influence our realities. These range from mundane details of everyday life to pervasive overviews of official politics. In fact, cognition research suggests that audiovisual sources such as film and television are particularly potent for politics.[3] Figures from films are prominent in the memories tapped by politics. Especially through popular genres of cinema, these figures help structure what we experience as political terrorism and responses to it.[4] In movies, popular genres are families of conventions for cinematography, *mise-en-scène,* story, dialogue, acting, editing, music, even marketing.[5] Thus popular genres are aesthetics: styles that tell us what goes with what else. As networks of figures, they have been shaping our senses of terrorist ends and means. They inform how we experience terrorist events and respond to them.[6] So they contribute to a "prefiguration of the phenomenal field" for political terrorism.[7]

The phenomenal field is the front edge of experience. It is the vague situation-and-event that can start to take specific shape in our awareness as we encounter it. Existential phenomenologists and social cognitionists suggest that, even before we consciously configure (let alone interpret) our experiences, we must prefigure them as initial kinds of occurrences.[8] As we walk into a room, does it look like a class with students lurking at the back to keep texting or a class with students crowding toward the front to claim attention? Does it seem like a gathering where friends clump together or where people work the room? Does it sound like a produce market for sampled wares and list prices or a bazaar for browsing then bargaining? The process is much the same as watching the first movie frames for the opening credits even as you start seeing the movie as horror, thriller, or romance.[9]

For cognition, the implication can seem paradoxical: before—or at least as—we cognize experience, we must recognize its elements. Otherwise cognition as form and dynamic must lack any content on which to work. Cognition depends on—more or less prior—recognition. To *apprehend* something in a firm (if mental) grasp, which is what the word means, we must discern something to grasp. We must (know to) turn toward it. Because form and content cannot yet be distinct, we do this with a "turn." The ancient Greek word for such a turn is *trope,* which the Greeks appreciated as a "figure" of speech, experience, making, perhaps even acting.[10]

As we've been emphasizing, even before we apprehend a particular movie, our culture provides templates for us to sense the whole. These are popular genres, which speed and shape our apprehension of a movie.[11] As families of figures, networks of tropes, popular genres work as wholes; but they also perform in parts. Thus they are subject to appropriation outside their usual milieus, as fragments when a familiar genre is in disarray or as remnants when an earlier genre has been dispersed. The recurrent elements of genres—as of aesthetics in general—are their conventional figures. Even as fragments and remnants, these figures inform our deeds, our words, our thoughts, even our sensations.

Genres and figures go together by elective affinity.[12] We connect like with like. Often we follow cultural paths of previous associations as we discern genres or choose figures. Prefigurations play a role, sometimes a decisive one. Yet we can make different affinities as we like, individually and socially. Popular genres work this way: like cultural myths and cognitive networks, they are dynamic webs of associations. The experiential activation of a node literally reminds us of linked nodes to spread activation throughout a web of memories, images, symbols, and the like. Each experience reinforces associations that otherwise atrophy, even as it subtly or significantly alters them.

Popular films can play prominent roles in our political cognition. Hollywood gives us figures for beginning even to sense events, personal and political. Popular cinema is far from our only source of prefiguration for any phenomenal field, including events of September 11, 2001, in particular or political terrorism in general. Yet even when their figures have not cohered into a singular genre, movies can help prefigure our political experiences and responses. What we bring with us to new experiences are less political facts than audiovisual tropes, many from movies.[13] Hence we do well to consider how Hollywood mythmaking, especially in the 1980s and 1990s, helped prefigure political terrorism prior to the trauma of 9/11. Here the interest is in what tropes of sight, sound, and story were available from popular films to shape American experiences of terrorist atrocities of 9/11 and later.

Myths and Genres

The aftermath of events on September 11, 2001, suggests the importance of cinema, television, and other electronic media in constructing our political realities.[14] Soon after, the Bush Administration was working with Hollywood screenwriters to anticipate possible targets and scenarios for future terrorist atrocities.[15] Yet the main Hollywood contributions had come earlier, before September 11, through popular films. These let audiences experience acts of political terrorism in vicarious, virtual, symbolical, and other modes.[16] In response to the dramatic escalation of terrorist attacks on U.S. citizens and institutions, Americans could call on cinematic prefigurations of terrorist strategies, the movements and states that use them, the regimes that support them, and the politics that reply to them. More than that, we could hardly help but prefigure events and settings of terrorism somewhat in Hollywood terms, because they were prominent in the figures that were familiar to us.

Hence we do well to consider how Hollywood mythmaking from the 1980s onward has helped us characterize terrorism, connections between American and Middle Eastern politics, attacks on the virtue or viability of western civilization, and so on.[17] Here the emphasis is on Hollywood aesthetics available to influence American experiences of terrorism and responses to it. The argument is that, especially through the aesthetic packages that we call popular genres, Hollywood cinema helps prefigure our experiences of terrorism. In the two decades prior to 9/11, Hollywood prefigures political terrorism in strikingly negative terms. Yet the specific figures for apprehending situations as terrorist might be even more helpful in suggesting how Americans came so quickly to a sense of astronomical stakes for an American "War on Terror."

Events in the decade before 2001 had shifted American sensibilities and Hollywood movies away from a Cold War conflict that had pitted the Communist Iron Curtain in the East against the Free World of Democracy in the West. As much as any administration or school of foreign affairs, popular movies had been helping turn American attention away from Villainous Commies out to undo Democracy in America. While Washington politicos worked overtime to follow Commies with other enemies of freedom, Hollywood joined in replacing the outdated villains of the Evil Empire with the Ruthless Terrorists who could range from the Middle East to Middle America.[18] Often, but not always, cinematic terrorists have hated western ways. Often, but not always in the movies, terrorists have declared total—if asymmetrical—war against America's hegemony as the world's only remaining military, political, and cultural superpower. Often, but not always in the movies, terrorists have been pointedly or vaguely Arabic in look and sound. (Many nationalities do surface on occasion in popular movies about political terrorism.)

As widely noted, these figures have become so familiar to Americans—principally from Hollywood films—that the journalistic and popular presumption at first was that terrorists with ties to the Middle East had obliterated the federal building in Oklahoma City. Although the American militia movement had not been ignored altogether by the popular media in America, Timothy McVeigh still came as a shock to the country. Furthermore his mythic figure has yet to become commonplace in popular films about political terrorism, although there are exceptions. Hollywood has filled most roles for terrorists with figures from afar, and its arsenals of terrorist plots twist mostly toward international machinations.

Fortunately for Americans, Hollywood in the twentieth century still supplied more numerous and sometimes more impressive instances of political terrorism than did the country's enemies. Neither America's political elites nor its mass publics sustained attention to political terrorism before the atrocities wrought in 2001 by al Qaeda. Not even terrorist bombings in the 1990s of the World Trade Center, the Murrah Federal Building, and American foreign embassies crowded out the sights and sounds of terrorism as genred by movie conventions increasingly global in their ambition and impact. This traces to the enormous artistic power, commercial success, and cultural reach of Hollywood products—distributed to audiences almost everywhere in the world. By September 11, 2001, the earlier terrorist acts mainly had become fuel for still more imaginative and graphic films. Consequently the phenomenal field for experiencing and responding to political terrorism remained wide open to prefiguration by Hollywood films.[19]

Many of these films have been "Hollywood thrillers." Let us include English-language films from Britain and Canada or elsewhere that enjoy wide release in the United States, for they use the same conventions and show in the same theaters. For present purposes, "Hollywood" is not just a place in greater Los Angeles. Thrillers span international intrigues, governmental and military conspiracies, foreign wars, police or social dramas, and others on the edges of the neighboring metagenre of action-adventure. Here we explore how thriller figures prefigured our senses of political terrorism for experiencing the attacks of 9/11. The aim is also to trace how these tropes established schemata for American experiences of the 9/11 aftermath and later acts of political terrorism.[20]

Tropes of terror do not constitute a singular genre or even a distinctive aesthetic, as I explore in more detail in Chapter 10. This situation leaves political terror especially open to presentation in diverse genres. The sense that terrorism takes us into the depths of political evil might encourage us to find horror or noir films especially fit for tales of terrorists. So far, though, Hollywood has seldom configured political terrorism in tropes from genres other than the thriller. The systematic exception is telling: Hollywood uses dystopia, which just is the political subgenre of horror, also is shared with science fiction, but uses dystopia only for dramas of regime terrorism. These show totalitarian regimes as exercises in terrorism, but they do not include terrorism as a device of rebellion or movement, let alone as an outgrowth of civil or holy war. Likewise war movies do not examine terrorism so much as tame and transform it. War movies treat terrorism as merely a tactic for victory, rather than as a sustained mode of politics; or war movies cram terrorism into their own dramas of residual honor in hellish conditions where anything goes and all's fair. In either event, figures familiar from war movies often overwhelm political aspects of terrorism rather than shaping terror politics in distinctive ways. Before 9/11, especially, this meant that political terrorism of kinds most relevant to plots from the likes of Osama bin Laden appeared mainly in generic thrillers.

Several other families of films are relevant but peripheral to this analysis. *James Bond* films are thrillers, and over half include acts of terrorism. The trouble is that Bond movies have been satires, spoofing international intrigues and Hollywood figures. At least this held until the first two films when the Bond franchise cast Daniel Craig as its title character. (His third Bond film revives aspects of the earlier mode.[21]) The Bond terrorists are caricatures mad for power and profit, or inane—more than insane—with evil. *Austin Powers* (1997, 1999, 2002) and company turn the Bond caricatures into cartoons. As a result, such films feature adult or adolescent play more than terrorism. Their effects on American templates for political terrorism probably remain marginal, even as the Bond films are numerous enough to skew forthcoming counts beyond use. (As a bone to those in Bondage, though, the analysis does tap the first *xXx* movie, which began to coalesce as a production before 9/11.) We also need to disregard superhero movies, where acts of political terrorism are conventional but almost completely cartoonish.[22] So here we do well to stress political thrillers and other popular films that might hype headlines and twist history but that stay linked to some semblance of serious attention to terrorism.

Different dynamics lead us away from documentaries, which seldom become popular films in America. Much the same goes for historical dramas with acts of domestic terror that go unrecognized as relevant to political terrorism of the 9/11 ilk. Americans seldom connect KKK cross-burnings, Pinkerton raids, presidential assassinations, and many other terrorist acts in the country's history to the political terrorism of Timothy McVeigh—let alone Osama bin Laden. Thus the figures of political terror available in such popular films as *Matewan* (1987), *Mississippi Burning* (1988), or even *O Brother, Where Art Thou?* (2001) probably do not contribute much to the popular prefiguration of political terrorism by Hollywood films. In principle, they could have a strong influence; in practice, however, our cultural connections seem mostly to ignore them.

Tropes and Politics

By this point, we are starting to see how Hollywood tropes can help configure political realities. In principle, the kinds of politics are innumerable; in practice, popular movies for the United States have been interested principally in a standard roster of politics. Some are modern and ideological: liberalism, conservatism, socialism, or democratism.[23] Others are postmodern and mythic: anarchism, existentialism, or perfectionism (loosely in the mode of Friedrich Nietzsche).[24] Most of these stem in part from the republicanism that begins even before modern times.[25] But in America, socialism seldom surfaces, and liberalism dominates democratism, so we can pare the roster for present purposes. All these politics came to the United States from Europe, where republicanism arises in ancient Rome and resurges in the Renaissance, modern ideologies started to form in the sixteenth century, and postmodern politics appear in the nineteenth century. Thus the political labels I use come from the field of political theory rather than popular talk, which is less clear and consistent in differentiating kinds of politics.

By these Eurocentric standards, please note, almost all of what Americans position on a Left-to-Right spectrum of politics is "liberal" in the terms of political theory. Otherwise it would not map so neatly onto a single spectrum. On the far left in America is not so much socialism in the European sense of political theory but welfare liberalism of the sort associated with Franklin Roosevelt and Lyndon Johnson. On the far right is classical liberalism linked of late to Barry Goldwater or the libertarianism of Ron and Rand Paul. Conservatives of European sorts stemming from Edmund Burke in eighteenth-century Britain are unusual in the United States. No more than full-fledged socialism is such conservatism prominent in American politics—or movies. The same goes for anarchism, yet we do well to keep that in the picture for movies that feature terrorism.[26] These days, the Republican Party in the United States is no more and no less "republican" in the lowercase than is the Democratic Party. Ideologically, at least, both are largely "liberal" in the lowercase. (When I capitalize Liberal or Conservative, Republican or Democratic, I am using proper names from the everyday discourse of American politics instead of technical terms from political theory.)

Still the need is for figural, more than conceptual, versions of these politics—although there is bound to be substantial overlap, since I am communicating the figures in words that political theorists and practitioners use often as concepts. (Icons or clips from films and TV ads could increase clarity, but that is an exercise for another occasion.[27]) To indicate how this can work, let me use two tables to evoke the six sets of political tropes that I argue to appear in Hollywood movies. In social-scientific terms, these are criteria for coding the overall politics of each film that features terrorism. In Table 8.1, I begin with tropes for republican, liberal, and conservative politics, to chart key figures for classical and modern politics in Hollywood films.

To characterize politics by contrasting these kinds of figures is to treat the politics as styles more than as ideologies, movements, parties, or policies. The advantage is that political styles surface in the conduct of movie characters across all their situations for action—and not just settings for election campaigns, government offices, international relations, or other arenas for the official politics of state. (In the concluding chapter, I return to advantages of attending to political styles when analyzing popular movies.) Thrillers and other genres differ in their main political styles.[28]

The earliest, classical politics in this first table are republican. Because we've been doing rhetorical analysis of movie politics, and rhetoric has been refined for two thousand years by the republican-rhetorical tradition, we've already been using lots of republican tropes. They cultivate the characters of citizens who seek

Table 8.1 Tropes of Classical and Modern Politics

Kind of Politics	Republican Trope	Liberal Trope	Conservative Trope
pervasive political purpose and dynamics	invention	representation	governance
mode of political and personal ties	responsibility	trust	respect
measure for action by ordinary members	emulation	consent	deference
model of political and personal ambition	leadership	sovereignty	regulation
sources and targets of political and personal thought and action	judgments and gestures	rights and institutions	rites and traditions
primordial identity of the individual	the citizen	the person	the place or role
ground or foundation for politics and backing for argument	lessons of history	states of nature	patterns of practice
characteristics principle of action	vigilance	fear	suspicion
standards and styles of communal memory	virtues	morals	mores
place to enjoy most the highest goods	public	private	family
keys to decision and explanation	characters	issues	stations
norm for reflection and distribution	deliberation	negotiation	demonstration
tenor and dynamic of cultural figuration	orality	visuality	conformity
grammar or rhetoric of political action	excel in contests	solve problems	restore order

to excel with one another in public affairs that rely on martial arts but more on oration, deliberation, and vigilance against abuses of power. Citizens develop virtues such as ambition, discipline, and magnanimity. By studying the lessons of history, while emulating the judgments and gestures of great leaders, citizens learn to be inventive contributors who take responsibility for their families, their communities, and themselves (in that order).[29]

As the name implies, liberalism develops the initially republican principle of liberty as the freedom of the polity from rule by tyrants or foreign powers. Liberalism extends liberty further to persons as free to fulfill themselves in private affairs. They are protected from the dangers of nature by a sovereign government with a monopoly on the legitimate means of violence to enforce laws for peace and prosperity. Persons can trust government to avoid tyranny when it can be seen to represent their ideas about rights and interests on issues of the moment, so political representation is crucial for liberals. Fear of government enforcement spurs individual persons to rational calculations that promote obedience of laws, negotiation of differences, and adjustment of institutions to solve any problems that arise in the civil society which results from keeping all people in awe of modern, sovereign, state power. For liberals, government is evil because it coerces us as individuals to obey laws for order; but it is an evil necessary for security and productivity.[30]

Whereas republicans prize political participation as the responsibility of citizens and the path to glory for some leaders, liberals see government activity as a rational but regrettable course that corrupts all too many attracted to it. In Europe, socialism reasserts a positive conception of community power and participation centered on the same modern state as liberalism. European styles of conservatism arise in alarm at socialist efforts to rationalize community and government. Thus conservatism favors the wisdom grown in social rites, traditions, and mores. It encourages demonstrations of respect for established patterns of practice and restoring order as needed. It is suspicious of political action and change. Instead it celebrates conformity, with deference to the person's organizational role, the family's social station, and the community's place in the world.

Table 8.2 diagrams tropes for three kinds of postmodern politics in much the same way, again with an eye to the myths of politics in Hollywood movies that turn on terrorism.

At levels of ideology, two kinds of anarchism have been prominent in the past century and a half, and both contribute features to anarchism as a political style of personal action. Anarchists agree with liberals that modern government is coercive and therefore evil, but anarchists deny that it is necessary or desirable. Libertarian anarchists emphasize rational self-management by individuals who do their own things, whereas communitarian anarchists promote mutual aid and support for individuals.[31] Existentialists doubt that individual rationality could or should determine personal choices, so they expect individuals to take responsibility for themselves and small communities akin to monasteries that might protect them from larger social systems and help them construct meanings.[32] On a similar basis, perfectionists toast the "genius" who turns away from criticism and reflection to act on vital impulses attuned to their settings. This sometimes attracts followers to cultivate a way of life for emulating the paragon of pathbreaking deeds and discourses.[33]

Table 8.2 Tropes of Postmodern Politics

Kind of Politics	Anarchism	Existentialism	Perfectionism
pervasive political purpose and dynamics	freedom	action	impulse
mode of political and personal ties	mutuality	meaning	success
measure for action by ordinary members	support	distance	attunement
model of political and personal ambition	collaboration	construction	culture
sources and targets of political and personal thought and action	reasons and practices	leaps and experiences	deeds and discourses
primordial identity of the individual	the decider	the self-maker	the doer
ground or foundation for politics and backing for argument	choices of people	horizons of becoming	deconstructions of perspective
characteristics principle of action	aid	resistance	inspiration
standards and styles of communal memory	truths	facts	tropes
place to enjoy most the highest goods	company	monastery	pinnacle
keys to decision and explanation	criteria	situations	paragons
norm for reflection and distribution	persuasion	conversation	path-breaking
tenor and dynamic of cultural figuration	individuality	particularity	uniformity
grammar or rhetoric of political action	do your own thing	resist systems	just do it

As I analyze political styles in thrillers about terrorism, I explain further some elements of each style. I use the full scheme, with all fourteen tropes for each mode of politics, to assess the movies. This introduces extra room for debate about the best way to classify politics in any case, but it respects the complexity of the politics at issue. To streamline the exposition, however, I focus only on the bottom row of tropes. These evoke the grammar or rhetoric of political action for each kind of politics, that is, the dynamic for each style.

Particularly in America, the pragmatic grammar of liberalism presents political action as solving problems.[34] Action in republican politics is agonal, with people going for glory by virtuoso performances in public. Thus republicans try to excel in contests.[35] Conservatives, especially of a Burkean sort, treat political action as restoring order, as healing communities that suffer diverse disruptions.[36] Anarchists oppose all governmental or hierarchical order. Their near neighbors, libertarians, oppose all but light touches of it; so I code these together for promoting political action as doing your own thing, not taking orders or following laws.[37] For existentialists, political action resists systems that regiment or otherwise oppress people.[38] And perfectionists are the Nietzschean charismatics who leap into action out of a successful feeling for their times: as the Nike slogan urges, they "Just Do It."[39]

The reason to focus on tropes of political action is that films from Hollywood rarely label their politics for overall ideology or myth. In contrast to propaganda films, few popular movies feature ideational dialogue, and popular audiences focus anyway on the dynamics of action. Distinctions among what screen characters do—solving problems, excelling in contests, and so on—can be accessible to viewers. They seldom analyze the films politically, but they can experience them as styles of action that tap the associated networks for politics.

The system of terror in *The Day After* (1983) shows how this can work. Its desperate straits of sheer survival after an exchange of missiles between nuclear powers trap people in a situation with no way out. Can individuals resist relentless depredations and degradations to survive in a humane way? This figure of action is existentialist. Action within the system yields no exit, no rescue; but it might maintain no capitulation through an insistent resistance.

Two other films with terrorist episodes configure themselves as system breakdowns. *Fight Club* (1999) vamps the sly disintegration of consumer society as a soft totalitarianism that atomizes humanity. The film's response is ecoterrorism. *Fight Club* encourages and enforces a system breakdown. Its injunction is to "hit bottom," eliminating compunctions and other complications of civilization, so that new perfectionist Overmen can "Just Do It!"[40] That makes political terrorism a perfect path to the annihilation of mores, credit histories, even personality structures. The tone is playful, and the terrorism is a little jokey; but it is clear that Luke Helder's spree of mailbox terrorism, now forgotten save for the communities in the Midwest that he hit, was prefigured in part by this film. Like the protagonist in *Fight Club,* Helder saw himself as the heroic liberator—of himself, if not always others—from subtle terrors inflicted by a system of domination that we do not readily recognize. Both try to satirize and deconstruct the system with its own smiley face: *Fight Club* burns this into the side of a skyscraper; Helder bombed it into the middle of his country. Villains and heroes of terrorist scenes in *Fight Club* fit the Nietzschean perfectionism in the film's focal trope of political action. Helder's libertarian rants against government are a far less perfect match (aesthetically and politically) for his teen idolization of Kurt Cobain or his smiley figure of Nietzschean action, yet the smell of nihilism is pervasive. As a mailbox bomber, Helder enacted a postmodern pastiche of terrorist ideas, images, and impulses. Then, adding in a way to his own weird pattern, Helder (properly) pled insanity. Go figure. Yet the pervasive sense of play keeps many viewers from taking the *Fight Club* terrorism seriously enough to be alarmed by it, and something similar seems to have kept most Americans from remembering the Helder terrorism at all.

The Sum of All Fears (2002), also in production before 9/11, presents the United States as a liberal society still trapped with Russia in a quasi-Cold War system of Mutual Assured Destruction. The American hero must solve problems to save his polity. Yet it is principally a republican subculture of honor and anger driving the leaders of America and Russia toward a nuclear war that neither wants but neither can figure out how to escape. Thus the film dramatizes a liberal diagnosis of systematic self-destruction by republican politics. It shows how republican reliance on codes of personal honor and communal responsibility can lead to disaster. As liberals see it, the results turn slights into offenses, grievances into grudges, and responses into feuds. These feudal politics become chaotic and, in our nuclear times, an-nihilistic: the upshot is a war of all against all where the strategy is to strike preemptively, to gain advantage in a globe-engulfing conflagration. As a matter of morality and prudence, *The Sum of All Fears* urges, like *War Games* in 1983, that "the only move is not to play."

Such examples may yield some sense of how the present analytical games are to be played. Anchoring the game boards are the fifty films in Table 8.3 that include acts of political terrorism. Forty-six were made more or less in America, four in other countries, and all for popular release in the United States. This film roster for analysis is surely not a census or even, in the strictest sense, a sample of movies *about* political terrorism. Many include an act or two of terrorism while focusing on other things. Yet this is how Hollywood often helps to prefigure politics. Before 9/11, "everybody" in Hollywood "knew" that overtly political films do badly at the box office; and producers steered clear of many scripts that centered on the high, official politics of state. Although it is likely that my list omits some of Hollywood's relevant efforts in the couple of decades just before 9/11, it includes all pertinent films I could recall seeing, with the analysis refreshed by another viewing or two. Hence the aim is not comprehensive coverage but a field for analysis varied enough to engage in productive detail.

Plots and Acts

Figures of political action connect with plots and tropes of action. Plots synopsize the turns made by a drama or told by a story. Stock plots are prominent conventions of popular genres. From the larger repertoire of a genre, a stock plot arranges a conventional subset of scenes, perhaps mixed with a few borrowed from the stocks of other genres or invented from other resources. The scenes are comprised of deeds, most familiar from the genre. A thriller scene in *The Sum of All Fears* is a standard fight to the death: a physical showdown between the hero and the most athletic of the villains. The hero withstands considerable punishment, since victory against a terrifying adversary could not come easily. Then he makes machinery at hand into a weapon that he wields to kill the bad guy. The symbolism in transforming the machine from a menace into a successful means of self-defense is an emblem of the movie's overall politics of technocratic liberalism in nuclear times. This act turns a problem into its solution. Likewise the plot converts a breakdown of the MAD system—with self-defense threatening to become self-destruction—into improved relations between Russia and the United States. The film shows this to be a step toward a world safe for individual problem-solvers who can learn to collaborate across countries to overcome crises.

There are eight to ten kinds of plots in the fifty films. For most purposes, let us combine **system-breakdown plots** and **dystopian plots**. Both show how terrible systems of society and government can sustain themselves indefinitely then fail unexpectedly. Their politics come more from the character of systems as systems than the particular ideology or myth that inflects a system with one of our six overall brands of politics. **Capers** are intrigues played lightly, but with the outcome in some doubt. **Conspiracies** focus on the machinations of people getting together in private to produce public acts (of terrorism). **Problem-solution plots**, already defined, include tales of detection. **Remarriage plots** might be genred as comedies or thrillers, but either way they trouble happy partners then bring them back together. **Resurrection plots** take someone into death or disaster, and beyond, then regenerate vitality; **sin-and-redemption plots** go beyond transgression to deliverance in much the same pattern, so they can be counted together with resurrection dramas. **Tragedies** do only the first part. And **spy-vs.-spy plots** pit heroes against villains in struggles with many episodes, *mano-a-mano,* until the heroes prevail.

Table 8.3 indicates the kinds of plots and political styles that characterize each movie with episodes of political terrorism. This table also records the principal projects of the focal villains and heroes in each film. These could be regarded as key motives for action by the focal characters in each film, clarifying how it

Table 8.3 Political Terrorism in the Two Decades of Films before 9/11

Movie	Year	Subgenre	Terror Mode	Villain Kind	Villain Motive	Film Stance	Hero Motive	Plot Type	Political Style
Air Force One	1997	political thriller	hijack, hostage	fanatical	revenge, power	discredit	protection	spy vs. spy	republican
Arlington Road	1999	political thriller	bomb	deluded	jihad	discredit	justice	conspiracy	republican
The Assignment	1997	spy thriller	bomb	pro	jihad	ignore	revenge	spy vs. spy	republican
Black Sunday	1977	police thriller	bomb	deranged	jihad	discount	protection	problem-solution	liberal
Blown Away	1994	police thriller	bomb	deranged	revenge	discount	protection	problem-solution	liberal
The Boxer	1997	social thriller	bomb	trapped	hatred	sympathy	rationality	resurrection	liberal
Cover Up	1991	spy thriller	chemical	pro	revenge	discredit	protection	spy vs. spy	republican
The Crying Game	1992	social thriller	bomb	trapped	seduction	sympathy	loyalty	tragedy	existentialist
The Day After	1983	war horror	nuclear war	ourselves	annihilation	discount	survival	dystopia	existentialist
Deadly Heroes	1996	spy thriller	hostage	fanatical	hatred	discount	protection	spy vs. spy	republican
The Delta Force	1986	military thriller	hijack, hostage	fanatical	jihad	discount	protection	problem-solution	republican
The Devil's Own	1997	social thriller	bomb	trapped	loyalty	sympathy	loyalty	problem-solution	liberal
Die Hard	1988	police thriller	hostage	criminal	theft	discount	protection	problem-solution	liberal
Die Hard 2	1990	police thriller	bomb	criminal	theft	discount	protection	problem-solution	liberal
Die Hard with a Vengeance	1995	police thriller	bomb	criminal	revenge	discount	protection	spy vs. spy	republican
Double Team	1997	spy thriller	bomb	pro	revenge	ignore	protection	spy vs. spy	republican
Executive Decision	1996	military thriller	hijack, biological	fanatical	jihad	ignore	protection	problem-solution	liberal

(continued)

Table 8.3 Continued

Movie	Year	Subgenre	Terror Mode	Villain Kind	Villain Motive	Film Stance	Hero Motive	Plot Type	Political Style
Fight Club	1999	satirical noir political thriller	vandal, bomb	ourselves	domination	empathy	liberation	system breakdown	perfectionist
Final Voyage	1999	guard thriller	hijack, hostage	criminal	theft	discredit	protection	remarriage thriller	republican
Fire Birds	1990	military thriller	chemical, drugs	pro	profit	discredit	protection	problem-solution	republican
The Fourth Angel	2001	spy thriller	hijack, hostage	pro	theft	discredit	revenge	spy vs. spy	republican
The Fourth Protocol	1987	spy thriller	nuke	fanatical	power	discredit	protection	spy vs. spy	liberal
High Crimes	2002	legal thriller	bomb, execution	pro	power	ignore	justice	problem-solution	republican
In the Name of the Father	1993	tragedy-triumph	bomb	fanatical	order	respect	justice	resurrection	republican
The Jackal	1997	spy thriller	assassin	pro	destruction	respect	protection	spy vs. spy	republican
Little Drummer Girl	1984	spy thriller	assassin	trapped	jihad	sympathy	protection	spy vs. spy	liberal
Missing	1982	political horror	regime	pro	domination	sympathy	justice	dystopia	republican
Mission Impossible II	2000	spy thriller	biological	criminal	extortion	discredit	protection	spy vs. spy sin-redemption	perfectionist
Navy Seals	1990	military thriller	hostage, missile	fanatical	jihad	ignore	honor		republican
The Package	1989	spy thriller	assassin	fanatical	power	discredit	vigilance	conspiracy	republican
The Patriot (Seagal)	1998	military thriller	biological	fanatical	liberation	sympathy	protection	problem-solution	anarchist
Patriot Games	1992	spy thriller	assassin	fanatical	revenge	ignore	honor	spy vs. spy	republican
The Peacemaker	1997	military thriller	nuke	fanatical	despair	sympathy	protection	remarriage thriller	conservative
Proof of Life	2000	spy thriller	hostage, bomb	criminal	extortion	discredit	honor	remarriage thriller	republican

(continued)

Table 8.3 Continued

Movie	Year	Subgenre	Terror Mode	Villain Kind	Villain Motive	Film Stance	Hero Motive	Plot Type	Political Style
The Rock	1996	military thriller	biological	deranged	revenge	discount	protection	problem-solution	liberal
The Siege	1999	political thriller	bomb	fanatical	jihad	sympathy	vigilance	conspiracy	republican
Speed	1994	police thriller	hijack, bomb	criminal	revenge	discount	protection	problem-solution	liberal
Speed 2: Cruise Control	1997	police thriller	hijack	criminal	extortion	discount	protection	caper	republican
Spy Game	2001	noir spy thriller	assassin	pro	bureaucracy	respect	justice	spy vs. spy	republican
Sudden Death	1995	police thriller	hostage	criminal	extortion	discredit	protection	spy vs. spy	republican
The Sum of All Fears, Nazi	2002	spy thriller	nuke	evil	domination	discount	vigilance	spy vs. spy	republican
The Sum of All Fears, CW	2002	political thriller	nuke	trapped	honor and anger	sympathy	escape	system breakdown	liberal
Swordfish	2001	noir police thriller	hijack, bomb	pro	revenge	respect	escape	caper	anarchist
Three Kings	1999	war satire thriller	bomb, torture	ourselves	profit	empathy	honor	satirical caper	republican
Toy Soldiers	1991	military thriller	hostage	familiar	extortion	discredit	protection	spy vs. spy	republican
True Lies	1994	satire spy thriller	nuke	deranged	jihad	ridicule	protection	remarriage thriller	conservative
Under Siege	1992	military thriller	nuke	criminal	extortion	discount	vigilance	spy vs.spy	republican
Under Siege 2	1995	military thriller	nuke	criminal	extortion	discount	vigilance	spy vs. spy	republican
Victory at Entebbe	1996	military thriller	hijack, bomb	fanatical	jihad	discredit	protection	problem-solution	liberal
Xchange	2000	science fiction	bomb	fanatical	power	respect	survival	problem-solution	liberal
xXx	2002	satire spy thriller	biological	criminal	anarchy	ridicule	action	spy vs. spy	perfectionist

configures its acts of political terrorism. But let us set them aside for now to address ties between the plots and the overall politics.

Some films interweave two or three main plots rather than hanging all the subplots from one central trunk. Multiple plots might contribute to one overall kind of politics for the film as a whole; or they might sustain more than one kind, perhaps pitting a first ambivalently against a second. *The Sum of All Fears* intertwines two plots. The vigilant hero (Ben Affleck) goes toe to toe with Nazis bent on world domination in a plot of spy-vs.-spy. This catalyzes a second plot, where a republican system of honor and anger breaks down into MADness, bringing out the problem-solving side of the hero. He helps us escape that terrible system into a liberal politics of contract and trade. That brings the present set of plots to a total of fifty-one, counting separately for most purposes these two main plots from *The Sum of All Fears.*

A third of the politics possible on this basis turn out to be liberal: fourteen out of fifty-one. To me, this is a surprise. If the popular cinema of political terrorism were dominated by an overriding disposition to defend the present liberal system in America, as critics who think popular movies simplistic might expect, the portion of films with liberal politics overall ought to be much higher. If Hollywood merely inserts acts of popular terrorism into the mill of action-adventure movies, which by genre favor republican contests between combatants, the portion of liberal films should be much lower. Twice as many of the films with political terrorism feature republican politics than liberal politics, at twenty-eight to fourteen. These results can be explained by elective affinities between kinds of plots and politics. By genre, more than four-fifths of these films are thrillers. Yet every genre, even when inclined overall toward one kind of politics, includes a considerable range of stock plots. Even within a single genre, different plots tend to implicate distinct politics. Almost any plot *could* be used to purvey almost any kind of politics, but elective affinities are the conventional practice.

Most of the liberal politics, where actors solve problems, arise from films with problem-solution plots. Among the films at issue, problem-solution plots seldom tie to other kinds of politics. Is the tie too strong? Four films with contrasting plots also pursue liberal politics overall. Moreover the sources of problem-solution plots are decently independent of liberal politics. In our films, plots stem mainly from a generic disposition to configure thrillers in important part as mysteries, even as tales of crime and detection. These proceed classically as plots of problem and solution.[41] Within the subgenre of classical detection, these problem-solution plots usually portend conservative politics, not liberal. Classical detectives come onto the scene after a crime has torn the moral and legal fabrics that drape society; then they detect the perpetrator (whodunit). Thus they restore order and decorum to the associations of privilege that keep social veils of illusion firmly in place.[42]

It cannot be surprising for the overall politics of a film that addresses terrorism through a problem-solution plot to be liberal, configuring the action as solving problems. But it can be informative. Problem-solution plots often implicate different politics; and a sizable portion of terrorism films with liberal politics might suggest that popular cinema prefigures the phenomenal field of terrorism in important part as one that pits terrorists against liberal institutions, styles, and values. Instead Hollywood provided twice as many terrorism thrillers with republican plots and politics. Both liberal and republican politics fit with the preeminence of protection among the overarching motives of heroes in these films. Yet the Hollywood disposition to see terrorism in terms of evil villains to be defeated more than social problems to be solved seems to have proved telling for initial responses of Americans and the Bush Administration to the 9/11 terror attacks.

Heroes and Villains

The third column from the right in Table 8.3 defines the overall project, aim, or motive of each focal hero in relation to the focal villain. A hero might pursue distinct projects for different villains in the same film. Again we have fifty-one plots to analyze. Our movies feature acts of terrorism that target civilians rather than soldiers or other professional participants in some military or political struggle. In its fourth column from the left, Table 8.3 identifies the main modes of terrorism for each film. Military and covert operatives might assassinate officials or leaders of their opponents, but terrorists assassinate the followers and bystanders—on purpose. In many ways, terrorists hijack civilians and take them hostage. Terrorists torture and vandalize innocents. Terrorists bomb indiscriminately. Terrorists wield weapons of mass destruction: chemical, biological, and nuclear.[43] Terrorists target civilians for injury, suffering, and death. This is enough to make the protection of civilians into the principal project for heroes who face episodes of terrorism.

To protect prospective victims from harm by violators of civil law is a defining mission of the modern, liberal state. This is why public officials worry that vigilantes might usurp or supplant the liberal state, with its law makers and enforcers. It is why protection turns out to be the heroic project most evocative of liberal politics in the terrorism films at issue. Nonetheless the project of protection is occasionally conservative: to protect or restore the status quo (which might be liberal, democratic, republican, or otherwise—but is not distinguished in those terms by heroes who act to conserve established institutions). If the protection is principally liberal but residually conservative, the principal project of republican heroes is vigilance. It is a disciplined alertness over long periods, a readiness to concentrate on secret or subtle dangers, and a willingness to sound alarms while interceding between threats and would-be victims. Vigilance can become the special responsibility of an order of unusually committed citizens. They wait and watch, acquitting a quietly heroic task, then spring into action when needed. Yet most of the plots at issue lean toward republican styles of action, so they feature the mission of protection but assign it individually to republican heroes who embody the community at twice the rate they assign it to liberal officials who represent the state. The main pattern, though, is that fully half of Hollywood's pre-9/11 movies on political terrorism emphasize projects of protection for civilians.

The Siege (1999) pursues a conspiracy plot with several dimensions. Conspiracies imply republican politics overall. But the hero, Anthony Hubbard (Denzel Washington), is engaged in protecting civilians menaced by terrorists. The film is careful to inform viewers that Hub (note the name symbolism) has long been waiting and watching for terrorists, since the 1993 bombing of the World Trade Center and even before. Vigilant in defense of a liberal republic, he protects its people. The film stresses that this republic respects liberal diversity and tolerance, even liberal individualism. Hub saves this from a particularly insidious and sinister brand of terror that disguises itself as a military rescue and martial law. Hence Hub's project is vigilance against abuses of power, even in protecting citizens from terrorist jihads.

In most of the twelve films with republican politics overall but heroes whose projects are protection, we meet the heroes too late in the day for vigilance; so their waiting and watching are done, and the time for protective action is at hand. Two of the movies are sequels, with projects of vigilance forming by the end of the previous films. Then the hero stands sentinel before new terrorism starts the sequel and invokes the hero's protection of innocents.

Of the twelve overarching projects for heroes across the full field of films, two others have strong ties in theory to liberalism. Only anarchism rivals liberalism in its emphasis on rationality in personal conduct. *The Boxer* (1997), our one film that moves its hero primarily by modern reason, does seem liberal overall—even though its tragic plot might sustain an elective affinity for Karl Mannheim's sense of "radicalism" and so anarchism.[44] To associate escape (particularly from an oppressive system) with personal freedom is to imply a tie to liberalism, even more than anarchism or existentialism. Those probabilities are born out by our two cinematic heroes whose principal projects are escape. Two of the other cases of heroic protection come in films with politics that are conservative, suiting the inclination of conservatives to quasi-parental care for common folk by people of privilege who act out of noblesse oblige to protect the innocent civilians who support the established order.

Table 8.3 shows in addition how there is a republican family of heroic projects. Honor, loyalty, and vigilance against tyranny are its principal virtues. Military situations cultivate these virtues and rely intensely on them. Liberation from oppression is the sort of freedom that republicans praise without qualification and pursue without equal.[45] Vengeance is mainly republican. Even justice is a more abiding concern for republican politics than for the other five political styles at issue. Of twenty-eight films with republican politics overall, sixteen have heroes with these projects. The twelve others give their heroes projects of protection, since protection is Hollywood's main idea about what we civilian viewers need from heroes who confront political terrorism for us.

The far-right column in Table 8.3 specifies the overall politics of each film, carried into action by the political style of its hero(es). These pre-9/11 films have an existentialist inclination toward heroes who survive the systems that can dominate and terrorize us. Existentialist resistance is equally apparent in foreign films on regime terrorism. As projects of heroism, these may seem less grand than the others. Survival and resistance lack the glamour of perfectionist action (Just Do It!) in *xXx*. For existentialists, that is the lesson for us: accept humble horizons for confronting difficult situations, where "the contemporary hero is not Lucifer; he is not even Prometheus; he is man."[46] When trapped in systems that would make us mere functionaries, it is heroic just to be human.

On occasion, a film features coequal heroes—or heroines. Then their interplay may be more important to the film's politics than any struggles between the heroes and villains. This is particularly true when a film taps conventions from such genres as romance, odd-couple films, or buddy movies. Take *The Peacemaker* (1997). Nicole Kidman enacts a liberal analyst, Dr. Julia Kelly, who is an academician transplanted into government; George Clooney plays a republican hero, Lieutenant Colonel Thom Devoe, not accidentally a military man. The film shows how they marry efforts to resist a terrorist act born of humanist despair unto nihilism.

Thrillers and Settings

Republican politics have no monopoly on heroes; but of our six styles of politics, the republicans invest the most in these figures.[47] Ideological politics such as liberalism, socialism, and conservatism promote modern, critical rationality so much that they find themselves debunking heroes as much as glorifying them. The same goes for anarchism. Perfectionists prize charisma rather than heroism. The masses will imitate and celebrate almost anyone who moves; and as a result, they get celebrities, not heroes. Republicanism accords honor to most heroes, even when they pursue other politics, like liberalism. (Since liberalism comes from ideologizing modern republicanism, this is nearly inevitable.) More than other sources of popular films, Hollywood relies heavily on thrillers to handle political terrorism. All but five—that is, forty-seven—of the pre-9/11 movie plots with political terrorism are thrillers. These are legal, military, noir, police, political, social, war, and especially spy thrillers. (*Fight Club* is multiply genred as a political thriller and a satirical noir; it, along with *The Sum of All Fears,* brings to fifty-two the cases available for classifying by subgenre in our fifty pre-9/11 films on political terrorism.)

Thrillers rely on heroism. They do not merely trace action in some setting; they thrill us with each deed and situation. They pump up the volume, vivify the events, and do this for the protagonists too. The use of thrillers for takes on terrorism is a strong reason to think that republicanism might dominate the overall politics of terrorism films. Duels to the death in plots that pit spy versus spy make this particularly easy to understand. These boil down to one-on-one contests between a terrorist and an antiterrorist. At stake are survival and glory for their causes and countries as well as the individual contestants. The scenes come straight from classical republicanism. It is easy to see how the preponderance of thrillers would favor republican politics in popular movies with acts of political terrorism.

As it happens, this is not fully right or wrong. Of our six styles, republican politics appear most often. Their twenty-eight films are just over half the total, even though ninety percent of our movies are thrillers. Notwithstanding the diffusely republican leanings of thrillers, liberal politics surface almost as strongly in terrorist thrillers. At fourteen of fifty-one plots, in the second column from the right in Table 8.3, more than a fourth of our films on terrorism turn out to be liberal in their politics.

These results make better sense when we take account of the settings that can be conventional for thrillers: military, police, political, and other settings indicated later in third column from the left within Table 8.3. This table enables us to relate thriller subgenres to the modes of terror, the film stances on terrorist grievances, and the sorts of villains in the focal films. Settings are so important to thrillers that they reproduce the genre's usual components as subgenres. Spy-vs.-spy plots need not involve professional espionage in an international arena, but they typically do turn on iterated contests between professionals of some sort in settings where the repeated confrontations create much of their own context. Once we recognize that spy-vs.-spy plots transpire in their own little worlds, we can notice that this holds for other types of thrillers. The name of each type tells the kind of settings conventional for each. Thus the military base and operation comprise their own little world.[48] The police beat, station, stakeout, and such construct a distinct realm of action.[49] Even the political practices of campaigning, governing, lobbying, and the like make for a special network of spaces for action.[50]

The special settings or subgenres of thrillers help explain the distributions of liberal and republican politics in Hollywood films with political terrorism. As Table 8.3 indicates, the films with spy-vs.-spy plots—and thus with settings defined by professional confrontations for extreme stakes—incline strongly to republican politics. *The Little Drummer Girl* (1984) is a good example. Its plot and setting of spy-vs.-spy pit Israeli spies against Arab terrorists, to be sure, but also one or two Israeli spies in particular against an American actress who works in Britain. Their nexus of personal contest—as usual over honor, ethics, politics, and heart even more than skills in the manipulative or martial arts—becomes for most of the movie its own universe of intricate interactions. The same pattern is evident for the political styles of thrillers, where we see that spy thrillers are more republican than liberal in their politics—by a proportion of five to one. The liberalism in thrillers comes more from other subgenres. Military thrillers are a minor surprise, though, for they divide almost evenly between republican and nonrepublican politics, when we might have expected them to prove mostly republican.

Particularly intriguing are thrillers with politics that are postmodern in comparison to premodern myths like republicanism and modern ideologies of liberalism and conservatism. These are the (relatively few) thrillers with anarchist, existentialist, and perfectionist politics. We may expect proportionately more of them in years ahead. They show a Hollywood move to discredit terrorists as anarchists or Nietzschean nihilists, yet pit them against perfectionist heroes who excel in the charisma and skill that thrillers require. How else, after all, could the heroes defeat the villains, not only in the thrilling plots but also in the hearts of viewers?

The spread of politics across plots can be telling. The premodern politics in these films on political terrorism are republican. (To be sure, republicanism can be recuperated in postmodern versions, and these can appear in popular movies.[51] Yet one-on-one contests are common in these terrorism movies, and their politics are amply premodern.) Thus the elective affinity of thrillers in general for republican heroism is apparent in twenty-eight, which is more than half of our fifty-one movie plots. The modern politics in our terrorism movies are conservative and liberal. Just shy of a third (sixteen) of our movies feature modern styles of political action, with most (ten) tracing to the association of problem-solution plots with liberalism. That leaves "radical" politics in the postmodern column, with seven of the fifty-one plots continuing as anarchist, existentialist, or perfectionist in its political style. Anarchism begins as a late-modern ideology among the likes of Rosa Luxemberg and Emma Goldman; but each of its two appearances for us, in *The Patriot* and *Swordfish,* is postmodernized as a style and a stand rather than enacted as a modern ideology.[52]

Overall the premodern politics of classical republicanism loom largest in our set of films, at almost twice the portion of ideological politics. Still the portion of our movies with postmodern politics is far from negligible at nearly a sixth. What might we make of this? The dispersion of plots is particularly impressive for postmodern politics. Elective ties of conspiracy to republicanism discourage taking such conspiracy in postmodern directions. A similar exclusion of postmodern impulses seems at work with the problem-solution plot linked to liberalism and the remarriage plot inclined to conservatism. Prior to 9/11, those three plots for terrorist films were less open politically to postmodern moves. But the other thriller plots seem likely to have been readily available for postmodern politics.

The perfectionist politics, especially, jibe with Hollywood's keen interest in stars and charismatic politics.[53] One of Hollywood's advantages in bringing the politics of terrorism into focus is their turn to charisma and spectacle. Political terrorism produces spectacles for some of its most potent effects.[54] Thus terrorism is theatrical, attuning it to what Hollywood knows best.[55] "Spectacle is one thing money really can buy," as Terrence Rafferty has observed.[56] In the pre-9/11 period, "Big-Budget" became Hollywood's middle name. In fact, this affinity for spectacle might be the single best reason to appreciate Hollywood's prefiguration of the phenomenal field for terrorism. The media dynamics crucial for political terrorism are central to Hollywood expertise. When government officials met with screenwriters to discuss terrorist scenarios in the aftermath of 9/11, this is a big part of the knowledge that Hollywood had and Washington needed. It is also why films that combine acts of terrorism with the sensibilities of postmodern politics can have special interest for the analysis.

Grievances and Responses

As a genre, thrillers go for energy and suspense more than mystery. As a group, they turn problems into crises to test the protagonists' skills of recognition and to develop our own. Thrillers also tap crises to intensify the motives of heroes, villains, and viewers. Then they turn crises into personal or professional contests, pressing toward catharsis and conclusion. Or they make crises into problems for solution—to (dis)solve them and dispel them. When Hollywood pours terrorism into these bottles, there are consequences for its prefiguration.

The Hollywood implication is that political terrorism holds civilians hostage, either in a direct and physical way or in some indirect fashion: moral, cultural, political, psychological, or the like. Even when an act of terrorism murders by-standing civilians, popular cinema has been interested in how the rest of that civilian population is held in thrall to the threat that they could be next. As popular movies know and show, victims of political terrorism extend beyond the first order of individuals killed, maimed, or intimidated. Second-order victims might include their families and friends. Third-order victims can encompass the government officials responsible for their safety and the political leaders who might have helped bring civilians into harm's way, however inadvertently. Fourth-order victims begin with media viewers and listeners who experience political terrorism as making them potential targets. Thus the targeting of "civilians," in the sense of people who lack focal responsibility for injustices cited by terrorists, becomes the key criterion for defining political terrorism in Hollywood films.[57]

Consider in this connection Table 8.4 on the targets, sites, and sources of political terrorism in the movies at issue for the two decades just before 9/11.

By targeting civilians, some terrorists try to provoke governments to dis-proportionate, irrational responses that spread the terror and alienate their populations. Getting proportions right is difficult in principle, because political terrorism typically is asymmetrical warfare that takes advantage of electronic communication to magnify the psychological (and therefore the political) effects of every attack. Governments and leaders lose legitimacy when they do not seem to be protecting ordinary citizens, because then they seem negligent in their duties. Go overboard in responding to terrorist acts, however, and these same figures lose legitimacy because they visibly become oppressors—sometimes of the very sorts that the terrorists have been claiming all along.[58] Popular films with acts of terrorism often feature these dynamics.

Hollywood films show terrorism as succeeding mainly by provoking dis-proportionate or downright irrational responses. Ignoring civil liberties and

Table 8.4 Targets, Sites, and Sources of Movie Terrorism

Film	Year	Target	Site	Source
Air Force One	1997	United States, Russia	Kazakhstan, Russia	liberation movement
Arlington Road	1999	United States	United States	militia movement
The Assignment	1997	the West	Europe	international terrorism
Black Sunday	1977	United States	United States	international terrorism
Blown Away	1994	United States	United States	Irish Republican Army
The Boxer	1997	Northern Ireland	Northern Ireland	Irish Republican Army
Cover Up	1991	Jerusalem	Middle East	aggrieved American spy
The Crying Game	1992	Northern Ireland	Northern Ireland	Irish Republican Army
The Day After	1983	superpowers	United States	nuclear war
Deadly Heroes	1996	United States	Caribbean	international terrorism
The Delta Force	1986	United States, Israel	Middle East	Islamism
The Devil's Own	1997	Northern Ireland	United States	Irish Republican Army
Die Hard	1988	United States	United States	crime
Die Hard 2	1990	United States	United States	crime
Die Hard with a Vengeance	1995	United States	United States	crime
Double Team	1997	United States	Western Europe	international terrorism
Executive Decision	1996	United States	United States	Islamism
Fight Club	1999	United States	United States	environmentalism
Final Voyage	1999	United States	Pacific Ocean	crime
Fire Birds	1990	United States	South America	drug cartel
The Fourth Angel	2001	United States, Britain	Cyprus, Britain	international terrorism
The Fourth Protocol	1987	NATO	Britain	nuclear war
High Crimes	2002	San Salvador	San Salvador	United States
In the Name of the Father	1993	Northern Ireland	Northern Ireland	Irish Republican Army
The Jackal	1997	United States	United States	international terrorism
Little Drummer Girl	1984	Israel	Germany	Islamism
Missing	1982	Latin America	Latin America	despotic regime

(continued)

creating concentration camps are disproportionate responses, but so are neglect and inaction. Popular films depict troubles in all these directions. Of the fifty-one Hollywood plots here, twelve debunk their terrorists as criminals, though not common ones. Thus the films discount or discredit terrorist grievances so profoundly that the usual issues of proportionality in response do not arise. Of the thirty-nine other plots, concerns of proportionality in response are plain in half or more. Therefore proportionality in response to political terrorism qualifies as a significant Hollywood theme.

Thus one effect from Hollywood prefiguration of the phenomenal field for terrorism is apt to be inoculation against impulses to respond thoughtlessly to

Table 8.4 *Continued*

Film	Year	Target	Site	Source
Mission Impossible II	2000	the West	Australia	crime
Navy Seals	1990	the West	Lebanon	Islamism
The Package	1989	superpowers	United States	international intrigue
The Patriot (Seagal)	1998	United States	United States	militia movement
Patriot Games	1992	Northern Ireland	Britain, USA	Irish Republican Army
The Peacemaker	1997	United Nations	United States	Yugoslavia
Proof of Life	2000	Ecuador	Ecuador	guerrilla movement, crime
The Rock	1996	United States	United States	crime
The Siege	1999	United States	United States	Islamism
Speed	1994	United States	United States	crime
Speed 2: Cruise Control	1997	United States	at sea	crime
Spy Game	2001	Communism	Vietnam, Lebanon	United States
Sudden Death	1995	United States	United States	United States
The Sum of All Fears, Nazi	2002	the West	United States	Nazism
The Sum of All Fears, CW	2002	superpowers	United States	nuclear war
Swordfish	2001	United States	United States	international terrorism
Three Kings	1999	Iraq	Iraq	Iraqi Republican Guard
Toy Soldiers	1991	United States	United States	Colombian drug cartel
True Lies	1994	United States	United States	Islamism
Under Siege	1992	United States	at sea	crime
Under Siege 2	1995	United States	United States	crime
Victory at Entebbe	1996	Israel	Uganda	Islamism
Xchange	2000	corporate CEOs	United States	guerrilla movement
xXx	2002	the West	Czech Republic	environmentalism

actual attacks by terrorists. Terrorists plan attacks to overwhelm onlookers, stun them in grief and horror, then derange them with outrage that cannot stop to think well about what to do.[59] For experienced populations, as Caleb Carr argues, terrorism loses some of its power to disorient. This is one of the reasons for Carr's claim that all campaigns of terrorism must eventually fail.[60] The vicarious and virtual experiences of terrorism in popular films may prepare Hollywood audiences for intelligent responses to terrorist acts.[61] Yet our movies imply that there is no guarantee or great likelihood that reflection prevents irrational, disproportionate, or otherwise unwise responses to terrorism.

How do popular films treat terrorist grievances? Positively with empathy, sympathy, or respect? Negatively by discounting their importance, discrediting their legitimacy, even ridiculing their assertion? Or do popular movies simply ignore justifications for terrorism, just putting viewers into the midst of thrilling action that never stops to ask about the animating complaints? The expectation may be that terrorist grievances get little attention from films, with that little staying mostly negative. Even before 9/11, America had shown little positive regard for terrorism. Moreover the rapid pace of thrillers elides motivations, and Hollywood viewers are not known for a love of political details. The obvious hypothesis is that thrillers tend to debase terrorists, debunk their politics, and discount or discredit their grievances.

In the fourth column from the right, Table 8.3 shows film stances toward grievances that terrorists claim to justify their acts. From the most positive to the most negative treatments, our films' stances on terrorist grievances stretch from empathy, sympathy, or respect for them—through ignoring them—to discounting, discrediting, or ridiculing them. The idea of degrees of feeling on a spectrum from positive to negative can seem fair in general, but there are complications. Ignoring grievances often can be a form of disrespect. Moreover empathy is feeling along with others—not necessarily feeling positively for them, which would be sympathy. Yet the dramatic function of such empathy in our films is typically to induce strongly positive identification with their terrorists. Likewise it's plenty possible that principled respect for grievances can be more positive than personal sympathy for terrorists. It's conceivable that discounting the significance of the grievances can wound terrorist causes more than discrediting their legitimacy. And there's the chance that targets of ridicule or condemnation can become sympathetic. For the movies here, though, these mostly prove small worries.

When a plot can fit more than one genre, the coding in Table 8.3 lets satire trump noir or thriller, noir trump thriller, and thriller trump war to produce what is probably the most telling comparison. Before 9/11, Hollywood could have prefigured terrorism as a tool or path for political liberation, as many Israelis treat the 1946 Irgun attack on the King David Hotel in Jerusalem. Or at least, it could have prefigured terrorism as a mark of oppression, even a measure of desperation, as many Europeans view intermittent acts of sabotage by Basque separatists or Chechen rebels. If so, our movies would show empathy, sympathy, or respect for terrorist grievances, whether or not the films see their terrorist acts as legitimate; but only sixteen out of fifty-one plots pay positive attention to terrorist grievances. The rest of the plots ignore (six), discount (fourteen), discredit (thirteen), or ridicule (two) terrorist grievances.

Hence for 9/11 responses, Hollywood prefigured political terrorism as not only unjustified but outrageous, despicable, beyond the bounds even of war. Yet is there less negativity than we might expect? The lone tragedy respects terrorist grievances: without respect all around, it is hard to get tragedy going. Satire is a resource for ridicule of grievances; but in the two movies at issue here, it spurs empathy in equal measure. Nonetheless thrillers pipe the Hollywood tune for political terrorism; and for thrillers only, the balance is categorically negative at twenty-six (or thirty-two) to nine.

Why are our movies open at all to appreciating terrorist grievances? The main reason is that a third of these movies have dramatic or political reasons to bring home to viewers the pains that animate terrorists. These films help viewers experience the grievances by cutting directly to sites and sufferings that spawn terrorism. These films show terrorists who want to make their targets feel the pains that the terrorists, their families, countries, or causes have suffered from sources tied politically to terrorist targets. Thus the principal terrorist in *The Peacemaker* tapes a television message on the motives for his desperate attempt to explode a nuclear bomb in New York. The film endorses the gravity of his grievances and the terrible reasons for his strategy to awaken westerners to terrors that their states inflict on others:

> I am a Serb, I am a Croat, I am a Muslim. You will look at what I have done and say, "Of course. Why not? They are all animals. They have slaughtered each other for centuries." But the truth is, I am not a monster. I'm a human man. I'm just like you, whether you like it or not. For years, we have tried to live together—until a war was waged on us, on all of us, a war waged by our own leaders. And who supplied the Serb cluster bombs, the Croatian tanks, the Muslim artillery shells that kill our sons and daughters? It was the governments of the West who drew the boundaries of our country: sometimes in ink, sometimes in blood—the blood of our people. And now you dispatch your peacekeepers to write our destiny again. We can never accept this peace that leaves us with nothing but pain: pain the peacemakers must be made to feel. Their wives, their children, their houses, and churches. So now you know, now you must understand. Leave us to find our own destiny. May God have mercy on us all.

Popular films with terrorism often take on themselves some of the burdens of communicating such grievances. This virtual terrorism is to punch home, not only the awful consequences of terrorist acts, but also the awful settings that provoke them. Striking sights and sounds from Hollywood seek to replace and render unnecessary the sights, sounds, and wounds of actual attacks on civilians. This subset of terrorism movies gives viewers fairly full-bodied access to grievances and attacks that they otherwise might not experience. And it does so in the hope that, as a result, they will not have to suffer such attacks. Hollywood also makes these moves for other settings and experiences. Then they not only prefigure but provide the phenomenal fields that bring viewers experiences that they cannot—or would not want to—have otherwise.

Only six films in our set pretty much ignore the political grievances of their terrorists. Viewers might develop feelings for or against the political causes of these terrorists, but these films provide so little information about specific grievances that viewers would need to add lots of information to specify their feelings. *Patriot Games* (1992) is the best-known example. It offers a glimpse of British military occupation of a neighborhood in Northern Ireland, and it makes clear that the American hero despises terrorists for the Irish Republican Army. But it doesn't detail the political grievances of its terrorists. To avoid taking any sides, it imagines a renegade group of ultra-terrorists disavowed and undermined by the IRA. As if this were not enough, its *über* terrorist—who targets the family of American Jack Ryan (Harrison Ford)—acts from a crazed compulsion to avenge the death of his terrorist brother. To escape controversy and enlarge the audience, it dumps or denatures most of the politics. It's easy to see why popular thrillers would do this, so it's telling that movies in our set so seldom try it.

The projects of terrorist villains in these films are diverse. I list the motivations of villains earlier (in moving from left to right in Table 8.3) than I do the motivations of heroes because the motivations of villains are the primary engines of the plots. Almost always these instigate the larger forms and ties for movies with terrorism. Projects of heroes take shape mostly in response to the villainy. This holds even though our films treat their heroes as acting from personal characters long in the making. *Three Kings* (1999) is a partial exception, since American heroes rather than Iraqi villains drive the plot. Yet the Americans begin as something like villains, setting out to steal for themselves gold taken from Kuwait by Iraqi invaders newly defeated by the Americans and their allies. The transformation of the Americans from liberal profiteers to republican soldiers of honor, who save a few Iraqis menaced by their own dictator in Saddam Hussein, is the trajectory of events featured by the film.

Most villainous projects of terrorists in popular films are political. In Table 8.3, which compares the projects of villains and heroes in our movies, "power" is specifically governmental by contrast with the leverage from money and other private resources or the political advantage from "jihad," "loyalty," "revenge," "seduction," and other projects with strongly political repercussions. "Domination" goes beyond greater resources within a fully political system to the anti-political exercise of control in totalitarian regimes. "Bureaucracy," "liberation," "honor and anger," "order," "anarchy," "destruction," and the more radical "annihilation" should be clear from earlier points about specific films.

"Theft," "extortion," and "profit" form an economic family of projects with money as their main aim: an aim that strongly discredits terrorists and their causes. Yet these three motives project different plots and networks of politics. Theft is stealing, taking the rightful possessions of others. Extortion is theft that plays on the failures of others to protect assets such as weapons, people, symbols, territories, or reputations; to fulfill commitments like loyalties, mores, and promises; to achieve aspirations such as peace, renown, or prosperity. In popular films, as specified by Table 8.3 in the column for film stances on grievances, these economic projects instantly debunk any terrorism, although the sting might be diminished by additional considerations. Psychological motives, including hate and despair, also debunk terrorism. If terrorism is a political project, it has a shot at respectability in our films; but if its motivation is economic or psychological, the terrorism is debased from the start. Eleven of the fifty-one plots in these films show economic motives for terrorism, and three are moved by extremities of psychology. But more than two-thirds of the plots take the projects of their terrorists politically—if not always seriously and often far from positively.

As villains, mostly in thrillers, all these terrorists appear in negative terms. Yet the versions of villainy can inflect our judgments about these figures. Five sets of terrorists have been "trapped" into villainy, encouraging our sympathy for them and their grievances. Likewise the ten "professionals" get sympathy or respect, and two of the three films that identify terrorists with us viewers promote empathy for them. Thus a third of the plots cast their terrorists as characters susceptible to some positive feelings from viewers, while roughly two-thirds of the plots condemn their terrorists categorically. Four give us "deranged" terrorists, and *Arlington Road* adds one who is "deluded." These act as madmen. One set of terrorists embodies unqualified "evil," fourteen are "fanatical," and twelve "criminal." With villains like these, popular films are in no danger of putting terrorists in too good a light. Even so, the films often contrast terrorists, who almost always appear as villains by Hollywood definition, to their political grievances. The grievances get respect or better in more than a third of the movies, they seldom fall beneath notice, and they often receive the backhanded respect of specific criticism. For Hollywood, terrorism and terrorists might be categorically wrong; but their political complaints are another matter.

Movies and Lessons

These are the mythic templates of political terrorism supplied by Hollywood before the al Qaeda attacks on September 11, 2001. In the aftermath, it has not been hard to see these figures in the continuing reactions of Americans. This starts with the very acts of political terrorism in our fifty films prior to 9/11. In light of these movies, apologists of the George W. Bush Administration sounded somewhere between odd and disingenuous when saying that nobody could have been expected to anticipate—let alone prevent—the kind of terrorism on 9/11. Not only have later reports, hearings, and books made clear that officials such as Richard A. Clarke were shunted aside when they tried to warn specifically of impending attacks by al Qaeda.[62] But popular movies already had made similar possibilities for terrorism on American soil all too familiar to millions of viewers.[63] These fifty films had helped shape the phenomenal field for Americans to experience the events of 9/11 and to configure the ensuing responses.

Consistent with Hollywood's thriller templates, Americans have been talking about 9/11 attacks and terrorism in the republican terms of villains and heroes more than the country's usual, liberal language of problems and solutions.[64] The Bush Administration did something similar by casting 9/11 terrorism in the context of an "Axis of Evil."[65] The vengeance, as well as protection, involved in striking back at al Qaeda (at first in Afghanistan) initially attracted general support in the United States; and it was the action required by honor in a field of largely republican options.

Putting terrorism outside America's normal, problem-solution province of policymaking reinforced other pre-9/11 dispositions in Hollywood treatments of terrorism to present political terrorism as a self-contained political fanaticism. The relative disregard for terrorist grievances in Hollywood films before 9/11 turns aside from seeing terrorism as a tactic or a strategy that serves more important politics; instead it treats terrorism as a kind of politics all its own. This helped position Americans to ask who had attacked them, what would avenge them, and what would protect them in the future—far more often and intensely than why they had been attacked.[66] It readied Americans to see terrorists of any kind as the enemy, regardless of grievances. It prepared Americans to accede to the "global War on Terror" soon declared by President George W. Bush then used implausibly by his administration to justify an invasion of Iraq.[67] Similarly the Hollywood stress on protecting civilians from terrorist attacks fit the frantic, strangely disproportionate efforts of government to make citizens safe in a few respects, even while weirdly neglecting other aspects less in the public eye.[68]

In his first term, President Barack Obama took to al Qaeda's remaining leadership the projects of vengeance and prevention-for-purposes-of-protection initiated by his predecessor. But Obama gradually backed away from the rhetoric and policy of the "global War on Terror." By his second term, Obama was ending the Bush wars in Iraq and Afghanistan. He also began to call for Americans and their allies to retire the concept of a "war on terror."[69] The Obama idea seems in part to be that Americans have been distorting their lives as well as their policies in ways at once perverse and unnecessary. Terrorist threats are nowhere near as apocalyptic as Americans have felt them to be, and deciding not to act as hostages is the main move that Americans must make to keep from being held in thrall even where and when terrorists have not attacked.

Already, before 9/11, Hollywood movies had agreed with experts that terrorism succeeds mainly by goading its survivors into responses that make their situations worse rather than better, helping realize terrorist ambitions. Of late, similar Hollywood movies on political terrorism have continued to foreground this lesson, while starting to adjust some of their other figures.[70] This raises the question how well Americans or others do to shape their senses of terrorism according to the conventions of popular thrillers. Could Hollywood movies readily do otherwise? Should they? The next chapter turns from thrillers to a subgenre of horror movies in order to reconsider the Bush War on Terror from the platform of a different genre. Then Chapter 10 compares thrillers with three other popular genres as possible forms for movies on political terrorism.

CHAPTER 9

MOVIES DISFIGURE POLITICS

HOW VAMPIRE HUNTERS PURSUED THE WAR ON TERROR (FEATURING BLADE AND BRAM STOKER'S DRACULA)

Bring 'em on![1]

—George W. Bush

So said a pugnacious president, forty-third in the lengthening history of the United States. Literally this was George W. Bush talking about retrograde Iraqis, who were not acquiescing in American rule but assassinating American soldiers instead. Mythically this might sound like Dirty Harry from Clint Eastwood movies, growling at a punk to "Make my day!" But because the president came from Texas, self-consciously mimicked horse operas more than other movies, and sometimes appeared to treat foreign affairs as a streamlined imperialism of cowboys over Indians, the press and the populace have tended to view his administration as a resurrection of the western matinee. The same has held since for foreign policy by so-called neoconservatives, a.k.a. neocons. This is not exactly wrong, but we can do better.

Prominent politicians invite us to view them as mythic figures, and American presidents make the exercise hard to resist.[2] My argument is not that we must refrain from interpreting the mythic dimensions of politics in general or presidents in particular. Susan Sontag might have thought that possible and moral, thus justifying her rejection of talking like John Dean about "a cancer on the presidency" of Richard Nixon; but what are the joys of a stringent and impossible literalism?[3] When myths are political arguments, symbolical stories of the whole, and musical words that rhythm our lives, we do not know which ones are true, which false, and which otherwise until we investigate them in detail.[4] We do know, though, that myths are inseparable from meanings. Consequently we do well to acknowledge that there is no way to ignore myths in politics, let alone remove them from politics, and there is no reason to try.[5] The point is crucial for comprehending the resonance of movies in American politics.

What I mean by saying we can do better is that figures in the Bush Administration mostly fit a different mythos. The alternative makes more sense of Bush foreign policy with respect to Iraq. To analyze mythic aspects of George W. Bush, Saddam Hussein, and others is not to debunk them. Myths inform, define, even pervade politics—from the exalted and respectable to the wretched and ludicrous. Of course, myths do the same for movies. Myth analysis can be light of heart and foot without becoming inaccurate or disrespectful. The ethos and enterprise here amount to a playful formalism. The project is to try out mythic forms for the insights of pattern and the pleasures of recognition they can yield.

Put the other way around, the purposes are fun and learning. As I explain the mythic alternative, please keep in mind that it—no more than the cowboy mythos—need trivialize the reasons for war in Iraq, the sacrifices in the war's conduct, or the consequences from its outcome. The same holds for the challenges in international relations at a time when the United States is arguably the only global superpower. When the French semiotician Roland Barthes can show how soap is sold through mythic associations with superhero powers, and the American political theorist Anne Norton can echo just about everybody in complaining that America sells its presidents like soap in political ads on television, spotting mythic figures in presidential administrations must be fair game.[6] Let us play this as a scholarly sport.

It is true that the second Bush Administration partly reprised the first, as well as the earlier Ford Administration. Donald Rumsfeld served again as Secretary of Defense, Dick Cheney shifted from powerful Chief of Staff to influential Vice President, George W. Bush moved from political point man and son-in-waiting to President. The list of Bush family associates and retainers with major roles in Republican presidencies from Ford to 43, as Bush the father calls W., is longer; but Bush, Cheney, and Rumsfeld are the figures ripe for analysis here. (I leave the likes of Colin Powell, Condoleezza Rice, and Paul Wolfowitz for readers to ponder at their leisure. The game can be too gruesome for dinner conversation, given the mythos of the moment. But it turns out to fit perfectly into talk in the early evening, when the sun is about to set. Atmosphere matters.)

Hence it seems appropriate to borrow from the western to declare mythically that "The Bush Gang Rides Again." Yet the question becomes: what kind of gang is it? Does it harken to the American Wild West of the late nineteenth century—with cowboys and Indians, gamblers, gunslingers, miners, sheriffs, cattle or railroad barons, ranchers, rustlers, and all the rest? Or does it appeal to the same period but draw instead from the European mythos of Dracula and other vampires? There are gangs of cowboys and others Out West, of course, but gangs also track vampires to mysterious locales like Transylvania. Many a movie has vampire hunters form gangs or teams to identify, find, and slay their villains. Dick Cheney might have been a foreign-affairs cowboy, but the production and conduct of the war in Iraq show Donald Rumsfeld and George W. Bush to have been more in the mythic mode of vampire hunters.

Rumsfeld reminds me of Professor Abraham Van Helsing from Bram Stoker's *Dracula*; and Bush recalls Blade, the comic-book character. These are the two vampire hunters best known from American cinema in the 1990s, more or less on the eve of September 11, 2001. The *locus classicus* for Dracula and his hunters is the novel by Bram Stoker.[7] But most people probably know Van Helsing from the quirky, charismatic portrayal by Anthony Hopkins in *Bram Stoker's Dracula* (1992), directed by Francis Ford Coppola.[8] Played enigmatically but charismatically by Wesley Snipes, Blade is familiar from the strong film of that name directed by Stephen Norrington (1998) and its weaker sequels: *Blade II* (2002) and *Blade Trinity* (2004). With apologies to fans of *Buffy the Vampire Slayer* (1992 on film, then 1997–2003 on television), *Vampire Hunter D* (1985, 2000), the *Dusk Till Dawn* movies (1996, 1999, 2000), or even such other takes as *Abraham Lincoln: Vampire Hunter* (2012), let us leave their analysis to the side for now.[9]

Cheney as Cowboy

To explain how Bush and Rumsfeld have acted in foreign affairs as vampire hunters more than cowboys, I need to detail both types. To start with cowboys means to start with Cheney. Evan Thomas notes for *Newsweek* that "Bush and Cheney are caricatured by Europeans, and not a few Americans, as 'cowboys.' The president, with his John Wayne 'dead or alive' metaphors, and the vice president, with his Gary Cooper terse-but-tough pronouncements, do sound like a couple of sheriffs, telling the bad guys that they have ten minutes to come out of the bar or 'we're coming in to get you.'"[10] This is the cowboy as the plain speaker.[11]

When Cheney endorses "the notion that the president is a cowboy," this is what he has in mind: "I don't think that's necessarily a bad idea. I think the fact of the matter is, he cuts to the chase, he is very direct."[12]

Like many people, Cheney praises the parts of his own character that he meets in his colleague, Bush, who began as his mentee and became his boss. In comparison to the taciturn and laconic Cheney, Bush can seem downright excitable and loquacious. Cheney is known as brief, abrupt, sometimes painfully direct. Bush prizes a reputation as plainspoken; but he can be smoother, eloquent (with the help of speechwriters) on formal occasions, and often charming. By this first measure, it is Cheney—more than Bush—who is the cowboy.

People who talk about "cowboys" in politics typically mean gunfighters more than cow punchers, so consider Cheney specifically as the Lone Ranger. Cheney's idea of foreign affairs has been to ride into town, impose his version of justice because nobody there has the strength or virtue for it, then move on. No nation-building for him. Just as Cheney stayed somewhat behind the scenes, especially from 9/11 until he left office, the Lone Ranger hides his personal identity behind the famous mask. As a gunslinger, the Lone Ranger has a faithful companion in Tonto (Bush), who is a "natural" in ways the gunslinger will never be and who has established common cause with him.[13]

As a group, gunslingers gravitate toward sensibilities of fate, destiny, tragedy, even fatalism.[14] The classicist Victor Hansen Davis professes admiration for "Cheney's 'tragic view of mankind,' akin to the ancient Greeks."[15] As "a man of few words," however, "Cheney might have more in common with the Lone Ranger than Pericles. 'It's more Wyoming, the code of the West,' said a top aide to the Vice President. 'It's "You're welcome around here, neighbor. But don't run your cattle on my land. I'm not going to sit back for that."'" "Whether ancient Greece or Old West," Thomas adds, "the vice president has a world view, and it is not the one shared by members of the East Coast foreign-policy establishment, men and women of moderation who believe in reason and dialogue, who think that problems can be talked out. Cheney believes that the world is a dangerous place, that diplomacy can be a trap, that force is sometimes the only choice."[16]

The gunslinger shows in response the kind of courage we call backbone and the sort of physical energy we term drive, even zip. He treats power as mechanical leverage—of the trigger, the hammer, the rifle butt, and such—because his are the politics of coercion, of forcing people to do what he wants.[17] The cowboy as gunslinger is manly, a man's man, even a mensch: each a term often applied to Cheney. The gunslinger's goal is to put a bullet between the eyes of the enemy. In the case of the Lone Ranger, it is a silver bullet, so maybe—mythically—he has just been waiting to join Blade in killing vampires: because Blade's vampires are hyperallergic to silver, he uses silver blades and bullets too.

Gunslingers embrace the Hobbesian war of all against all in a State of Nature that lacks sovereign governance.[18] This condition is shared by the Wild West and the international realm.[19] Cheney has said that "war is the natural state of mankind."[20] Cheney, not Bush, has been the Hobbesian. "With his strong religious faith," says Thomas, "President Bush has a more upbeat, soul-saving Christian take on life than his somewhat Hobbesian vice president."[21] The gunslinger senses sins and calculates interests, and this is the mode of realism apparent in Cheney's politics. Inflected by Hobbes, it is an authoritarian mode of command at home more in business and military settings than electoral or legislative politics.

Bush as Blade

Bush declared in the 2000 campaign that his favorite political theorist is Jesus; then he called on Billy Graham in the wake of 9/11. Bush has been a moralist, confronting Evil with the force of his personal convictions. The sensibility is romantic, not tragic; religious rather than militaristic, let alone businesslike; medieval (especially feudal) more than classical. "Bush had something like a conversion experience after 9-11; he went from a politician who was glad, and perhaps a little surprised, to be president, to a war leader with a providential sense of duty and destiny."[22] That week, before speechwriters could put words in his mouth, Bush vowed a "crusade" against terrorism. In that missionary spirit, his administration regarded the Americans abroad from Afghanistan to Africa as "paladins of democracy."[23] To people outside the United States, for the most part, his international politics seemed even more imperial than authoritarian.

Personally as well as politically, Bush has been depicted as the alpha male: at times, macho to the point of being a bully. His courage summons guts and balls, but his energy stems more from spiritual zeal. On such figural kinds of political energy for the major players in the Bush War on Terror, see Table 9.1.

Imbued with moral conviction, graced by a sometimes preternatural sense of certainty, Bush has pursued political enthusiasms through campaigns against enemies such as terrorists and appeasers. Beware if silver bullets are not enough to undo these enemies, because the blazing sunlight of his True Belief might burn them all to ash.

Who is this mythically? Not the Lone Ranger but Blade, who blends the gunslinger with the vampire hunter and the superhero to produce a vampire killer of

Table 9.1 Four Kinds of Political Energy

Players	Cheney	Rumsfeld	Bush	The French
characters	cowboy	vampire slayer	vampire killer	easterners
exemplars	Lone Ranger	Van Helsing	Blade	Vamps
energy principles	**zip**	**zest**	**zeal**	**Zen**
logical levels	mechanical	biological	spiritual	mental
personal modes	physical	visceral	moral	intellectual
cultural signs	force	vitality	enthusiasm	(self-)possession
political powers	coercion	charisma	grace	seduction

superhuman powers. He is "the Daywalker," who knows the fallen enemy in his blood but keeps himself from descending to that despicable level by force of will and dedication to his cause. Bush has talked about his dissolute past that way, trumpeting his salvation by faith and the love of his strong-willed woman. Blade was born in vengeance. His crusade became to rid the world of the vampires, who prey on people and took his mother even as she was about to deliver him.

Infected from birth with the vampire craving for blood, Blade represses it chemically, but mainly he sublimates it to the cause of killing vampires. He does this with the technology and tutelage of Abraham Whistler (Kris Kristofferson), his mentor and eventual sidekick. Together Laura Bush and Dick Cheney can make a composite Whistler for Dubbya. Nonetheless Blade is a loner in combat and clean-up operations, scorning most collaborators as feeble and deficient in moral fervor. In the first film, Blade finds himself cornered into working with Dr. Karen Jensen (N'Bushe Wright). More sophisticated by far than Blade, she is nonetheless all too human. Still she contributes crucial pieces of semireliable information to the cause, and her help in the ensuing battles is somewhat symbolical but significant, making it hard to miss the parallels to Tony Blair and Britain.

Whistler wants to purge the world of vampires, but he works equally hard to make Blade safe for the world. This is the conventional challenge in taming superheroes to take advantage of their superpowers. Thus Ma and Pa Kent must raise Superman in Smallville for him to learn the commitment to "Truth, Justice, and the American Way." Otherwise *Übermenschen* are not safe for humans, let alone democracies. Blade, like Bush, could come across as an ordinary guy; but critics complained that he did not care enough about ordinary people.[24] Blade's passion is to kill vampires; if he protects humans along the way, so be it. To make Blade constructive, Whistler must somehow keep him connected to humanity. With George Bush presiding over the world's one superpower, and the Chief of

State standing for the government and the country, the political challenge clear to Europeans—of keeping America safe for the world—comes readily to mind. Then Bush was Blade, the superpowered vampire killer, rather than a merely human slayer of vampires, because he was the President of the United States of America. Mythically Bush embodies the military, economic, and cultural super powers of the United States of America. For the earlier time that faced the self-proclaimed *Übermenschen* from Nazi Germany, he might have been Captain America.[25] But lately the enemies are more overtly vampirical, and Bush could become Blade.

Saddam as Dracula

In the first *Blade* movie, Deacon Frost (Stephen Dorff) is the vampire who strikes at Blade's mother just before she gives birth. Subsequent superpowers make Frost into La Magra, the "Blood God," a supervampire to rule the world. Undoing the Blood God becomes Blade's consuming passion and crowning feat. In our world, Saddam Hussein tried to assassinate the elder Bush in retaliation for the Gulf War. That along with Saddam's early penchant for waging war and terror with weapons of mass destruction seem to have made undoing him into an overriding priority for the younger Bush. "Together, Bush and Cheney have presented an unwavering determination to rid the world of Saddam Hussein. Almost messianic in their conviction, Bush and most of his top advisers have frightened or perplexed their European allies and many opinion makers in the United States."[26] Bush and his administration cast Saddam as Dracula, *the* vampire. Earlier Saddam had been despicable but human. After 9/11, in a move mystifying to many outside the administration, Saddam became for Bush the demonic embodiment of Evil: preying cynically and outrageously on the people within his sinister reach.[27]

In words and deeds, the Bush Administration in general and the President in particular came to treat Saddam far less as the ruthless authoritarian found in westerns than as the supervillain, the monster, straight from scenes of horror. For Bush, Saddam's was not the outlaw regime of an oil baron, exploiting his people and invading others. Instead it was a totalitarian reign of terror that sucked his people dry and threatened the apocalyptic destruction of others. Even later, with Iraq invaded again but no stockpiles or even programs for weapons of mass destruction found, veterans of the second Bush Administration repeatedly portrayed themselves as going to war to undo totalitarian rule by Saddam.

For Blade, vampires and the Blood God are outrages—as were terrorists and Saddam for Bush. Saddam often reinforced this mythmaking by portraying

Table 9.2 Saddam as Dictator or Demon

Identities	Saddam the Dictator	Saddam the Demon
rulers	oil baron	Dracula
realms	outlaw regime	totalitarian reign of terror
activities	oppressing his people and invading others	terrorizing his people and sucking them dry
politics	authoritarianism	perfectionism
motives	vengeance	reckoning
roles	vigilante	quasi-aristocratic prince
acts	taking the law into his own hands	putting himself above the law
crimes	extralegal	super-legal
modes	violation	predation
statuses	outlaw	monster
resources	violence	superpowers

himself in corresponding terms. He did not defend himself as an international vigilante, taking corrupted law into his own hands to protect Iraq against the lawless violence of others. He offered himself rather as a perfectionist prince, rising above mere law to show others the way. Table 9.2 on Saddam's villainy schematizes these contrasts.

For the Bush folks, the Saddam shell games with weapons of mass destruction mimicked the shape-shifting of Dracula. Under frontal assault, that formidable figure might disperse into a cloud of bats or a scurry of rats. Then he can coalesce anew into a concerted threat on the other side of the room, the wall, the country. This feat shocks victims, rocks unprepared adversaries, and mocks unsophisticated heroes who foolishly take such a foe to be susceptible to diplomacy or defeat as usual. Dracula and the Blood God are no ordinary vampires, let alone ordinary villains. Merely to stymie such an enemy requires extraordinary determination, coordination, intelligence, virtue, strength, guile, and more. Actually to terminate such a perfectionist monster necessitates a coalition of heroes willing to heed a master of vampire lore and war: a Whistler or a Van Helsing. But it might also demand a superhero: enter Bush as Blade, with casting by Karl Rove.

Terrorists, who stay permanently dispersed, can be a worse challenge still. Striking from many angles at once, they bewilder as well as wound. Always already beheaded or otherwise undead, they cannot be killed by a single stroke, no matter how swift or symbolical. Anyone who wants to be a superhero does better to face the Blood God or track Dracula to his lair than to confront the myriad cells of al Qaeda or contest the caves of Tora Bora. (Eventually Bush and the Army bearded Saddam in his hole and helped eliminate the terrorizer of Iraqis;

but it took Barack Obama and Navy Seals to slay the terrorizer of Americans, Osama bin Laden.)

For the second Bush Administration, Saddam became not just any old demonized foe, but the Super Vampire who coddled al Qaeda and who threatened the United States (and the world) with mass destruction. Down-home demonizing, such as likening Saddam to Hitler, as the regime of the senior George had done, could be good enough for liberating Kuwait. Apparently a more powerful motive would be needed for eradicating Saddam's rule in Iraq, especially with Osama bin Laden and his scattered minions drawing attention to many other parts of the globe. Nonetheless the administration of the junior George was equal to the task, even when it faced unexpected opposition from Gulf War allies of the elder Bush.

Rumsfeld as Van Helsing

These former allies, especially from what Rumsfeld called "the Old Europe," participate in the vampire mythos. Had this episode occurred during the Cold War, Rumsfeld and colleagues would have excoriated France and Germany in particular as "fellow travelers" who give aid and comfort to enemies of America and the world. Not even Rumsfeld wanted to condemn these continuing collaborators of America as full members of the company of vampires.[28] For the second Bush Administration, it made more sense to view them as vamps: vampire sympathizers, tolerators, or wannabes. Like cowardly intellectuals, these effete easterners play with vampire ideas, identities, and familiars—if not the vampires themselves—becoming their minions. Many vamps revel in vampire chic. Others have become too sophisticated or world-weary for their own good: no longer able to see where evils start and Evil ensues. No wonder they want endlessly ineffective diplomacy rather than a final reckoning.

Even before there is a Blood God, Blade accosts the corrupt city as a conspiracy among vampires, vamps, familiars, and politicians. They make preying on humans into a cynical game. If vampires are the predators of the night, vamps are their twilight enablers. Vamp raves, salons, nightclubs, and other cultivated diversions lure unsuspecting people and set them up for the kill. As Blade sees vamps, and the second Bush Administration portrayed the Old Europeans, they are Machiavellian manipulators who sell ideals for profit. In part, these Europeans are self-possessed seducers who lead others astray, even when not preying directly on them. And especially the Old Worlders are craven practitioners of

Realpolitik, who put narrow and momentary interests of trade or state ahead of defending humanity against terrible troubles. Only proximate outcomes matter to them; they show no compunctions about means.

As vamps, by the reckoning of Bush and Rumsfeld, the French and Germans literally demoralize. They diminish goods and evils into mere contrasts to be savored: *vive la différence.* Stylish European vamps leech the mental energy of others and convert it into wiles of seduction. Their cunning is sharp and circuitous, their action dilatory and deceptive, their honor so refined and gentled that they might as well be aesthetes, dandies.[29] In fact, many are. (If "vamps" are vaguely female by gender, then "dandies" are pretty much their male counterparts.)

The one notorious for denouncing Europeans this way is Donald Rumsfeld. Even in his seventies, the secretary of defense made himself the television equivalent of a matinee idol through dashing midday briefings on American military operations around the world. To cross storylines but stay within roles, Rumsfeld was the generally suave, occasionally crass, but always virile man of modern science, technology, and intellect: Van Helsing, the vampire slayer. I say "slayer," and not simply vampire "killer" as with Blade, because vampire slayers seem to relish the contest with their opponents as a test of invention, discipline, and audacity. Blade is more a no-nonsense executioner when it comes to vampires.

Van Helsing seems to relish almost everything. He is the sort of nineteenth-century enthusiast of science poised on the edge between genius and crank. His implicit politics seem republican, likewise poised on the edge between virtuosity and imperialism. Brimming vitality makes Van Helsing charismatic, and his zest for the hunt is elemental, biological. Yet he has a clinical, analytical eye for the evils and operations of the supervermin he has vowed to purge. In striking contrast to the laconic gunslinger and the plainspoken vampire killer, Van Helsing is voluble, even glib. All this reads like a review of a Rumsfeld press conference. On television, Rummy notoriously came across as a Type-A personality and then some. As Gary Trudeau joked in *Doonesbury,* Rumsfeld didn't just finish other people's sentences for them; he posed the questions for them, preemptively, before he answered them forcefully and often dismissively.

Van Helsing organizes, goads, and outshines the three suitors to Lucy Westenra (Sadie Frost), turning them into a team that rides to the rescue of heroine Mina Murray Harker (Winona Ryder). The resemblance is uncanny to relations between Rumsfeld and the Joint Chiefs of Staff as titular heads of the three branches of America's military forces. Like Van Helsing, Rumsfeld appears congenitally pragmatic and optimistic, confident of overcoming troubles that might intervene before a happy, comedic outcome. Their mission is to protect civilization against the *outré*, the offensively improper. To make good on that mission, they go so far as to stalk the night, Van Helsing literally and Rumsfeld figuratively with nighttime raids to strike at Saddam and his sons. To slay vampires, Van Helsing pounds wooden stakes through their hearts and cuts off their heads. To slay terrorist regimes, Rumsfeld pounds the soldiers with bombs to shock, awe, and dishearten them, even as he conducts decapitation campaigns against their political and military leaders. In myth, Rumsfeld is Van Helsing: the first of the fully modern, laboratory-tested, politically disciplined, technologically enhanced vampire slayers. So Whistler resembles Van Helsing as the comrade in arms suited to Blade as he dispatches the Blood God then returns to ridding the world of vampires, if not vamps. The full argument appears in formal terms in Table 9.3 on contrasts among cowboys, vampire hunters, and vamps.

A critic of George W. Bush might complain that comparing him to a cowboy in foreign affairs is enough to give cowboys a bad name. A defender of Bush might be pleased at the comparison. An apostate Texan of my acquaintance says that the cowboy connection is figural shorthand for the political culture of Texas. Before we mess with Texas, though, maybe we should let cowboys *and* Texans off the mythic hook. Where the second Bush Administration—and persistent neocons—operate in foreign affairs, let the sign say instead: Vampire Killers at Work.

Table 9.3 Four Characters in Foreign Affairs

Players	Dick Cheney	Donald Rumsfeld	George W. Bush	The French
characters	cowboy	vampire slayer	vampire killer	easterners
exemplars	Lone Ranger	Van Helsing	Blade	Vamps
figures	gun slinger	night stalker	day walker	fellow travelers
sidekicks	Tonto	Three Suitors	Whistler	familiars
relations	companion	aides	mentor	minions
allegories	Bush	joint chiefs	Blair	Old Europeans
weapons	silver bullets	stakes (in the heart) and decapitation	silver bullets and sunlight	dark blood (oil?)
sites	trail in the wild	laboratory	factory	salon
settings	sunset	night	day	twilight
genres	western	horror	western horror	western horror
motives	interests and sins	evils	Evil	perspectives
words	laconic or taciturn	voluble even glib	plain spoken	sophisticated
actions	determined	disciplined	dedicated	dilatory
periods	classical	modern	medieval	postmodern
sources	business	science	religion	politics
practices	military	technology	crusade	diplomacy
energies	zip	zest	zeal	Zen
trajectories	fate	vocation	destiny	fortune
rationalities	calculation	intellection	conviction	cunning
masculinities	manly: a man's man, even a mensch	virile: a woman's man, even a heartthrob	macho: an alpha male, even a bully	gentlemanly: a gentled man, even a dandy
plots	tragedy	comedy	romance	satire
politics	authoritarianism	republicanism	imperialism	cynicism
theorists	Hobbes	Arendt	Graham	Machiavelli
principles	realism	pragmatism	moralism	Realpolitik
ambitions	backbone	audacity	balls or guts	craven profit
ambiences	war	totalitarianism	terrorism	difference
projects	justice	protection	reckoning	teaching
targets	outlaws	outrés	outrages	outcomes

CHAPTER 10

MOVIES CONFIGURE POLITICS

How Horror, Dystopia, Thriller, and Noir Shape Terrorism (Featuring Fight Club, Spy Game, and Swordfish)

The strategy of terror is a spectacularly failed one.[1]

—Caleb Carr

Terror, like panic, might be almost impossible to sustain. It strikes and spikes with virtual simultaneity; it decays nearly as fast. It consumes personal and historical moments that might last beyond minutes and hours to days and weeks, but it rages too hot and ranges too far to leave fuel for durable burns. This, unfortunately, is the good news. The bad news is that terror all too readily recurs; and when it doesn't, it echoes—in some settings, seemingly without end.

As a strategy, terrorism targets bystanders, civilians, "innocents" in a still decent sense of the word. That is why Caleb Carr, a military historian and popular novelist of note, argues that sustained terrorism does not succeed.[2] Outrageous violence against noncombatants spurs people to resist terrorists categorically. It mobilizes whole populations to extraordinary resolution, even desperation, so that they do whatever it takes over the long haul to destroy terrorist forces while discrediting terrorist causes. Not once in history, claims Carr, has a terrorist campaign in war or insurgency succeeded for long. This leads Carr and others to teach that individuals and governments must not overreact and respond in kind to terrorism. For the main hope of terrorists is to provoke self-defeating terrorism in return.[3]

150

Government terrorism might be another matter. In people, terror spirals into psychosis and breakdown; or it atrophies into anxiety. In politics, terror some-times takes the iron enclosure, utter domination, and systematic inefficiency of the totalitarian regime as a method for turning the perversity inward, leaving terror to feed indefinitely on itself. Yet experience suggests that actual totalitari-anisms fall after a few years or decades into a malaise of immorality too placid and pragmatic to count as terror, even though it is stoked by terrorist devices like concentration camps, death squads, and secret police. These are endurable, more or less, because they rarely reach for most people the fever pitch of full-fledged terror. At least in a world providing external political alternatives, we have learned, regimes of terror gradually routinize themselves into more traditional patterns of oppression and exploitation. Eventually a pervasive corruption can erode further the rigor of any terror, opening such regimes to reform, liberaliza-tion, or dissolution from within—and invasion from without.[4] Most terror stays local in space and momentary in time.

This happens in part because terror depends on unpredictability so radical that it undoes itself, preventing even a pattern of surprise. Dread can ensue instead, but it differs considerably from terror. Conducted in dread, everyday life expects catastrophe but plods timidly or doggedly ahead.[5] Terror shocks so deeply and stuns so decisively that we feel recovery is impossible, only to find ourselves unable later to tie its awful trauma to ordinary affairs. Terror disrupts routines apparently beyond repair, but dissipates rapidly into daytime amnesia.[6] The strange injunction to "return to normalcy" so as "not to let the terrorists win" testifies to the discombobulation intended but not always induced by terror.

In the aftermath of terror, such exhortations go overnight from absurd and undoable to simply unnecessary. The resulting routines might differ in detail from earlier days, and the echoes of terror might unsettle us for decades in some places or practices, yet the terror itself can dissipate rapidly in sensation and recogni-tion, if not consequence. Air travel "will never be the same" for Americans after 9/11, but how much different does it feel from before? The national-security state has expanded exponentially in apparent response to 9/11, yet do we pay much attention to it in our everyday lives? Even so, long wars have been fought and justified in response to 9/11; and the related rhetoric animates us.

Like other politics, terrorism is theatrical, performative, thus rhetorical.[7] Still aspects of terror can be so evanescent by comparison with other political experi-ences that terrorism can rely for political effects exceptionally on the rhetoric in its aftermath. Rhetoric in response to terrorist acts can construct enduring meanings and effects for them, inflecting their details in relatively lasting directions. The first terrorist bombing of the World Trade Center, in 1993, attracted momentary attention in America but generated scant rhetoric in response and next to no public memory. The embassy bombings soon to follow in other countries did not create in this one the echoing waves of terror sought by al Qaeda. Popular rhetorics of response seldom connected those dots with any sense of clarity or urgency in any political direction.[8] By contrast, the Beltway Snipers kept the nation's capital in turmoil on the edge of terror for days, and the Anthrax Assassin for weeks, because our rhetorics helped their deeds echo al Qaeda's. This continued even after conventional wisdom became that neither set of attacks tied organizationally or even motivationally to Islamic fundamentalism turned anti-American.

In the aftermath of terror, our rhetorics produce the dots or don't, then connect them or not. Far more than the words in our moments of terror, let alone the raw violations or feelings in such overwhelming experiences, our rhetorics in response define the perspectives and resolutions that emerge. The injuries of victims, the grievances of terrorists, the obligations of governments, the strategies of media, the responsibilities of citizens: all take clear shape only in the ensuing rhetorics. And our movies are important parts of those rhetorics.

So in the aftermath of terror, our movies help tell the tales, pipe the tunes, make the memories, shape the politics. What some movies might lack in box-office bang, they still can make up in political reverberation. Most terrorism is too volatile in detail and precarious in duration to define even its own meanings long term. The one regime of terror that so far has engulfed the globe for many decades is not so much political as military and apocalyptic. It is the shadow of the doomsday weapon, one not merely of "mass destruction" but potentially of total annihilation. Yet in the twenty-first century, our preeminent terrors take different forms than in the second half of the twentieth century. No more do we face the MADness of a superpower showdown between the United States and the Soviet Union. The new specters include the sabotage of civilization by "suitcase bombs" that provoke longer-range missiles through a profusion of regional conflicts that might escalate beyond all restraint. The terror of nuclear annihilation endures—now augmented by doomsday germs, poisons, and climate changes. Maybe this is why we still find it challenging to invent effective rhetorics for facing terrors of a humanly imposed apocalypse. So far, these are the stuff of nightmares and movies more than campaigns or policies. They stay repressed in everyday politics and foreign affairs, yet express themselves in profound disturbances of music, image, language, and cinema.[9] It is good that we try, in movies and more, to give our terrors actionable figures and faces.

Terror and Meaning

Americans have been making sense of terrorist events and concerting themselves to action with the help of Hollywood aesthetics. This is happening even though these popular styles are being disrupted in various degrees by the emerging politics that they have helped to prefigure. As Chapter 8 on how movies prefigure politics explains, we may observe that popular movies in recent decades have been helping construct "the phenomenal field" for political terrorism—as we are coming to know and contest it in the wake of 9/11.[10]

The political mythmaking of movies also helps us make retrospective sense of our experiences, and recent dynamics of terrorism are no exception. Through a Hollywood war movie, we could re-experience Mogadishu in Somalia with a *Black Hawk Down* (2001) years after the dust had settled from the disastrous moments of an aid mission in 1993. Through a political thriller, we could anticipate the experience of New York City under *The Siege* (1998) of terrorist attacks, years before the fall of 2001. Through a foreign dystopia, set in *Bab El Oued City* (1994), Americans could feel the effects of individual moves to resist or escape the encompassing system of regime terrorism in Algeria. Through the experimental cinema of *The Tornado* (1996), we could do the same for the anarchist system of civil-war terrorism in Lebanon. And through the blockbuster entertainment of *The Sum of All Fears* (2002), we could sense the frustrating complications in endeavors to resist the residual system of Cold War suspicions when trying to avert nuclear war spurred by rogue acts of nuclear terrorism.

As myths, popular genres are stories and dramas that share kinds of settings, events, and characters. As aesthetics, popular genres are conventional affinities among figures that help define one another. Thus the resurgent genre of noir need not link night and rain, but typically it does, and we know it in part from such figures.[11] Conventionally a noir protagonist encounters some dark night of the soul and needs a purging deluge. The figures of night and rain enact or embellish such meanings through the "pathetic strategy" common in popular genres.[12] And this holds even when both the night and the rain might be, well, more figural than literal: *The Matrix* (1999) give us neon-green figures that rain down the black screens of computers like the deluge down a window pane at night.

The families of defining conventions for popular genres are far more numerous—and sometimes far more complicated—than any two or three figures such as night and rain. The relationship is not one of necessary conditions: there are many noir films with no rain and now at least two with no night.[13] Nor is the logic one of sufficient conditions: there are innumerable movies with night and rain but no noir aesthetics. The connection among a genre's conventions is not even one of separate causes to contingent effects, as in behavioral paradigms for the social sciences. Not even in noir does night often cause rain or vice versa.

Rather than atomistically mechanical, popular genres are interdependently systemic. They do not specify directions or degrees of causation. Instead the correlations worth tracing among a genre's figures, styles, themes, or other aspects can help us appreciate its patterns of meaning. If Hollywood films have been helping prefigure our experiences of terrorism, they also have been helping us make sense of particular terrorist events and terrorism in general. So we may ask how figures from popular cinema help inform our political sense of what to say and do about terrorist acts, tactics, strategies, and consequences. And we may ponder how genres of popular cinema help coordinate and illuminate our senses of terrorism.

Chapter 8 specified how thriller conventions had shaped our sense of terrorism prior to 9/11, and Chapter 9 noticed how vampire movies fit several figures from the War on Terror. In this chapter, let us compare thriller tropes for terrorism with political figures in horror, dystopia, and noir as popular genres. One remarkable development is that mythic figures of terrorism do not exactly constitute a singular genre or even a distinctive aesthetic. That leaves political terror especially open to exploration in diverse genres with contrasting styles. To make decent sense of political terrorism, we might need all four of these popular forms.[14] Therefore we do well to explore the genres of horror, dystopia, thriller, and noir as contrasting political mythoi. This also enables us to revisit such figures from earlier chapters as shadow conspiracies, everyday evils, and fractal films. Together they suggest how the conventions of popular cinema continue to make important myths for American politics.

Horror and Evil

Apocalyptic reactions to 9/11 might imply that the generic home for terrorism could, even should, be popular horror. President George W. Bush soon denounced all terrorism as unqualified "evil." Thus the enduring phrase from his next State of the Union Address became a condemnation of Iran, Iraq, and North Korea as "the Axis of Evil" for pursuing weapons of mass destruction and sponsoring international terrorism. As Chapter 3 explains, horror is *the* popular genre of facing evils, especially evils of everyday life. Yet the conventions of popular horror do not figure prominently in any Hollywood treatments of what Americans recognize as political terrorism. This probably implies that popular cultures in the United States do not regard terrorism as an everyday evil but as an exceptional, even apocalyptic event.

Arguably there are two kinds or contexts for political terrorism that do appear in our popular films, yet neither Hollywood in particular nor America in general sees either as part of political terrorism. Thus Americans separate regime terrorism and war categorically from both "international terrorism" and "domestic terrorism." The genre for regime terrorism has become dystopia, an outlying form of political horror analyzed in the next section. War has a cinematic form of its own; and as Chapter 7 observes, war movies argue generically that war is (not so much terror as) hell—with heroism.[15] But when it comes to terrorism, the Hollywood dog that has not barked is horror. Hence it helps to contrast terror with horror, as both a family of feelings and a popular genre of films.

Terror is the fraternal twin of horror. As emotions and conditions, the two share most of their genetic material, yet they present distinct faces to the world. Together terror and horror form a complex of action and feeling that can figure momentarily in almost any kind of drama or film. Yet "horror" names a popular genre of movies, a whole family of conventions, whereas "terror" surfaces only in a few conventions of film. And "terrorism" characterizes a prominent form of politics, while "horrorism" remains only a possible word in waiting, with no referents for politics or other realms. Perhaps an implication is that the intertwined trajectories of horror and terror can be teased apart in the popular operation of politics and possibly in the generic apparatus of cinema. How does Hollywood handle them?

Terror is the overwhelming dread-and-despair that puts us (or our movie stand-ins) at the categorical center of assault. Or it does much the same by dispersing specific assaults into a continuing condition. Terror radicalizes anxiety. It projects death or degradation as immanent possibilities from almost any angle at any time in any place. Therefore terror disables us from action. It diminishes personal movement into mere behavior. It makes people flee or freeze in blind, frantic, unthinking aversion. Terror overflows fear. It overwhelms the appeal of fear to cognitive calculation of punishments and alternatives. It shoves aside the calm, cool apparatus of rationality. It panics people and destroys their identities as individual, responsible beings. It escalates and coagulates anxiety. Terror preempts escape. It prevents hope.[16] Thus political terrorism resists becoming recognized as an everyday evil because it insists on bringing an end to any sense of everyday life.

Horror is the overwhelming dread-and-disgust that initially puts someone or something else at the center of assault. Horror happens at first to us as onlookers.

We see atrocities that mock any possibility for goodness, truth, or beauty to remain unmixed with monstrosity. Later in horror, however, we look around to realize that the source of perversion is turning to get us, the circle of corruption is coming to encompass us, or the sinister system has swallowed us whole. Horror is revulsion for awful acts; it is repulsion from terrible entities. It stems from natural boundaries eradicated or cultural standards transcended. Hence it springs from the strange territory of the uncanny and the sublime, where awful abominations and awesome absolutes turn into one another with each twist in perspective. We might freeze in horror. Or we might refuse to recognize the horrors we glimpse, and go back to daily routines that pretend nothing major is awry. Yet we also might turn to face horrors, making human sense of their threats and finding good ways to resist them. Horror appalls and revolts; yet horror also can revolutionize, provoking fresh perspectives and effective inventions. For good or ill, horror provokes extreme responses that range from willful oblivion to apocalyptic reckoning. Terror disrupts and stops action by the victims; horror interrupts and radicalizes it.[17]

Terrorism can stem from criminals, from corrupt governments, from political or religious movements. Sometimes it serves strategies of war, sometimes oppression, sometimes protest or resistance or rebellion or liberation, sometimes revenge and redistribution; other times, it serves psychosis, sheer destruction, or the emergence of some new kind of civilization. At times, terrorism can operate through big-lie and brain-washing techniques. It can use tactics of random death and disappearance. It can impose iron discipline, work through mass hysteria, propagate paranoia, or rely on surveillance. It can anonymize people beneath notice, let alone contempt.[18] It can debase or humiliate most abjectly. It can concentrate citizens like pigs into pens. It can isolate individuals like pigeons into holes or compartments. It can drive parties, interests, even families underground. It can incarcerate whole populations. Nevertheless terror has stayed surprisingly separate from horror, with episodes of political terrorism as rare as a vampire's reflections in the popular genre of horror.

There is an obvious objection to these contrasts between terror and horror. It is the same objection that might be made to the claim that popular movies seldom, if ever, treat political terrorism through the popular aesthetics of horror: is the claim too literalistic? In other words, does the claim allow for the defining symbolism of generic horror? Relentlessly the existentialist conventions of this genre disguise the daylight dynamics of psychology, society, history, economy, polity, and more within the nightmare figures of vampires, werewolves, witches, zombies, demons, ghosts, and myriad monsters; haunted houses and hidden lairs; magical spells and satanic rituals. "Just as science fiction stories are popular science," remarks horror writer Dennis Etchison, "then horror stories are popular existentialism."[19] Who is to say that episodes of political terrorism are not amply and specifically evoked by Hollywood uses of existentialist symbolism in the genre of horror?

Yet film after film, intriguing glints of horror do not turn into sustained illuminations of terrorist politics. Nor do possible hints develop into detailed subtexts of political terrorism. These would be the ways to seek signs of political terrorism in horror movies, as Chapter 3 suggests. The few exceptions, where the symbols or subtexts do evoke political terrorism, leave us more with diffuse ideas than specific actions. To me, at least, these possible turns to political terrorism remain too fragmentary, too momentary, to make many contributions to our sensibilities for terrorist events. At most, these cinematic signs in horror give mere glimpses: neither articulate nor imaginative enough to prefigure a field of political terrorism addressed far more amply in thrillers (as Chapter 8 argues) and perhaps increasingly in noirs (as the last section of this chapter envisions).

Unsurprisingly the (counter) examples of political terrorism that surface in the popular genre of horror tie most to regime terrorism. The most vivid example I know is from *Interview with the Vampire* (1994), a cinematic allegory for horrors of the modern state. Its figure for the fire-bombing of Germany and probably also for the nuclear holocaust suffered by Japan is the poignant pose of a vampire "mother" and "daughter" who hold each other in their arms while the sun burns them into an ashen monument that soon blows away on the breeze. The scene and its encompassing sequence evoke acts of totalitarian terrorism that induce the response of a terrorist campaign in war. Notwithstanding considerable attention to these episodes of political terrorism before and after seeing the film, its imagery is acutely affecting. Horror, like terror, can be overwhelming.

If this were an exercise in the cinematic psychology of terrorism, we might try to probe the existential conventions of horror movies. How might the seductive gaze and glamour of the vampire suggest how situations of terror draw us into self-destruction, even as they horrify and repulse us? How might the dull gaze and crude appetites of the zombie show how terrorism takes away capacities for intelligent, truly political action? How might the haunting chill of the ghost evoke the abiding hatred and corrosive guilt that keep terrorist acts from much success? Horror might be ripe for use in probing dynamics of political terror; in fact, however, it has not been turned often toward overtly, officially political acts. In *Danse Macabre*, Stephen King talks of "the horror film as political polemic." But it is telling that his examples are entirely from the regions where horror overlaps science fiction; and King's own forays into political horror seem to me to be science fiction first, horror only second.[20] The single most visible exception associated with the current meisters of horror probably is *The Dead Zone* (1983), directed by David Cronenberg from a King novel of political apocalypse and assassination.[21] (In the context presently at hand, the movie's assassination of a political leader would not count as terrorism because it does not target civilians or other bystanders, a consideration emphasized in the King novel. If there is an act of political terrorism in the novel and movie, it is when the monstrous politician tries to avert his assassination by holding a baby between himself and the assassin, but that is too impulsive and momentary to justify seeing *The Dead Zone* as a work on terrorism.)

Even so, it is intriguing to notice that the recent westerns I know to include dynamics of political terrorism all appropriate figures of horror in this connection.[22] *Unforgiven* (1992), *The Quick and the Dead* (1995), and *Jonah Hex* (2010) turn in important part on regime terrorism—in all three cases as a figure for state terrorism. The tastes of horror in *Unforgiven* are subtle, but *The Quick and the Dead* includes a moldering black mansion and nightmare riders from the most horrific pages in *The Lord of the Rings,* and Jonah Hex is an avenging demon able to revive the dead and compel them to answer truthfully.[23] Both *Tombstone* (1993) and *Wyatt Earp* (1994) show how Earp took the modern politics of enforcement and revenge beyond the bend into political terrorism, and both movies borrow visual and verbal devices of conventional horror to brand his departure from any stern, proportionate, or otherwise defensible endeavor.[24] Likewise the relentless killer played by Javier Bardem in *No Country for Old Men* (2007) is a terrorizing agent of chaos especially at home in horror.[25] But do not expect to see these westerns in rosters of films that feature political acts of terrorism. As talk with diverse viewers keeps reminding me, few recognize Earp's acts as terrorism, even in glimmering ways. In all these movies, moreover, western conventions overshadow figures of terror and horror. Yet these films still merit mention here, since they suggest some cinematic routes to addressing political terrorism through figures of popular horror.

Dystopia and Totalitarianism

In regime terrorism, the political system targets its own inhabitants almost willy-nilly for atrocities such as arbitrary arrests, tortures, disappearances, poisons, bombings, or other radical disruptions. The aim—insofar as there is a coherent idea at work—is to subjugate, humiliate, and dehumanize the population.[26] In other words, the antipolitical purpose of regime terror soon turns into power and cruelty for their own insanely sadistic sake. Picture, wrote George Orwell, "a boot stamping on a human face—forever."[27] This is the totalitarian nightmare of systematic regime terror that drove the democratic imagination to war throughout most of the twentieth century.[28] By the twenty-first century, events and Hollywood had begun to supplement totalitarian control and regime terrorism with terrorism by movements and insurgent conspiracies as the western template for political hell on earth.[29]

Regime terrorism virtually defines its own (sub)genre of dystopia.[30] This articulates the horror archetype of the Bad Place into an intricate and far-reaching web of figures that remains even today America's primary epitome of political horror.[31] Hollywood seldom produces films in this mode, in important part because relentless downers do not draw lots of viewers or make much money. (The exceptions so far are the recent dystopias based on best-selling novels for tweens and teens.) As far as Hollywood is concerned, dystopia is less a genre in its own right than a subgenre. Yet it is even more a subgenre of science fiction than horror, and it tends to omit specific acts of political terrorism. Two of the best dystopias that focus on terrorist acts are popular Middle-Eastern, rather than Hollywood, films: *Bab el Oued City* and *The Tornado*. Remarkable as well is *The Day After*, one of the more sensational movies made for television. Its terrorizing regime is the international system of nuclear deterrence during the Cold War. When the system of Mutual Assured Destruction breaks down, the resulting nuclear holocaust becomes an act of political terrorism that produces an unremitting nightmare. Yet none of these three films seems likely to be important, at least for Americans, in configuring political terrorism or in explaining specific terrorist acts by insurgents or antiwestern movements.

When Hollywood does venture a dystopia, it is apt to shift from terrorism that targets bystanders to ruthless regimes of surveillance, torture, and punishment. These identify dissidents and do them in. To be sure, all people subject to totalitarian regimes in a way would be bystanders rather than empowered or responsible citizens; and all are targets of terrorism. Yet dystopian films on regime terrorism focus on dramas that feature dissidents. Presumably the judgment is that this makes motivations more comprehensible, plots tighter, and settings more plausible for viewers used to people and practices that calculate interests for efficient means to given ends. *Brazil* (1985) and the 1984 version of *1984* are examples.

Accordingly the political terrorism crucial for dynamics of totalitarian regimes—and apparent also in the actions of some authoritarian polities—seldom surfaces in Hollywood dystopias. Many dystopias regiment their societies by means other than terrorism, as we ordinarily would recognize it. Dystopias that lack or at least do not feature acts of political terrorism include *The Handmaid's Tale* (1990), *Gattaca* (1997), *The Lathe of Heaven* (2001), *A Scanner Darkly* (2006), and *Never Let Me Go* (2010). All of these films are science fiction, yet the telling point is that none are also full-fledged thrillers. Recent dystopias that do feature acts of political terrorism are not only science fiction but especially thrillers: *Twelve Monkeys* (1995), *The Island* (2005), *Children of Men* (2006), *V for Vendetta* (2006), *Babylon A.D.* (2008), *Repo Men* (2010), *In Time* (2011), and *The Purge* (2013). In each, the terrorism ties strongly to its film's thriller aspects of conspiracy, spectacle, and action. If anything, this observation holds even more strongly for recent cyberias—cyber dystopias—which often work so prominently as thrillers that viewers do not even notice the important ingredients of terror, horror, and science fiction in the likes of *Strange Days* (1995), *Virtuosity* (1995), or *Gamer* (2009). These comparisons indicate that Hollywood's elective affinities between dystopian tropes and terrorism remain weak and erratic by contrast with its links between thriller conventions and terrorism.

For political theorists, terrorism by totalitarian regimes is arbitrary in many particular instances but still endemic to the system. It is, in a word, systemic. For popular movies in America, political terrorism is occasional and instrumental. It usually springs from specific grievances, even though it targets civilians who lack focal roles in producing the grievances. As we have just started to notice, though, there is a complication. For reasons of dramatic economy and punch, as well as ideology, popular movies seldom portray political or other systems overtly as systems, in fully literal terms. Popular films rely instead on a convention of conspiracy that is more familiar from the thriller.

Thriller and Conspiracy

By convention, conspiracies have their primary Hollywood home in thrillers. Not by coincidence, as we have seen, thrillers are the principal genre for films that feature acts of political terrorism. Thrillers typically give viewers unqualified heroes, heroines, and villains. Yet thriller settings are more familiar, realistic, and up-to-date than those for the far-larger-than-life figures in action-adventure films, let alone superhero movies. In fact, such settings define subgenres for thrillers. These span international intrigues, foreign wars, governmental and military contests, criminal connivances, political potboilers, police stories, legal dramas, medical sagas, business tales, and others at the edges of neighboring genres like detection or action-adventure. The Hollywood disposition to emplot political terrorism in thrillers has several implications for the figures of terrorism widely available to Americans in making sense of terrorist events in the wake of 9/11.

As Chapter 2 argues, the academy and the press share an unfortunate penchant for literalistic criticisms of the Hollywood fondness for conspiracies. The frowning equation of conspiracy with crackpot politics surely creeps into American notions of terrorism when popular films insistently show political terrorism as conducted by conspiracy. We all know the refrain: how epistemically implausible, how social-scientifically unsophisticated, and how politically irresponsible it is to portray some cabal as running the world from behind the scenes.[32] Political scientists have wondered in print whether such Hollywood scripts are written by political rubes who know little about systems or art—and hence personalize everything simplistically—or by political extremists from the left and right who compulsively demonize a few foes as responsible for all the things that go wrong with their worlds.[33]

But as Chapter 2 also argues, Hollywood rhetorics of conspiracy are more sophisticated and defensible than these criticisms conceive. Conspiracies in thrillers are typically figures for oppressive or exploitive systems. Major characters and elements of a conspiracy can stand for major components or dynamics of a system much too complicated for a feature-length film to dramatize in literal detail. As explained earlier, *The Parallax View* (1974) presents an assassination conspiracy to trace symbolically how America's two-party system squelches political dissent. *Power* (1986) presents a conspiracy to show how American elections are being corrupted by big money from special interests. *Conspiracy Theory* (1997), *Enemy of the State* (1998), and *Shooter* (2007) dramatize conspiracies to probe oppressive aspects of the political system of the national-security state. *The Skulls* (2000) evokes Yale's notorious secret society for the Bushes and their buddies to suggest how political elites systematically extend themselves in democratic times. *From Hell* (2001) also deploys a secret society to indict how Victorian culture systematically exploits and represses middle-class dreams and personal freedoms. And *The Ghost Writer* (2010) explains the staunch but unpopular support by the British government for America's war in Iraq with a literally far-fetched conspiracy that illuminates symbolically how the United Kingdom depends politically, culturally, and commercially on the United States. In popular cinema, conspiracies abound.

This is not to say that popular cinema would err in connecting literal conspiracies to terrorist acts. As Chapter 2 cautions, conspiracies in a literal sense can be prominent devices of political struggle, especially in republics. For a group to conceive and conduct illegal acts without preemption by any regime that enforces its laws, secret communication is crucial: actual conspiracy is then a must. Even the peculiar acts of political terrorism that do not primarily target a state or regime tend to attack both secondarily. Such terrorism impugns the legitimacy of states and regimes by demonstrating that they cannot meet their responsibility to provide domestic tranquility—by protecting civilians from violence.

Yet if conspiracies appear in many films with political terrorism, and if conspiracies can be Hollywood figures for political systems, how can we say with confidence that few popular movies so far have addressed regime terrorism—even in contrast with the run-of-the-mill devices of political oppression portrayed at least in passing by thousands of popular movies? Might the terrorist conspiracies in Hollywood cinema often turn out to symbolize terrorist systems—and thus regime terrorism? Possibly, but concerted efforts to think through the symbols in many of the popular films potentially at issue leave me without a single clear example. It is not that regime terrorism never surfaces at all in Hollywood films. Rather it appears seldom and mostly as a sideshow, not as the focus, except in a few dystopias.

Conceptually and politically, it helps to distinguish occasional conspiracies within larger plots from plots that are conspiracies overall. As Chapter 8 specifies, the many hundreds of thrillers in the two decades just before 9/11 include fifty that feature political terrorism. At least thirty include some sort of conspiracy in their plots, although it is often the merest kind of criminal conspiracy. Yet only three of these films have conspiracy plots overall. The ratios are telling: three-fourths of the plots with acts of political terrorism *include* conspiracies, but less than a tenth *are* conspiracies. *The Package* (1989) offers an assassination conspiracy at the end of the Cold War. *Arlington Road* (1999) sounds an alarm about the American militia movement, and it shows how terrorists can use benign politics within America against the government. Then *The Siege* (1999) warns that foreign terrorism can happen here, might elicit an authoritarian and racist response, and could go so far as to provoke something like regime terrorism.

To emplot terrorism in thrillers is to endow the films' politics with clear heroes and monstrous villains, both acting from motives more personal than ideological. Thrillers treat terrorism as political violence against bystanders—by contrast with military combatants and public officials. This accords with a classic definition of political terrorism.[34] (And it suggests that we set aside for now the many thrillers about actions against overtly political figures.) In thrillers, this puts terrorists unarguably in the wrong: thrillers seldom face the complications in how one cause's terrorist can be another's freedom fighter. To do that might take tragedy of a classical kind. This is rare in popular films; but among the movies on political terrorism, perhaps *The Crying Game* (1992) and *The Boxer* (1997) come closest—and it is notable that neither is a usual Hollywood product, with both being written and directed by Irishmen for filming in Britain and Ireland to address terrorism by the Irish Republican Army.

The notion of terrorism as attacking innocents for political gain does not fit the genres of horror and dystopia. In horror, adults are guilty, secretly if not originally. That is how they can know and combat (but also be) the monsters. Children might begin as innocents, yet they must develop the moral and political sophistication born of facing their own eventual evils if they are to survive monstrous attacks. The systematic, encompassing corruption of dystopias means that the civilians targeted by the regime share responsibility for its terrorism. As theorists have made painfully clear, people subject to totalitarianism can contribute to terrorizing themselves.[35] Hence there is little room in horror or dystopia for the dynamics of political terrorism that turn on victimizing bystanders. In the systems of transgression and guilt that both those genres present, nobody is a bystander. Of course, that argument is congenial to political terrorists who take themselves to attack oppressive regimes where, if you are not part of the solution, you are part of the problem. To date, though, terrorists have not made many popular movies, let alone Hollywood releases.[36] Accordingly the thriller has become the Hollywood genre of choice for facing political terrorism.

But we misestimate the craft of popular movies if we infer that Hollywood merely turns terrors into thrills. Critics and scholars do complain that Hollywood thrillers cheapen the politics and denature the terrors.[37] That happens in some thrillers, but it is not the generic pattern. Part of this misunderstanding arises from the modern inclination to treat politics as exhausted by the operations of government and ideology. Not even thrillers about political terrorism show much interest in political ideologies, although the films do give considerable attention to machinations of government in combating terrorism.

Fortunately for us, there are many other kinds of politics, they are amply evident in electronic times, and they play signal roles in thrillers on terrorism. These are the classical politics of republicanism plus the postmodern politics of anarchism, existentialism, and perfectionism evoked in Chapter 8; and they surface in the political projects attributed to the terrorists as villains. That their politics seldom fit such modern ideologies of politics as liberalism, socialism, and conservatism (or even the likes of fascism, nazism, and communism) should not surprise us. Most terrorist politics have been postmodern or antiwestern, and many terrorist thrillers do engage such politics literally or figurally.[38] Thrillers also attend to the political projects enacted by the heroes who resist assaults by terrorists. Again this becomes easier to recognize when we encompass subtexts and when we open our eyes to politics that exceed the political forms most familiar to modern scholars.[39]

The Peacemaker (1997) is comparable to *The Siege* in suggesting that the United States needs to work as a liberal republic in order to survive, whether as the lone superpower taking primary responsibility for a nuclear world or as the leading ally in a multilateral effort with the United Nations. Otherwise neither the United States nor the United Nations can withstand the asymmetrical warfare from terrorists with access to weapons of mass destruction. In *The Peacemaker,* it is telling that the liberal analyst must persuade the republican military man to take seriously the political motives, especially the ideological causes, of terrorists. In the military, he has learned scorn for the supposedly political reasons of most people, including terrorists, who operate in an increasingly globalized world of would-be profiteers. Maybe he has read too many books about the onward march of globalization.[40] Or maybe he has watched too many Hollywood thrillers like the *Die Hard* movies (1988, 1990, 1995, 2007) and the *Speed* films (1994, 1997), where apparent terrorism turns out to be a smokescreen for garden-variety robbery.)

Stanley Cavell provides a beautiful analysis of the mid-twentieth-century "Hollywood comedy of remarriage," explaining (among many other things) how these romantic comedies enact the conservative politics of restoring order and healing communities.[41] *The Peacemaker* might be more or less a thriller of remarriage. It starts logically from the destroyed marriage of the eventual villain, a professor of music and a political activist who has lost his wife and daughter to warfare when the United States and its N.A.T.O. allies attempted to impose order on the disintegrating Balkans. The wife and daughter were civilians caught in the crossfire. As the professor experiences it, they were by-standing victims of semiadvertent, busybody terrorism. Acting from despair about any decent future, with his marriage and his community gone, the professor contrives to bring the terror home to its careless perpetrators in New York City. In diagnosing then responding to his terrorist project, the movie weaves a replacement marriage. Step by step, the film intertwines the components initially pitted against one another in the pairing of Lieutenant Colonel Thom Devoe (George Clooney) with Dr. Julia Kelly (Nicole Kidman).

Devoe is a military male who focuses on economics; Kelly is a civilian female whose specialty is politics. Devoe is a practical, low culture, but trusting man

of action who polices realities of crime; Kelly is a high culture, distrusting bu-
reaucrat, who is a thoughtful scholar of terrorism. Initially Devoe favors brute
force, whereas Kelly promotes civilized negotiation. To face and defeat the world-
destroying powers soon to be in the possession of terrorists, *The Peacemaker*
suggests that America must reunite these long-alienated identities and capacities.
That is a pretty tall order, but if anybody is up to the task of remarriage, Hollywood can help.

Indeed it can call its current hero of heroes, whomever he might be, to
the task.[42] *True Lies* (1994) is a remarriage thriller that is equally a comedy of
remarriage. The matrimonial union of Harry Tasker (Arnold Schwarzenegger)
and his wife, Helen (Jamie Lee Curtis), drifts then begins to unravel piece by
piece in the first half of the film. So the second half reweaves it. Along the way,
of course, the political terrorists get identified and defeated, while the Taskers
and the audience share comic thrills from James Cameron. The system of the
national-security state achieves respect, rescue, and restoration. Overall the politics are ideologically conservative: no great surprise with Arnold in the lead. But
again aesthetics trump ideologies: comedy devolves into farce, thriller heroism
escalates into superheroism, and the conservative outrage at terrorism turns into
the sly romance of bystanders striking back. Nuclear annihilation of the Florida
Keys begins as a terrorist atrocity, but it becomes merely a colorful prelude to
fun on the dance floor.

The Sum of All Fears is complicated because there are two sets of obstacles
for the hero. The overt villains are Nazis who crave world domination, and they
provoke the crisis typical for thrillers. Yet the crisis would not occur were there
no quasi-Cold War confrontation remaining between Russia and the United
States as the world's two nuclear powers of greatest note. The government officials in Russia and the United States are driven in conventional thriller fashion
by personal and political imperatives that boil down to upholding the honor of
their own sides.

Jack Ryan (Ben Affleck) must exercise a cool calculation of interests based
on a mastery of information about characters and conditions in order to take
the Russians and Americans out of their escalating showdown over national and
individual honor. In regard to the Russians and Americans, therefore, Ryan is
a critical historian who promotes the liberal politics of a larger rationality of
knowledge and human interests. This averts disaster from the republican dialectic
of honor and anger, where affronts escalate into all-out war. Thus it replays the
political lessons promoted by arguably protoliberal theorists such as Thomas
Hobbes and John Locke, centuries ago in England.

In response to the international gang of resurgent Nazis, by contrast, Affleck's figure is the dashing hero familiar from spy-vs.-spy thrillers. He shows his excellence in action through daring, perseverance, improvisation, and martial arts. The Nazi terrorists instigate the crisis, but the nuclear powers complicate it. Thus the first skein of the plot is republican, and the second is liberal. Ryan helps America and the world limit Nazi terrorism and avenge Nazi evil. He also helps Russia and the United States escape from the terrible system of escalating grudges.

The academic caricature of thrillers would take their conventions of heroism and villainy to mean especially short shrift for the grievances of terrorists. That is what *The Sum of All Fears* gives us for the Nazi terrorism: little sense of what grievances the gang might have or why, and no sympathy at all for its politics. The larger part of the movie, however, concerns motivations for Russian and American acts that provide chilling parallels to the Nazi terrorism. These receive careful exposition in words as well as colorful articulation in symbols both aural and visual. The film cultivates some sympathy for grievances on each side, even as it criticizes every turn toward terrorism.

The genre does much the same. Roughly a tenth of the time, as Chapter 8 indicates, pre-9/11 thrillers with political terrorism ignore grievances altogether. More than half of the time, those thrillers criticize terrorist grievances emphatically and perhaps one-sidedly. But even before 9/11, more than a fourth of the thrillers on terrorism delve more respectfully into the motivations for political terror, and post-9/11 thrillers seem to be building on that.[43] Thrillers condemn terrorism as violence against more or less innocent bystanders; yet this does not keep the genre from detailed, and sometimes supportive, consideration of troubles that generate political terrorism. Hollywood thrillers have been more subtle and intelligent than we might expect in configuring terrorism. In movies such as *The Siege*, the genre even ventured early warnings against accommodating terrorists by responding to their attacks with misdirected or disproportionate retaliation, suspension of civil liberties, and regime terror. Thrillers show more than a modicum of sophistication about political terrorism.

Noir and Sophistication

It makes sense, then, that Hollywood has started blending thrillers with noirs in order to tackle political terrorism with even greater flair and sophistication. In some Hollywood quarters, noir films seem little more than thrillers become acutely stylish, self-aware, and sophisticated. In others, the mark of noir is realism, in a strongly stylized sense.[44] This realism encompasses seedy settings, grainy colors, and many shadows. It also means moral malaise, political hardball, and rhetorical savvy in social systems that ensnare people left and right. Noir is a genre ready-made for the complexities of political terrorism along with attempts to preempt, repudiate, or punish it.

As political terrorists began targeting the United States more intensely in the 1990s, film noir was returning to the fore in popular movies.[45] Early examples of the genre had flourished in the 1940s and 1950s. Then noir subsided so much in prominence that many scholars defined it as a delimited period rather than a continuing genre. When you look for them, of course, there turn out to have been more than ten noir films released every decade in the 1960s, 1970s, and 1980s. Nevertheless the Hollywood proportion of noir films had declined, and a few shining exceptions like *Chinatown* (1974) showed how marginal noir had become to the aesthetics of Hollywood in this interregnum. By the second half of the 1980s, however, film noir was making a comeback. The 1990s viewed some eighty new noirs, and the resurgent genre once more became a prominent Hollywood source of sights, sounds, and stories.[46] If we reckon that the new century began in 2000, we may say that it already has contributed some two hundred neo-noir films.

Accordingly noir aesthetics have been amply available to help Americans make sense of terrorist acts, and this Hollywood genre is making an impact on our political sensibilities. When Maureen Dowd, the national weathervane of the *New York Times,* addressed the attacks on 9/11, she took her title, "Touch of Evil," from a famous noir film by Orson Welles. Recently this noir had been rereleased in a "director's cut," based on rediscovered requests that Welles had made of the studio, which had edited his footage into a logical mess. His movie still was powerful enough aesthetically to attract popular attention half a century later. Dowd used the film's theme to evoke her take on the world in the wake of September 11. She began a commentary with the look and feel of a genre renowned for painting gray on gray: "I've always loved film noir. The grays, the shadows, the mysterious webs of murder, deception and corruption, the morally ambiguous characters." Nonetheless, she wrote, "I never expected to see a noir shadow fall on the white marble hive of Washington. The film noir hero, as Nicholas Christopher wrote, descends 'into an underworld, on a spiral.' The object of his quest 'is elusive,' and he is beset 'by agents of a larger design of which he is only dimly aware.'"[47]

Like most fans, Dowd seems to have thrilled to the genre's ambiguities, its sophisticated sense of foggy complications that make for steamy mysteries and stories of the American dream undone by its own ambitions. Even by October of 2001, Dowd could observe how "Sept. 11 was a day of crystalline certainty. Thousands of innocent people were dead. We had to find the murderers and unleash hell." Soon there were complications. "But after that things got weirdly muddied. We would have been prepared for a conventional war outside our borders. But we were not prepared for the terrorists' unconventional war inside our heads. We went from never imagining the damage the barbarians inside our gates could do to imagining little else." Noir contributed to the imagining. Even before the United States became superserious about political terrorism, noir had started to edge into the field of popular films about it. *Fight Club* (1999), *Spy Game* (2001), and *Swordfish* (2001) feature the looks, sounds, and structures of film noir made into the popular genre of neo noir, and they are three of the more provocative treatments of political terrorism to issue from Hollywood.

Fight Club and *Swordfish* pay special attention to spectacle, a shared concern of terrorism and cinema.[48] Gabriel Weimann and Conrad Winn maintain that "the essence of terrorism is the actual or threatened use of violence against victims of symbolical importance in such a way as to gain psychological impact for the purpose of achieving political objectives."[49] Spectacle is what terrorists promote for this purpose, and spectacle is the stock-in-trade of popular cinema.[50] As a genre, neo noir has developed an acute concern for the engines and dangers of spectacle.

The terrorists who star in *Fight Club* and *Swordfish* both pursue the politics of spectacle. In doing this, these characters claim superior realism, yet neither film is the least inclined toward mundane realism in story or cinematic style. Instead they share the sophisticated realism of noir, and they use the genre to expose the corruption of spectacular societies as systems that invite the politics of terror. Such stylish realism stems from their attunement to the cinematic construction of political realities in America—and the world that its media have been busy globalizing. The two movies' cinematic devices of terrorism display this knowledge, though playfully in both cases. This locates them in the family of films such as *Mad City* (1997), *Wag the Dog* (1997), *Pleasantville* (1998), *The Truman Show* (1998), *EdTV* (1999), *15 Minutes* (2001), *S1m0ne* (2002), and *Idiocracy* (2006) that play reflectively and prophetically with media construction. Most of the films with political acts of terrorism show some awareness of such media dynamics and their postmodern politics. Yet among these, only *Three Kings* (1999) and possibly *Spy Game* also might qualify for the family of films that emphasize dynamics of media construction.

The specific brands of postmodern politics in *Fight Club* and *Swordfish* are especially debatable as to types. *Swordfish* has an antiterrorist terrorist named

Gabriel and played by John Travolta. By the end of *Swordfish,* Gabriel's terrorism is financing his own foreign and military policy of counterterrorist vengeance. This radical, perhaps satirical adjustment of domestic and international politics seems somewhat anarchical in ideology but even more in style. The later politics of terrorism in *Fight Club* also might be categorized as anarchist—or nihilist, since its movement named Project Mayhem claims to pursue a fanaticism of destruction. Its obliteration of civilization by bombing credit records is to plunge the world into a kind of chaos. This echoes the expectation of Giambattista Vico, a republican theorist in the Italian Enlightenment, that the humans in sophisticated cities would descend through a corrupt "barbarism of reflection" where supercritical lawyers and commentators tear people to shreds with sharp tongues and teeth to a noble "barbarism of sense" with unrefined humans living in true attunement to nature.[51] Western civilization knows the barbarism of sense, as a situation without government as hierarchical order, to be anarchy in the meaning so unsettling to Thomas Hobbes.

Yet the charismatic project of liberation by Tyler Durden (Brad Pitt and Edward Norton) as the protagonist in *Fight Club* is devoted less to eliminating all hierarchical order than to reviving pure, impulsive, perfectionist action by uncivilized Nietzschean nobles in a setting before the west was won. The movie makes such a masculinist trajectory at least borderline patriarchal, hence incipiently hierarchical, though cultic would be a better category. There is in *Swordfish,* by contrast, no perfectionist celebration of impulsive action or primitive cult-ure. Its violence of terrorism is not a Dionysian rite, as in *Fight Club,* but a hardball device for trumping violent terrorists. Gabriel is a planner who leaves few probabilities uncalculated. His enterprise is eminently sophisticated, if fatally cynical—at least to others. Therefore the politics of *Swordfish* are "anarchist," whereas the politics of *Fight Club* are "perfectionist" and Nietzschean. In neither film, though, is any ideology half so detailed or influential politically as the aesthetics of noir. The protagonists' political styles are what matter. Neither film offers a sober, respectable take on terrorism; and both mobilize noir in similarly playful ways. Yet both have become cult favorites by featuring noir conventions for configuring our senses of political terrorism.

Spy Game uses the stylish realism of noir to indict terrorist tactics by covert operatives for the United States. It moves good-hearted but hard-boiled protagonists played by Brad Pitt and Robert Redford from CIA assassinations during the Vietnam War, Cold War betrayals in Berlin, and political bombings in Beirut, to ruthless trade struggles with China. The film fully acknowledges that American enemies also terrorize, but it suggests that many of America's hard choices have come mainly from being all too hard-headed and heavy-handed in foreign policies. Noir tropes sophisticate the thriller politics until, by the end, personal ties lead the protagonists to renounce the room that *Realpolitik* makes for sacrificing bystanders to larger political causes.

Like horror and dystopia, noir suspects that systems entrap us even in the most ordinary of everyday activities. The leading figures in noir films are nothing like innocent. When they try hardest to be bystanders, stepping aside from the fray or pretending that they can stay aloof from the systematic corruption, their ignorance ruins their own efforts and other people's lives. Yet the wake-up calls that rouse noir protagonists to recognize their perils and responsibilities activate their residual virtues. These reconstruct the shadows and mirrors of politics into rights and wrongs that make human sense in fallen worlds far from pure innocence or absolute evil. In some ways, we all participate in the regime, the system, the transgressions, even the terrors. But in other ways, there can be bystanders, civilians, victims outside any proper scope of violence—notwithstanding their real contributions, conscious or not, to acts that outrage others. In noir, we can learn how war, terror, freedom-fighting, and all other politics face complications that should induce a sense of limits along with a capacity of self-criticism.

Noir sprang from the literary subgenre of hardboiled detection. In the 1920s and '30s, the "roman noir" had turned the upper-crust amateur detective operating in the milieu of the country manor into a sometimes suave but always hard-bitten private eye who scrambles to make a living from the seamy side of the city.[52] Like hardboiled detection, classical film noir situates itself in the gritty night of an endlessly corrupt city under siege in every direction from criminals and political manipulators.[53] As a "lone knight of justice," the noir detective cannot hope to restore order or impose justice on the model of the classical detective. He is in over his head, and his interventions in the ongoing dynamics of crime are more likely to aggravate the harm than heal even a small part of the city. Even when the protagonist of classical noir is not exactly a detective—but more a minor-league Faust who blunders toward personal, moral, social, and political catastrophe—the most he can manage is to leave behind a lesson: his cautionary tale about how things went wrong.

Dowd observed that "The last thing this country wanted was to be pulled into another hostile, unfamiliar landscape or more political quicksand. Even in our national discourse, we rejected ambiguities, preferring the thumbs up–thumbs down, who's in–who's out, box office winner–box office loser sureties. But now we're enmeshed in ambiguity. First we wanted to bomb Afghanistan. Then, when we saw the suffering of the people there, we wanted to send food. Now we may bomb them with missiles and care packages." This fits the chiaroscuro complexity of noir. "President Bush is struggling with geopolitical jujitsu. Our old enemy Russia is our new ally. Our old ally Israel is accusing us of appeasing the Arabs. We have to now trust countries we distrusted, like Pakistan. We have to hand out bribes and play footsy with those who tolerated and sheltered and exported terrorists—and may again." As Dowd concluded, "Our desire for justice remains unambiguous. Beyond that, as Keats wrote, 'there is nothing stable in the world; uproar's your only music.'" The classical sensibility of noir finds abyss and chaos just below the surface. It experiences ruin and corruption perceptible through the pretty pretensions and petty sophistications of the city.

Classical noir always favored Los Angeles as its sin city. As a city, however, L.A. was always already decentered and postmodern: more a ramshackle network of suburbs in search of a city than a gleaming beacon on the hill of western imagination.[54] Film noir establishes L.A. with shots from the mountainside. These look down on the basin below as a tangle of freeways, aqueducts, and subdivisions in a valley that shades into smog and night. The Hollywood sign of celebrity culture and politics labels a neighboring hill. Hollywood films show Arab terrorists in particular as coming from the dark warrens, bright deserts, and sun-washed cities of the Middle East, and the L.A. of film noir manages all three at once, as well as unreal downpours of rain that can never wash the city clean. When we witness a New York suffocated in ash and smoke and grit, or we look upon the ruined-coliseum façade mimicked by fallen fragments from the twin towers of the World Trade Center, we see with Dowd a noir city left in the twilight of the idols.

Resurgent noir turns the fatally sophisticated city not only into suburbs but also into the abstracted systems of domination and corruption long excoriated by the existentialists.[55] The targets, dynamics, and consequences of political terrorism find themselves in—and lend themselves to—noirish figures that include rather than excuse ourselves from the picture.

Not long after reading Dowd, I attended a symposium sponsored by the University of Iowa Project on Rhetoric of Inquiry about responses to the terrorist attacks of 9/11.[56] The conference guide to art exhibits, academic panels, and original performances runs almost forty pages, and its cover shows in noirish silhouette an airplane flying into the soft gray air over a New York skyline that still featured the twin towers. For the first day, the conference organizers projected this grim, funereal image in grayscale on a big screen behind the stage for symposiasts. Throughout the second day, participants watched video ruminations on the 9/11 aftermath, photographs of Ground Zero and the informal memorials taking shape around it, and a drama on naming the dead: the victims in New York, Washington, and Pennsylvania. Every one of the videos, pictures, and performances glowered with shadowy-gray sensibilities of noir. More ominous even than the stark blacks, whites, and reds of horror, the chiaroscuro sophistication of noir gave the occasion a somber sense of the fatal, fateful perplexities of political terror. Similar effects can be seen in the Hollywood turn to noir as a generic setting for coming to terms with terrorism.

It is in our capacity to envision consequences and project possibilities that our pasts, our presents, and our futures emerge. With them, emerge our exalting—if also corrupting—politics of construction, criticism, and struggle. For us after 9/11, sophistication means recognizing these dynamics as our politics. For us still early in the twenty-first century, popular movies are potent forms of political imagination. For us as a civilization still learning more than it ever wanted to know about the politics of terror, noir is a popular genre that has much to recommend it. The shadowy shapes of twin towers at the World Trade Center collapsed into a flash of fire, a rain of ash, then a darkness of more than night and rubble. Rebuilding has proceeded, yet these can become influential figures from film noir for the terrorisms now emerging in Hollywood's politics and our own.

CHAPTER 11

CONCLUSION

POLITICAL STYLES IN POPULAR MOVIES (FEATURING ELYSIUM, IN TIME, UPSIDE DOWN, AND THE HUNGER GAMES)

One should not underestimate the effect, at once extravagant and insidious, of popular entertainment on the political imagination.[1]

—Anthony Lane

As forms of life, our cultures are systems; and as systems, our cultures are nonlinear. Thus their aspects or components—such as entertainments and politics—are strongly, sensitively interdependent. Effects are not just distant and disproportionate but indistinguishable at times from causes, and vice versa. So it is hard to say at times whether popular entertainments affect political imaginations, or vice versa. Yet we need not draw causal lines in order to ascertain strong associations and mutual influences. Hollywood movies and American politics meet in the rhetorical dynamics of mythmaking that shape and interpret our daily lives and governing deeds.

Our politics concern our communities, and our communities take their forms and contents from our communications. Rhetoric constructs and analyzes these forms and contents, especially with respect to their politics. For a century, already, popular movies have remained prominent in the culture and politics of America. Continuing technological innovation so far has been keeping movies on the forefront of political mythmaking by reproducing them in myriad electronic

173

media. Therefore rhetorical analysis of the politics in popular movies can contribute significantly to our comprehension of politics and communications in the United States and beyond. Film takes can help do this; and these takes on horror, thriller, war, and science-fiction movies can show how.

More than mere entertainments, popular movies operate as virtual realities. They give us reservoirs of new experiences, and they practice us in repertoires of political actions. As Connie Willis writes, "That's what the movies do. . . . They give us lines to say, they assign us parts: John Wayne, Theda Bara, Shirley Temple, take your pick."[2] Accordingly the virtual realities of popular cinema enter into our venues of private experience and public action. Popular movies often provide virtual realities to augment—as well as affect—our political realities. They furnish forms of imagination, interpretation, and action. Film takes can appreciate these contributions.

Movies as Memories

Popular films also influence political realities by making some of our memories of them and reconfiguring others. Ancient Greeks and Romans recognized that memories can be crucial platforms for action and pervasive standards for achievement in politics.[3] For their classical civilization, community memories were the stories told in public about notable deeds and words that they or their forbearers had witnessed. These were their myths, their symbolical stories of the community: its founders, members, enemies, and destinies.

For our postmodern civilization, community memories include the movies that we see and discuss, time and again, throughout our lives. "Novels, plays *and films* are filled with references to, quotations from, parodies of—old movies," Kenneth Tynan argued. "They dominate the cultural subconscious because we absorb them in our formative years (as we don't absorb books, for instance); and we see them again on TV when we grow up." As Tynan added, "The first two generations predominately nourished on movies are now of an age when they rule the media." Tynan experienced it as "frightening to see how deeply—in their behavior as well as their work—the cinema has imprinted itself on them." He explained that "Nobody took into account the tremendous impact that would be made by the fact that films are *permanent* and *easily accessible from childhood onward*." Tynan even anticipated that, "as the sheer number of films piles up, their influence will increase, until we have a civilization entirely molded by cinematic values and behavior patterns."[4] And by now, a further generation or two down the road from Tynan's observations, we have every reason to recognize popular movies as some of our most pervasive networks of myths, especially about our community's coherence in politics and everyday life.

Neuroscience and cognition experiments provide diverse evidence that memories are just as important to political realities as ancient scholars had inferred.[5] Shared stories are our shared storage. Audiovisual sources like cinema and television are particularly potent for politics.[6] Thus the mythic figures from popular movies stand to be especially significant for rhetorical analysis of their politics. Yet popular films also influence realities by making or disseminating many of the aesthetics that configure electronic societies. Especially through popular genres of cinema, these styles help prefigure the fields of events that we experience and the forms of responses that we rehearse. Famous episodes when presidential words echo popular movies are small indications: "Make my day!" "Where's the rest of me?" And "all things considered, I'd rather be in Philadelphia."[7] Movies also help configure governmental plans, improvisations, and criticisms. Mainly, though, prefiguring, disfiguring, and configuring our fields of political experience involve the larger looks and sounds of popular movies that permeate our ordinary modes of everyday life. As film takes suggest, these political dimensions and dynamics of movies appear less as overt topics than dispersed subtexts, less in formal ideologies than informal aesthetics, and less for any film analyzed alone than taken in terms of its cultural background of popular genres.

Persuasions as Politics

In ancient Greece and Rome, rhetoricians emphasized distinctive modes of persuasion that they associated with different psychological "faculties." Aristotle's classic trio of logos, ethos, and pathos has informed rhetorical analysis ever since.[8] More than two millennia later, though, we do well to reach beyond western trichotomies toward more ample networks of devices for analysis. We could amplify the ancient trio in two ways: we could recognize additional modes of persuasion that come to the fore in electronic communication, and we could recognize more dynamics in each mode.[9] The film takes in this volume have been working with the possible supplements summarized experimentally for four periods of western civilization in Table 11.1 to display six—not just three—modes of persuasion and their associated mental faculties.

Table 11.1 Six Modes of Persuasion

Persuasion	Faculty	Classical	Medieval	Modern	Postmodern
logos	**reason**	topics	stases	rationality	cognitions
(logics)	(self-identity)	dialectics	arguments	calculation	intellections
ethos	**spirit**	characters	authorities	credibility	moods
(ethics)	(will, honor)	standings	offices	expertise	ambience
pathos	**desire**	passions	senses	emotion	styles
(pathologies)	(appetite)	feelings	sensibilities	sentiment	aesthetics
mythos	**memory**	tales	epics	history	stories
(myths)	(meaning)	narratives	parables	series	novels
tropos	**imagination**	turns	figures	charts	icons
(tropes)	(invention)	symbols	illustrations	diagrams	emblems
athos	**language**	laws	maxims	rules	slogans
(aporia)	(criticism)	letters	handbooks	textbooks	aphorisms

Such angles of analysis enable us to pursue rhetoric—and thus the politics in popular movies—in ways that can be more inclusive and adventurous than the classical categories on their own.

Scholars love logos as (loosely) the written and rational word, and I am a scholar, so my film takes all try to respect and explore the political logics of their movies. Nonetheless Chapters 6 and 7 pay special attention to logics of cinematic argument. In its classical aspect as character, ethos is an emphasis of Chapters 6 and 9; in its western connection with ethics, ethos is a focus of Chapter 4; and in its postmodern sense as mood or atmosphere, ethos is a preoccupation of Chapter 7. As persuasion through emotion, pathos is crucial for the fourth and fifth takes. Mythos as symbolically charged storytelling looms large in Chapters 3 and 4, and this last take returns to story forms further ere it is done. Attention to tropos as the configuration of sight, sound, talk, and action is central to Chapters 1 and 2 as well as the three takes on political terrorism. Even the fascination of athos with rhetorical gaps, criticisms, and devices for dealing with them surfaces at times in the fourth, fifth, and sixth takes. Although the book at hand is an introduction to film takes, not a treatise on modes of persuasion in general or even in cinema, we do well to acknowledge these key means.

Popular cinema is far from the only electronic medium that invites enhanced devices for rhetorical analysis. Programming and advertising on American television turn time and again to persuasion through mythos.[10] Innovations in verbal and visual rhetoric through electronic politics depend on tropos.[11] If *athos* designates our deconstructive attention to aporia, the gaps that lurk inevitably in communications of every kind, any medium is ripe for analysis attuned to it.[12]

And if we continue to borrow names from the Three Musketeers, *porthos* could label our strained but indispensable communication across contrasting rhetorics, paradigms, disciplines, institutions, languages, and the like.[13] Willingness to develop rhetoric with such concepts can suggest hosts of enlightening exercises, and film takes are fine places for many of them.[14]

Genres as Generalizations

In our ordinary talk about movies, such modes of persuasion point to popular genres and the conventions that define them. None of the film takes here ventures a comprehensive account of any popular genre. In other words, no treatment here of war, horror, thriller, or science-fiction movies pretends to provide a political theory of its respective form. Instead the goal is to engage us in thinking about the politics in popular movies, and the means are hit-and-run comparisons of the politics in film uses of a few conventions at a time. Ultraviolence on screen can have other effects—and thus other politics—than grossing out some viewers and revving up others; instead it can spur empathy that moves us into ethical action. Or so Chapter 5 explains. The Bush War on Terror can be seen less as gunslinging than vampire hunting, suggests the ninth take. And "the new disorder" in cinema could turn out to be the emergence of a popular genre of fractal films fit for "a new order" of nonlinear politics in global systems, as Chapter 4 argues.

Although not the business at hand, political theories of popular genres are possible and useful. In fact, they inform several of this volume's takes on popular movies. A foundation for Chapter 7's analysis of recent war movies is the political theory of war films in general as evocations of how war is hell with heroism. The chapter does not detail or justify that theory; it simply uses it to advance a distinct perspective on Hollywood's post–Vietnam War movies on war. Similarly the third take sketches (ever so summarily) a political theory of popular horror, as facing evils in everyday life; but again, this merely provides a platform for the quick case that some horror films focus provocatively on political communication. The ragged, ramshackle, cultural character of popular genres keeps any political theories of them from exclusive validity or primacy. As political theories of cultural forms, generic accounts of war, horror, thriller, or science-fiction movies need not discredit competitors. Often they do well instead to complement some contrasting theories.

Since popular genres are cultural forms, it can be fun and instructive to play with their political relations. The forms remain immensely flexible, so any

Table 11.2 Kinds of Politics Prominent in Popular Genres

Popular Genres	Political Topics	Political Antinomies
detective tales—classical	social disorder	conservatism vs. liberalism
detective tales—hardboiled	political corruption	socialism vs. liberalism
epics	oppression and liberation	republicanism vs. imperialism
fantasies—adult	identity and responsibility	existentialism vs. republicanism
fantasies—juvenile	death, sex, and identity	existentialism vs. perfectionism
fantasies—sword and sorcery	honor, anger, and interest	feudalism vs. capitalism
fantasies—talking animals	western civilization	conservatism vs. perfectionism
fantasies—urban	postmodern civilization	existentialism vs. capitalism
horror stories	crises in everyday life politics	existentialism vs. perfectionism
neo noirs	social and political spectacle	democratism vs. perfectionism
romances—feminist	the personal as political	feminism vs. patriarchalism
satires—political	dispossession and exploitation	populism vs. elitism
science fictions	science, change, and society	perspectivism vs. absolutism
superhero sagas	ambition, identity, and justice	democratism vs. perfectionism
thrillers—legal	law and justice	conservatism vs. capitalism
thrillers—police	law and order	liberalism vs. anarchism
thrillers—spy	bureaucracy and Cold War	republicanism vs. totalitarianism
war dramas	character and calculation	realism vs. idealism
westerns	enforcement and forgiveness	liberalism vs. republicanism

comparisons may be prized for the insights they yield; but their possibilities must not be pushed toward literalist, essentialist, or foundationalist claims about the necessary character or politics of particular performances. Just as a matter of actual, elective affinities, though, Table 11.2 offers a preliminary sense of political topics and antinomies especially strong in their recent associations with several popular genres.

Occasional consideration of these affinities can evoke the lay of the land for takes done and takes yet to come. But of course, we need to remember that many popular works of cinema, literature, and television twist their conventions; and some works are multiply genred. Thus *Blade* (1998) and *Se7en* (1995) are both horror and noir; *Blade Runner* (1982) is science fiction and noir; *Déjà Vu* (2006) is a time-travel thriller; *Three Kings* (1999) is a war caper; *The Peacemaker* (1997) is a military thriller of remarriage; while *Pacific Rim* (2013) is a scifi-horror flick that is also a war movie. The generalizations are almost ridiculously rough—but useful even so.

The table takes on aspects of only twelve of the popular genres of movies at this moment in the history of Hollywood, and this book targets only four of them for specific analysis: horror, war, thriller, and science-fiction films. So let me not leave the impression that any of these is somehow "more popular" or "more political" than the many other candidates for genre-oriented analysis of popular politics. Pick a personal favorite from popular genres of cinema, literature, or television; and the odds are overwhelming that specialists in those media have devoted many articles and at least several books to some aspects of your genre's politics. Such studies suggest irresistibly that popular genres of entertainment are major arenas of political communication.

Yet media specialists such as film scholars often stay fairly abstract, denatured, or even deflected in their treatments of politics. When horror scholars write about the existentialism in *28 Days Later . . .* (2002), *The Wolfman* (2010), or the five-part *Twilight Saga* (2008–2012), they are apt to sociologize existentialist politics as alienation in mass society, psychoanalyze them as aberrations of mourning, or philosophize them as perplexities of personal resistance. There is plenty of political importance to learn from such angles of analysis.[15] But they do not preempt examination of the micropower structures, the linear and nonlinear systems, or the construction of protective communities in such horror movies.[16] When experts in literature or cinema analyze politics in westerns, they feature frontier myths, American virtues, models of individuality and masculinity, or Cold War echoes.[17] Yet films such as *Unforgiven* (1992), *Appaloosa* (2008), *True Grit* (2010), and *The Lone Ranger* (2013) can also inform political theories with strategies of environmentalism, feminism, state making, and public formation.[18] Overall there is lots of room for specifically political takes on Hollywood movies and political theories of popular genres.

Styles as Sensibilities

Popular movies engage our politics more as personal styles of action than as parties, policies, ideologies, or even institutions. The politics featured by these takes on horror, war, thriller, and science-fiction films are mainly styles of republicanism, liberalism, perfectionism, and existentialism. The politics of anarchism and conservatism are readily visible too, but even they operate more as styles than as ideologies in popular movies distributed widely in the United

States. Hollywood movies include many additional kinds of politics: feminist, environmentalist, idealist, populist, realist, and so on. All these politics take cinematic shape primarily as styles.

Personally and communally, styles coalesce the many modes of persuasion into action. This is why republicans since ancient Rome have taken gestures to epitomize personal characters and political styles. It is why republicans have sculpted busts and statues to monumentalize the lessons of history. And it is why rhetoricians from Greece and Rome onward treat figures of speech-in-action-in-public as fundaments of community life.[19] Public action is performance, especially for republicans. Even we ordinary citizens act through-form—in our uses of gestures, genres, conventions, institutions, rituals, styles, and such.[20] Movies show politics principally as styles of action, and movies do politics through inflecting these styles.

Styles are aesthetics.[21] Here I do not mean aesthetics mainly as studies of art or beauty—but more as their cultural and personal practices. They are the full-bodied capacities of feeling that help us sense what goes with what else, to what effect, and with what responses. They are the looks, the sounds, the tastes, the touches, the auras and aromas that become our senses of situations. Then they settle into popular conventions of expression and experience.

Thus styles can be reproduced or appropriated from one setting to another. The elements of a style can change remarkably from one time to another; yet they can connect, complement, or otherwise coordinate to tap similar complexes of feeling. Aesthetics in architecture include the classical, neoclassical, modern, art deco, pop, and postmodern. Styles of clothing, even of life, among teens have ranged in my times from hippie or yippie to nerdy or preppy to goth or grunge and so forth. All are "fashions" or "fads" because they come in and out of favor. Yet many manage to become lasting "looks" and "tastes" or sometimes even "sounds." Film takes often focus on the stylistic aspects of politics, because they predominate in our everyday action.

Styles are sensibilities and practices more than creeds.[22] Styles do not consist primarily of doctrines or principles, though sensibilities can be evoked in part by the sorts of principles that could serve as mottoes of action for the particular people who epitomize those styles in action. To characterize a style, we often do well to settle first on a gesture or other figure that epitomizes it. This lets us specify how the figure embodies or enacts the style. Then in doing so, film takes can analyze how these components work together in practicing the style.

Often the name of the style says how it coheres. Minimalist aesthetics rely on a few, subtle signals of meaning. Expressionist aesthetics press out "internal," personal feelings into "external," shareable sights and sounds so vivid that others are hard-pressed to miss them. Tracing to rocker Kurt Cobain, grunge gets down and dirty in the dissolute suburb and the disillusioned city. Goth retrieves and streamlines the gothic aesthetics going back to the nights, if not exactly the days, of Edmund Burke—who has been better known in political precincts for defending the American Revolution when he was in the British Parliament and for theorizing the kind of conservatism favored in parts of Europe.[23] Film takes often analyze the politics of these styles and others. But of course, the names of liberalism, republicanism, conservatism, and socialism also signal respectively how each of those coheres as a style too. And of course, the popular genres at the hub of the preceding exercises in rhetorical analysis are themselves styles—in some respects, political styles—of movies.

Critics often trace the vices and virtues of works by performers in any art or practice to their distinctive, enduring styles. Is it any wonder that styles reach from aesthetic forms to moral characters, from rhetorical arrangements to political judgments, or even from our manners of civilization to our modes of argument? There are likely to be dimensions and dynamics of style for every sustained practice, ideology, institution, or other form of politics.[24] Robert Hariman, for example, has analyzed political styles from recurrent settings of international relations, courts, republics, and bureaucracies.[25]

Popular genres of movies depend similarly on distinctive practices that connect with recognizable styles of politicking. As Chapter 8 specifies, eight kinds of movie thrillers include political terrorism in the two decades before 9/11: bodyguard, legal, military, police, political, social, spy, and war thrillers. But there are also movie thrillers focused on medicine, journalism, finance, science, business, and church politics. Likewise the academic novel, although seldom a thriller, is apt to probe professorial styles of politicking; whereas even romance might trace political styles of the heart. At least some styles of action come into their own as ways of crossing boundaries between practices or situations. That holds for styles of detection in crime or mystery movies. Their solutions conventionally depend on detectives learning enough about embedded settings for the target transgressions to configure clues that can stand out from the background dynamics of their places and politics. We can even create new forms of movies to examine different kinds of politics, as Chapter 4 shows for the fractal films that try to come to terms with nonlinear politics of globalization, terrorism, or sinister systems. Film takes attuned rhetorically to political styles as sensibilities for engaging distinctive situations can come to revealing terms with the diverse politics in popular movies.

Perspectivism and Populism in SciFi Films

We began this book with my favorite popular genre of science fiction. Chapter 1 culminates in a brief film take that projects how, in the second half of the twentieth century, the looks of successive scifi movies helped prefigure our futures. They have given us technological, cultural, and political senses of where we are heading for the twenty-first century and beyond. In the middle of this book, Chapter 6 analyzes a later science-fiction movie to show how media of electronic communication are remaking the political foundations of our postmodern communities. Let us end, then, with a few political motifs favored by scifi films in recent years.

Table 11.2 on political topics and antinomies of popular genres recognizes the affinity of science fiction for politics of perspectivism.[26] These test or undo putative absolutes—such as God, Man, Truth, Evil, and Reality—by attuning us to further horizons of experience and imagination.[27] In general, as a genre, science fiction centers on science not as a royal road to any Reality, Truth, or Control but as a community committed adventurously yet humbly to learning.[28] It is less declarative than debate-oriented, less authoritative than inventive, self-critical, and self-correcting. It can help us experience the virtues in several perspectives, almost no matter how opposed they might seem at the moment. It is not that works of science fiction take no political positions or favor no perspectives over others; it is that science-fiction works appreciate the diverse validities of competing positions almost as much as the sometime necessities of choice and virtuosities of action. (This take is informed by a political theory of science fiction as *syzygy*—as a tense and transient alignment of things past, present, and possible, from the ancient Greek word for *spouse*; but that is a tale for another time.[29])

After America's election of President Barack Obama in 2008, the political headlines soon featured surges of populism: first from the right with the Tea Party then from the left with the Occupy Movement.[30] Together these helped focus the next two national elections, in 2010 and 2012, on populist themes. By 2010, the leftist populism against class exploitation—of the 99% by the 1%, as Occupiers put it—was becoming a more pronounced concern of Hollywood films, especially in the genre of science fiction. Right-wing populism lately finds more movie homes in American thrillers (worried about unconstitutional usurpations of power by sinister governments) and chillers (where beings that do not belong are invading Earth or at least the United States).

Populism is more movement and sensibility than creed, which is how it emerges as a style on both the left and the right of ideological spectra in American and European politics. As a popular genre of politics, especially as a political style from the nineteenth century onward in the United States, populism embraces a network of stock characters, settings, and events. Populists resent dispossession and exploitation of the people by elites, establishments, experts, and the like. They hate upstart minorities or outsiders who threaten to steal the people's spotlight and thunder. They rally to charismatic champions of the people who promise to take back resources and restore the people to power or at least prominence. Populists expect these champions to go behind the scenes of power to expose the machinations of bosses, special interests, and leisure classes. Or at least, they delight in populist champions sticking it to rulers, snobs, and cynics by lampooning their elite pretensions and political correctness. Populists love honest sentiment and passionate conviction. They celebrate us little people, who work for a living and do the country's hard, dirty jobs. They follow celebrities with fascination but also scorn. They privilege common sense, subordinating the authoritative truths of republicanism and the expert truths of liberalism to the popular truths of feeling. Above all, populism prizes the voice and the approval of the people.[31]

In many respects, populism in the United States is an updated, movement version—or better, offspring—of modern republicanism. Populism intensifies the republican emphasis on the *vox populi,* the republican inclination to resent disrespect, the republican vigilance against abuses of power, and the republican opposition to vast disparities in wealth and privilege. This sharing can make populist and republican upheavals indistinguishable at times, especially at early stages and when their grievances amount to flagrant exploitation of the many by the few. That is the key Occupy complaint, of course; and it is even a concern of Tea Partiers, although not as severe for them as taxation, regulation, and secularization.

Populist-republican rebellion against dispossession and exploitation of the people by an (alien and manipulative) elite is also the focal concern of a surprising number and portion of scifi films from 2010 through this writing in the summer of 2013. In this period of the Tea Party and Occupy movements, a few Hollywood films in other genres trace the terrible harms from gross gaps in resources, as in *The Great Gatsby* (2013). Some even show popular uprisings against the exploiting elites, as in *Robin Hood* (2010), *Tower Heist* (2011), and *Les Misérables* (2012). Still the extent and detail of attunement by scifi films to rising against elite exploitation of the people is remarkable. Two-thirds of the way into 2013, I count forty-seven scifi movies released from Hollywood since the start of 2010. This is similar to the forty-five I count for the full four years previous, from 2006 through 2009. Those earlier scifi films include only three that feature elite exploitations, and they also dramatize popular rebellions in response: *V for Vendetta* (2006), *Avatar* (2009), and *District 9* (2009). The later scifi films include three that foreground elite exploitations, especially for vital organs and violent urges, but without popular rebellions: *Never Let Me Go* (2010), *Repo Men* (2010), and *The Purge* (2013). (In other words, these three are indubitably dystopias.) The later films also include seven more that show populist-republican uprisings against elite exploitations: *In Time* (2011), *Rise of the Planet of the Apes* (2011), *The Hunger Games* (2012), *Total Recall* (2012), *Upside Down* (2012), *Elysium* (2013), and *Oblivion* (2013). Once the Tea Party and Occupy movements are in full swing, science-fiction movies focused on elite exploitation of the people triple. Since 2010, it is eminently possible that most of the Hollywood movies with this populist-republican emphasis are science-fiction films.

The Adjustment Bureau (2011) and *Perfect Sense* (2012), the two other dystopias from 2010 to 2013, are neither populist nor republican but existentialist and perfectionist instead. To keep the counts cautious, neither set of scifi films includes superhero movies, which get regarded by fans and critics as a genre unto themselves as well as a subgenre of science fiction. Supervillains often exploit and oppress the people, but seldom do superheroes lead populist uprisings. Instead the generic politics of superhero movies are primarily perfectionist. (Even secondarily, superhero movies turn to democratic equality and participation rather than populist productivity and imitation.) In 2010–2013, there were at least fourteen superhero flicks. But only two, *The Amazing Spider-Man* (2012) and *The Dark Knight Rises* (2012), show much concern with populist politics; and neither focuses on populist characters, settings, or movements.

Of 2010–2013 movies that do appear in the scifi count, the largest contingent features alien invasions of Earth. Do those thirteen movies play to nativist unto populist fears of immigration? Maybe, but they work harder at motifs of environmental catastrophe. Almost all are scifi-horror flicks that echo the Japanese monster movies with Godzilla, Mothra, and other icons of postwar anxiety about nuclear weapons and radiation.[32] Subtexts of environmental politics are prominent also in several of the period's other scifi-horror films, including *Priest* (2011) and *World War Z* (2013). To clarify our populist moment in scifi films, let us concentrate instead on the uprisings, looking quickly at four of the recent movies that use distinctive conventions of science fiction to draw out telling characteristics of populist politics of late in the United States.

The production summary for *Elysium* leaves unmistakable its populist politics. "In the year 2154, two classes of people exist: the very wealthy who live on a pristine man-made space station called Elysium and the rest who live on an overpopulated, ruined Earth." In personifying the ruling elite, Secretary Rhodes (Jodie Foster) "will stop at nothing to enforce anti-immigration laws and preserve the luxurious lifestyle of Elysium." Yet this "doesn't stop the people of Earth from trying to get in by any means they can." Eventually Max (Matt Damon) from Earth "agrees to take on a daunting mission that ... [not only saves] his life [but also brings] equality to these polarized worlds."[33] (Name symbolism in this film is seldom subtle in its politics.)

To champion the people of Earth in taking on Elysium elites, Max becomes the fractured, transformative scifi figure of a cyborg. Literally a cyborg is a cybernetic organism; and usually in scifi, it melds a machine with a man.[34] Some feminists have appropriated the cyborg as a mythic identity fit for an exceptionally self-aware, even ironical pursuit of fundamental change.[35] Such a political psychology plus the cyborg's superhuman powers complement the charisma of Max as a character and the popularity of his cause to epitomize a populist champion, at least for America. In symbol as well as personality, this scifi figure gives *Elysium* an edge peculiar to populism. For in America, the common sense of populists includes self-awareness as a streak of ironism (unto a touch of cynicism). Such a cyborg sensibility protects the people and their champions from any deep surprise and disillusionment—if their fondest dreams or greatest expectations go somewhat awry on the road to "re-form," let alone revolution. It also keeps the people and their champions ready for "rascality," as self-aggrandizing behavior that ironizes elites even as it limits reform.[36]

In Time is written and directed by Andrew Niccol, who has become Hollywood's go-to guy for science fiction in the last two decades. It imagines a near-future or alternate southwest for a two-tiered America where individuals can continue to live biologically as 25-year-olds, as long as they keep gaining time implanted in them. To keep resources from exhaustion, time gets rationed to control the population. This life time is interpersonally transferrable and becomes the currency. Most folks barely manage to keep lives going by hard jobs, including the manufacture of life time, and exploitative exchanges that all too soon have them timing out. A few families accumulate huge stocks of time, and live in luxury in separate zones with the favored servants who help run the show. Timekeepers police the time exchanges and zones.

When worker Will Salas (Justin Timberlake) gets a time windfall yet loses his mother to the expiration of her time clock, he impulsively leaves his run-down industrial zone for the city center of New Greenwich. There he woos Sylvia (Amanda Seyfried), daughter of the richest man around. Like *Bonnie and Clyde*

(1967), also populist icons, Sylvia and Will are soon racing around the territory, just ahead of the Timekeepers. The two rob time banks to return deposits to the people, restoring the times of their lives as expropriated by Sylvia's father and his associates. Using Sylvia's insider status and knowledge, the outlaw couple empties the central bank in New Greenwich. Sensing that their system is doomed, the Timekeepers abandon the chase. And by the movie's end, Sylvia and Will are taking down the rest of the system, one bank at a time.

As a Robin Hood fable of redistribution, *In Time* is even more populist than republican. Its focal complaint is the elite expropriation of time from the little people who actually make it. By the populist template, Will is a charismatic champion *of* the people in coming from them as well as fighting for them. That Will converts Sylvia from the exploitative elite to the populist cause is what clinches success for the rebellion, at least in the short term; and it follows a usual populist script for the successful champion. What distinguishes *In Time* as a populist movie is its specifically science-fictional twist on time.[37] At least in capitalist America, populists keep trying to contest the elitist denigration of feelings, efforts, and products of ordinary people. To exploit the people, elites convert these personal energies and tangible assets into social abstractions such as credit and status, which get used to stigmatize and step on the people as mere underlings. By treating personal time not just as commodity but currency, *In Time* gives itself many advantages in showing how the elite exploitation of the people is pervasive and personal, not just economic.

Upside Down takes similarly populist advantage of scifi's distinctive trope of space. This is the genre's most visibly perspectivist figure.[38] The idea of *Upside Down* is that a solar system positions two Earth-like planets so close in their orbits that they almost touch, supposedly making a gravitational system where material from each planet is drawn to it. Of course, the film's hero (Jim Sturgess) is from the under planet that produces goods to sustain an elite lifestyle on the upper planet. His boyhood best friend turns out to be a girl (Kirsten Dunst), who then climbs/descends to him from a mountain peak in the wilderness, where his own tree is at times only a rope's length from her. Events part the two then reconnect them as inventive adults, when they flout laws of government (but not nature!) to end exploitation of the people on the bottom planet by the elite on the top planet.

With many a wrinkle linked to aspects of populism, the plot is about what you would expect. What makes *Upside Down* entrancing and provocative are its spectacular images of the hero navigating this visually stunning planetary system which elite exploitation has turned upside down for him. Therefore the film *spatializes* the perverse, disconcerting inversions that populism indicts, so that we can *see* how the people suffer them and imagine what could be done to reform them. *Elysium* makes similar use of the same scifi trope in having its title *space* station epitomize the corrupt elevation of an exploitative elite over an oppressed people confined below, on Earth.

Across all three novels by Suzanne Collins, *The Hunger Games* is a republican epic about overthrowing an empire.[39] Yet it is even more fiercely a populist argument against "politics as usual." The first film, like the first novel, begins with the populist rise of a charismatic champion of the people. Katniss Everdeen (Jennifer Lawrence) is like Dorothy in the American allegory of populism presented by L. Frank Baum as *The Wizard of Oz* (1939).[40] She is not exactly leading anybody, and she seldom knows as well as others what is happening. Yet she attracts everybody's attention, even as she epitomizes personal resistance to elite exploitation and oppression. As her fans and followers snowball, her rebellious gestures spark larger rebellions.

Also like Dorothy and her little dog, Katniss almost inadvertently tugs aside the system's curtains of concealment, to expose the bosses' selfish and cynical machinations for all to see. The main scifi figure in *The Hunger Games* is a postapocalyptic empire called Panem.[41] It has come from a capital in the Rocky Mountains subduing rebellious districts around North America. Now the districts must pay tribute to Panem and its president every year in the form of a preteen or teenage boy and girl selected by lot to fight the other tributes to the death in a spectacular and changing arena. The one who survives becomes a celebrity who coaches the next "contestants." The capital televises these Hunger Games for all to see; and they are the circuses to go with the sometimes scant "breads" available to districts that must send most of their products to sustain a luxurious, high-fashion, dissolute style of life for the ruling elites in the capital.

Volunteering as a tribute, to spare her young sister, Katniss has only her prowess as an outlaw archer for the black market (Robin Hood again) plus her impulsive powers of charisma to take to the capital. Once there, in populist fashion, Katniss more stumbles than steps behind the scenes. There, she glimpses the bosses conspiring against the people; and soon, in ways oblique at times but blatant at others, she starts signaling what she sees. Meanwhile Katniss also stumbles into the midst of the elites and their entertainments. Again she not only learns for herself but displays for the rest of us how almost everybody in the system gets puppeteered, with spectacles and fashions as well as peacekeepers and rations. Hers are mostly populist contributions made in mainly charismatic and populist ways. Her political style in action can repay careful scrutiny.

Katniss is a striking figure with an instinct for the crucial deed; but otherwise she shows little talent as a leader, a strategist, or a politician. Katniss is no George Washington or Benjamin Franklin.[42] To her, Sarah Palin (for Tea Partiers) or possibly Elizabeth Warren (for Occupiers) would be a better comparison.[43] Katniss works reluctantly with Haymitch Abernathy (Woody Harrelson), but he—not she—is the film's republican survivor and strategist. She pairs with Peeta Mellark (Josh Hutcherson), but he—not she—is the movie's natural-born politician and maybe even its republican statesman. Still it is Katniss who draws crucial support from Cinna (Lenny Kravitz) and many, many others. It is Katniss who strives to protect young Rue (Amandla Stenberg) then salutes her resonantly in death. It is Katniss who is too obstreperous not to be believable, almost despite herself, in beginning to love Peeta. And it is Katniss who knows instantly that changed rules for the last two survivors of her Hunger Games must be challenged—and how to do it. Katniss is as complicated and compelling a charismatic champion of the people as the screen has shown since Lonesome Rhodes (Andy Griffith), whom Elia Kazan directed to a deservedly worse end in *A Face in the Crowd* (1957). An advantage for Collins, and thus for Katniss, is the vast repertoire of science-fiction tropes that comprise *The Hunger Games*. They give her character, her world, and its events one of the most colorful, subtle, and provocative palettes in all our popular genres.

A GLOSSARY FOR ANALYZING POLITICS

Anarchism is a movement with two main ideological branches. By modern standards, both are "radical" in holding that modern states are bad and unnecessary. If **libertarians** insist on the smallest, least adventurous government possible for peaceful association, libertarian or **individualist anarchists** share the principle that markets and other nongovernmental institutions can accomplish any social coordination we need while maximizing personal freedom for each human. And if **socialists** treat government as constructive and political participation that is good for people, **mutual-aid-and-support anarchists** share the belief in ample participation, even though they hold as anarchists that government gets in the way of people taking proper care of each other and taking adequate part in their communities.

Classical times in western civilization stretch from the consolidation of the polis by ancient Greeks in the sixth and fifth centuries BCE to the decline and fall of the Roman empire a millennium or so later. (Such periodization is loose and rough, but the times and terms recognized by theorists of politics can differ from those prominent in other fields.) After another couple of centuries of transition, the medieval times, or middle ages, coalesce.

Conservatism is a family of modern ideologies and postmodern movements. It names several ideologies in Europe, including the reactive governance of muddling-through promoted by Edmund Burke. In the United States, it often labels strongly procapitalist versions of liberalism, including what much of the world these days calls "neoliberalism." Unhappy with many residual elements of liberalism, some Americans who lately call themselves "conservative" are "libertarian" in ideology. Others have yet to detail much of a social logic beyond vehement rejections of liberal moves, yet their cultural and electoral efforts cohere at least enough to recognize them as "movement conservatives."

Ethos is the classical mode of persuasion that features the persuader's character as known by other people in public interaction. It is the source of ethics as our standards and practices for appropriate interaction with community members. Its main modern version is the narrower notion of personal or institutional credibility. Yet people often respect ethos these days as the public spirit, community mood, or situational atmosphere that can induce belief and further action.

Existentialism is a life philosophy, more than a political ideology, that has become a political style and occasionally a political movement. Existentialists see modern ideologies, institutions, practices, even societies as inclined to rationalize, bureaucratize, and become totalizing systems that corrupt their many functionaries. Existentialists want people to recognize such systems, large or small, and resist them when overthrowing or undoing them seems impossible for now. To resist is to take personal responsibility for your own ethical, social, and biological well-being yet also for the well-being of at least some other people too. But the power and coverage of late-modern systems is often so great that the individual must seek small gaps, fissures, or interstices from which to take a stand against the rampant corruption. There people can form small, intense communities where they at least participate and help protect each other from some of the corruption, until times more favorable for open, large-scale rebellion. Largely in this mode, European existentialists participated in underground resistance against German Nazi domination of their countries during the Second World War.

Idealism is a family of political styles that take themselves to respect principles as the proper guides to action, even when holding to ideals is difficult or costly. Idealists say that the means make the ends, that most politics respect rules and ideals, that the road to hell is paved with sidelined principles, and that at times we must lose right today in order to win right tomorrow. Idealists urge firm, fervent explanation of aims and measures. To climb mountains and slay dragons, idealists are high-minded, pure-hearted, and fair dealing.

Ideologies are, in a loose sense, systems of belief and practice. They are creeds and deeds of culture, economy, polity, and more. In these pages, though, ideologies are specifically modern sciences of society that are pursued as logics of ideas, with societies treated as a texture of ideas. Ideologies begin with European analysts and activists in the seventeenth and eighteenth centuries: authoritarianism partly with Thomas Hobbes, liberalism with John Locke, conservatism with Edmund Burke, and socialism with Robert Owen. In the second half of the nineteenth century, ideologies started to be academized into the late-modern social sciences: socialism into sociology, liberalism into political science, capitalism into economics, liberalism and conservatism into psychology, and other combinations into fields of additional disciplines. This specific take on ideologies can stand in clearer contrast to political movements, myths, policies, and styles.

Liberalism is the modern ideology that dominated politics in the United States in the nineteenth and twentieth centuries. It treats the modern state as the crucial contributor to conditions for individual peace and prosperity in the private matters of civil society. The state does this by defining key terms, making and enforcing laws, respecting individual rights, and representing citizen interests. Modern states are needed for individuals to have effective freedoms, but governments are still evils because enforcing laws is coercive. What Americans call **"Liberalism"** is mainly an activist-government take on "liberalism" in the initial, European, small *l* sense used here. What Americans call **"Conservatism"** is mostly a reactivist-government version of "liberalism." But both distrust government and politicians, and both camps have extensive lists of things for government to do—and not do. Further figures of liberalism include contracts, reasons, moderation, tolerance, and institutional tinkering.

Logos is the classical mode of persuasion that explains meanings or implications and provides evidence or other reasons for people to accept beliefs, claims, and arguments—or reject them. Its main modern versions are logics, whether formal or informal.

Medieval times in western civilization run roughly from the ninth through the twelfth centuries CE. Looking back, early moderns came to regard medieval politics as "feudal," that is, as more or less literally dominated by feuds, raids, civil wars, crusades, and such.

Modern times in western civilization begin with the Renaissance and the Reformation in Europe during the fifteenth and sixteenth centuries CE. They include the Enlightenment, largely in the eighteenth century, and the nineteenth century Victorian culture that spurs much of the twentieth. Distinctively modern ideologies and institutions continue to be prominent into the twenty-first century, coexisting with postmodern or even postwestern initiatives.

Movements are typically less organized than interest groups or political parties. They are less coherent in creed than are ideologies, so they seldom map well onto any ideological spectrum from left to right. Usually they rely more on direct action within civil societies than on indirect action (through governments) to change daily lives. Thus movements promote different associations, ethics, habits, lifestyles, and rhetorics (along with laws, policies, or implementations) in order to achieve their political ambitions.

Mythos is the classical mode of persuasion that evokes cultural commonplaces and familiar figures or themes to coalesce people around kinds of experiences that spur shared courses of action. Modern cultures often condemn myths as shared exaggerations or falsehoods. The present-day versions are the myths that people enact in everyday events, special occasions, even world-turning crises.

Pathos is the classical mode of persuasion that appeals to emotion, imagination, and volition to move people into action. Modern cultures often caution against mobilizing passions, preferring supposedly dispassionate (and somehow singular) logic instead. Yet latter-day specialists in persuasion, such as advertisers, appreciate pathos as a fully legitimate and particularly powerful aspect of persuasion. With *pathos* as the root from ancient Greek, **sympathy** is a feeling for others, **empathy** is a feeling with (or as) others, and **apathy** is an absence of (or resistance to) feeling about others.

Perfectionism is a political philosophy and movement against western civilization as meek, mediocre, massifying, and debilitating. Stemming from Ralph Waldo Emerson and Friedrich Nietzsche, perfectionist politics inform many indictments of mass society as homogenizing and oppressive. The "men's movement" associated with Robert Bly's *Iron John* is one example. Likewise environmentalists such as Michael Pollan inform their green politics with Nietzschean deconstructions, while others such as Gary Snyder turn to the perfectionist insights and practices of Zen Buddhism.

Perspectivism is a philosophy unto a movement that deconstructs metaphysical grounds of God, Nature, Reality, Science, Truth, and such to recognize that humans make their meanings and construct their foundations for reason, action, and community. Thus perspectivists acknowledge natures, realities, sciences, truths—inflected by human interactions with what they would know or learn. Many existentialists and perfectionists participate in perspectivism, as do artists in many media. With Ralph Waldo Emerson, they see all language as "fossil poetry"; and with Friedrich Nietzsche, they see all truths as tropes. The foundationalist philosophies of modern and western civilization see perspectivism as a radical relativism that leaves judgments impossible to make intelligently and standards impossible to defend rationally. But perspectivists reject Rationality in favor of reasons, and they say that human practices show that reasoning among people is usually sufficient for defensible standards and judgments.

Populism is more a family of styles and movements than an ideology of politics. Its figures feature the common people and their charismatic champions, who rise from humble beginnings to sweep the corrupt system momentarily clean and take power back for the people. Populist figures also include ambiguous celebrities, exploitative elites, bosses behind the scenes, dispossessing upstarts, and ready scapegoats. In America of late, the Tea Party understands itself as right-wing populism; while the Occupy Movement takes itself to be left-wing populism.

Postmodern times in western civilization take shape with electronics and the formation of what the twenty-first century sees as popular cultures. Hence it reaches from the nineteenth century CE to the present. Although there are several substantive takes on postmodern times as "postindustrialist," "late-capitalist," "globalist," or the like, it suffices here to say simply that postmodern times start self-consciously to overturn or sideline modern ideas and devices. It remains to be seen whether postmodern times merely transition us to a further, yet unnamed period of western civilization, actually form such a period in themselves, or even take us beyond western civilization as a whole.

Postwestern times might begin forming in the second half of the nineteenth century CE, when philosophers deconstruct the metaphysical foundations of western civilization arising with the ancient Greeks and Romans. If so, the radically greater interactions of East and West abetted by dynamics of globalization after the Second World War are contributors. So are political movements of environmentalism, existentialism, feminism, LGBT rights, and others that contest long-defining practices and categories of western civilization. Whether postwestern movements will lead to postwestern arrangements that coalesce as some new civilization (or postcivilization), only time will tell.

Realism is a family of political styles that take themselves to face hard facts and consequences, adjusting principles to realities. Realists say that the ends justify the means, that anything goes in most politics, that the road to hell is paved with good intentions, and that, at times, we must do whatever it takes to prevail. Realists urge cool, calm calculation of costs and results. To make hard choices and play hardball, realists are hardboiled and hard-headed.

Republicanism is the family of political styles associated with republics, whether classical, modern, or postmodern. Classical republics predate modern states, so their politics are not activities in, by, and with respect to governments in the modern sense. Whether tied to government or not, republics provide public places for citizens or their representatives to deliberate and decide courses of action for the community. In the sense that traces to Europe, therefore, republicanism (with a small *r*) celebrates such political participation as needed for people to develop fully as humans. Tropes of republicanism include reluctant, virtuous leaders invited to serve as officials in times of corruption or crisis, when time-honored institutions and traditions of the republic are threatened by demagogues and crowds from within or imperial powers and unpolitical peoples from without. Citizens are to be informed followers who stay eternally vigilant against abuses of power; and leaders are to show ambition, courage, and prudence in political action. Rhetorics take shape in proto-publics and early republics, producing a republican-rhetorical tradition of political practice and analysis now more than two millennia in the making.

Rhetorics practice and study our communication in action in public. They arise with the Sophists in ancient Greece as the arts of persuading communities to act and the sciences of analyzing such political moves. Rhetorics began with oral speech; but they concern all media of communication, especially each medium's political devices and effects.

Styles are sensibilities and practices, personal and cultural. They are the full-bodied capacities of feeling and doing that inform our judgments of what goes with what else, how, with what effects, inviting what responses. Styles are the elective affinities that cohere sights, sounds, tastes, touches, aromas, thoughts, and gestures into personal or cultural packages. Thus popular genres are styles for making or viewing movies, while political styles can extend to daily, performative versions of modern ideologies and postmodern movements.

Systems are self-sustaining interactions, often among components that are many and diverse. **Natural systems** individuate their own boundaries, elements, and dynamics for humans to trace. **Analytical systems** come from humans positing boundaries, defining elements; then investigating dynamics to understand things in system terms. **Linear systems** are mechanisms, with parts specified separately from each other so changes in independent variables may be shown by to cause (by particular paths) changes in dependent variables. **Nonlinear systems** are flows, with sensitive interdependence among mutually defining elements that do not sustain mechanical causation but instead involve phase changes and cusps, thus explanations but not predictions, roughness or turbulence, strange attractors, coherence through self-similar figures across levels of magnitude, and "butterfly effects" as "disproportionate" consequences "at a distance." In politics, it can make sense to treat institutions and other formal organizations as linear, whereas movements and fashions as informal waves of social change seem nonlinear or, in the sense used by mathematicians for systems of nonlinear equations, "chaotic."

Terrorism is violence that targets civilians or other bystanders. It is a political tactic, a strategy, or a striking out in desperation. It is not mainly a political ideology, movement, or style, but instead a tool, a method, or a spasm associated with some (more substantive) version of politics. Campaigns of terror seek to incapacitate, panic, or scapegoat people rather than induce rational responses by them.

Totalitarianism is a kind of political movement that thoroughly atomizes, mobilizes; then regiments the populace with an extreme ideology and a cult of personality. Both urge imitation of a leader presented as a radically advanced embodiment of some purified race, class, creed, party, or history. When in power, a totalitarian regime expects inhabitants to follow the leader even when he exceeds any laws. So there is little or no rule of law, and any apparatus of the regime matters less than the leader's example. This is not a tyranny in the ancient sense of illegitimate and forceful rule by one, nor is it a dictatorship in the modern sense of a ruler's oral word as law because it trumps any process for writing and publicizing legislation. As an ideal type, totalitarianism is intrinsically dystopian; and it's probably impossible to practice strictly. Yet it differs categorically from classical politics and modern governments of all kinds.

Tropos, from the ancient Greek, is literally a *turn*: a change in course or condition that directs our lives individually and communally. These turns trace recurrent shapes, so that **tropes** are figures of experience, speech, and deed. When we "figure out" something, we track its persistent turns, that is, its characteristic shapes and changes.

A Glossary for Analyzing Movies

Allegories, in the loose sense, are narratives that emphasize figural layers of meaning beyond the literal significance of their characters, settings, events, or other details. In the strict sense favored here, however, allegories regiment their layers of meaning so that most of their literal details map one-to-one onto figures at any other level. In political allegories, the privileged layer(s) of meaning are overtly political in some official sense. Based on an allegorical novel that harkens to the Cold War, the title figure in *The Iron Giant* (1999) just is the Soviet Union, symbolically, and the paranoid responses to its friendly efforts to protect a boy track some specific individuals, institutions, and events of the period. Even though it's not usually taken this way, it can be seen as a reply to the far more famous, anti-Soviet allegory of George Orwell's *Animal Farm,* later in two movies (1954, 1999).

Codas conclude musical compositions with passages unlike but somehow complementary to the preceding ones. Cinematic codas do much the same in ending scenes that depart from the main dramatic currents of their movies. Typically they add twists that provoke larger or contrasting perspectives on the main action. Epics are especially apt to include codas, which resemble epimyths as lessons at the end of fables or epilogues as speeches after plays seem finished.

Conventions in movies and other media are widely recognized figures that help supply social meanings and coordinate social practices. Among the many conventions of popular horror are monsters, graves, and hauntings. War films typically include soldiers, ruins, and battles, whereas thrillers focus on maverick heroes, exotic locales, and chase scenes.

Detective movies treat crimes as puzzles to be solved. The focal investigators who try to figure out identities of criminals come in several kinds. Most prominent in the beginning were **classical detectives**, who conventionally arrive to collect clues and interview suspects after crimes that victimize elites. Often classical detectives are amateurs with wealth enough for such an avocation, and their efforts usually end with determining whodunit. **Hardboiled detectives** are professionals who arrive as crimes continue to occur. Often they are thick-skinned, lower-middle-class professionals working in the undersides of cities; and their work is not done until criminals have been brought to justice or readers recognize how the crimes symbolize systematic corruption led by elites left untouched. **Police procedurals** often include classical detectives, while **police thrillers** favor more hardboiled heroes. **Noirs** typically turn their hardboiled characters into protagonists.

Dystopias are literally dysfunctional places; thus they name a subgenre of political horror and science fiction exemplified by *A Clockwork Orange* (1971), *1984* (1984), *Brazil* (1985), *Gattaca* (1997), and *Repo Men* (2010).

Elective affinities are personal and cultural inclinations to connect distinct things that instead could be linked to other, sometimes contrasting things. As affinities, these say what else can be expected to come with any particulars or types. As elective, these acknowledge that the matches are conventional, preferential, and readily subject to rearrangement. To violate a elective affinity is to risk leaving expectations unmet, sensibilities offended, or meaningful associations underutilized. Yet unconventional matches sometimes prove enlightening, provocative, otherwise enjoyable, or early steps toward new conventions.

Epics feature heroes or friends who lead and epitomize communities that form, free themselves, or face other challenges to their identities and legacies. The episodes that compose epics often are emblems of their heroes and communities, so their stories sometimes depart from linear chronologies or modern histories. As a popular genre, the epic is typically spectacular: with vast casts and vistas that traverse many lands, generations, and crises. Examples include the *Godfather* threesome (1972, 1974, 1990) from Francis Ford Coppola, the *Star Wars* films (1977, 1980, 1983, 1999, 2002, 2005) from George Lucas, the *Back to the Future* trilogy (1985, 1989, 1990) by Robert Zemeckis, plus *The Lord of the Rings* (2001, 2002, 2003) and *Hobbit* films (2012, 2013, 2014) by Peter Jackson. Single-film epics include *Ben-Hur* (1959), *Places in the Heart* (1984), *Titanic* (1997), *Gladiator* (2000), and *Troy* (2004).

Exotic cameras set scenes or show actions from unusual, extreme, even estranging perspectives. Often they seek to unsettle viewers, although exotic cameras are conventional for several popular genres, including horror and noir, which typically try to disconcert or defamiliarize viewers.

Fantasies evoke imaginary worlds somewhat parasitic on the worlds of their listeners, readers, or viewers. J. R. R. Tolkien called these "secondary creations." Among their many tropes are imaginary creatures, legendary leaders, magic kingdoms, supernatural beings, talking animals, and events on the sublime cusp for differentiating awesome from awful. Arguably all fairy tales are fantasies, but it's far from the other way around, and many fables don't involve secondary worlds. Many blockbusters in our time are fantasy films like *Harry Potter, The Hobbit,* and *The Lord of the Rings.* Other striking fantasies of late include *Edward Scissorhands* (1990), *Clearcut* (1992), *Stranger Than Fiction* (2006), *Stardust* (2007), *Hugo* (2011), plus *Snow White and the Huntsman* (2012).

Film takes employ devices of rhetoric to analyze how movies help shape our communities and experiences. Often they feature the politics implicit in film uses of genre conventions.

Fractal films explore recent practices as nonlinear systems that seem to fracture modern time, space, action, or causation, replacing these with strange discontinuities, dependencies, and possibilities. Such movies jump abruptly among characters, settings, and events in challenging viewers to make sense of the various social systems that configure our lives. In this century, fractal films might be emerging as a popular genre from the five others most implicated so far in fractal cinema: conspiracy thrillers, neo noirs, time travels, mosaic movies, and epic films.

Genres are forms of communication that cohere as networks of recurrent conventions. These conventions are neither necessary nor sufficient conditions for their genres. Sheriffs are conventional characters in the western as a genre, yet a western centered on a cattle drive or a mining camp could easily omit this figure. On the other hand, detective tales and police thrillers often include sheriffs without working otherwise as westerns. Genres of specific works come from the relative prominence and cohesion of their conventions in making the works meaningful. **Popular genres** are forms widely recognized in a culture that helps make their distinctive families of conventions. **Analytical genres** are forms defined by commentators to clarify developments not (yet) recognized culturally.

Horror movies can be regarded as dark fantasies that draw from an ever-expanding stable of figures such as boogeymen, cannibals, demons, ghosts, graveyards, haunted houses, infested vessels, mad scientists, morgues, mummies, portals of hell, psychics, serial killers, stalkers, torture chambers, vampires, werewolves, witches, and zombies. That master vampire Dracula might have appeared in more movies than any other fictional character, and the American Film Institute cited Anthony Hopkins' version of Hannibal Lecter in *The Silence of the Lambs*

(1991), *Hannibal* (2001), and *Red Dragon* (2002) as the top movie villain in its first hundred years.

Media are devices of communication distinguished by particular technologies and conventional uses. Electronic (and now computing) technologies figure in many media, including the telegraph, telephone, radio, television, video game, Internet, and cinema. Each medium can seem especially well suited to some kinds of communication by comparison to others fit more for contrasting media. Still many media can share diverse senders, receivers, contexts, and uses but also messages, genres, icons, speech acts, subtexts, tropes, and other "content-forms"—as we can call what appears when we "look inside" such media.

Mosaic movies seem to jump abruptly among dramatic moments presented apart from any usual, largely linear order in space and time; yet as viewers experience and sort more and more of these apparently disjoined scenes, they cohere into distinct dramas that are meaningful in themselves while interacting to form an encompassing drama more meaningful still. To view them can be similar to pulling slowly back from a field of photos, so that you appreciate more and more of images individually while you eventually see an overall, photomosaic image snap into focus. Examples include *Jacob's Ladder* (1990), *Vanilla Sky* (2001), *Babel* (2006), *Before the Devil Knows You're Dead* (2007), and *The Tree of Life* (2011).

Myths are symbolic stories of the whole community, institution, or individual. Whatever their literal truths, the details of myths also symbolize the kinds of characters, settings, and events that recur to configure the whole. Holidays rehearse such myths—in America, of settlers in a new land sharing harvests and thanks with its natives, of founders leading a revolution for independence, of tricksters roaming the night for treats, of students fleeing the winter for spring moments of madness, of a culture part-Christian and part-capitalist learning year-end rites of getting and giving. For a century, American myths and movies have helped make each other, while shaping American senses and practices of politics.

Noir films show protagonists awakening to resist corrupt systems. **Classical noirs** of the 1940s and 1950s were grouped mostly by analysts, often long after those films were released, but **neo noirs** from the 1980s onward form a popular genre fairly prominent of late. Noir protagonists are almost always males but not exactly heroes, because they are too corrupt. Other neo-noir tropes include hardboiled detectives, spider women, system bosses, and system fixers; mean streets, purging rains, and gritty realisms or garish distortions; plus plot frames, plot loops, voiceover narratives, and wake-up calls. Classical noirs reach from *The Maltese Falcon* (1941) and *Casablanca* (1942) to *Sunset Boulevard* (1950) and

Vertigo (1958). Neo noirs stretch from *Blade Runner* (1982) and *Blood Simple* (1984) to *End of Watch* (2012), *Trance* (2013), and beyond.

Phenomenology analyzes the elements and dynamics of experiences by individuals in societies. This sets aside questions about physical, biological, or cultural realities in order to parse how such realities appear to people, and why. Since cinema is an art of appearances, its instances and their politics encourage appreciation in terms informed by phenomenology. The **phenomenal field** is the initial, typically diffuse sense of situation that we encounter as we enter scenes and start to specify experiences. Thus it is an early apprehension of our surroundings and selves that draws especially from previous experiences and learned figures to help us recognize what is happening and how.

Prefiguration, specifically of the phenomenal field arising from movies or other experiences, is the anticipatory shaping of sensations by prior figures, cultural and personal, that help to make them meaningful and sometimes memorable.

Science fiction extrapolates from scientific concepts to project technologies, settings, characters, and events that help explore change and humanity. This popular genre is also called **scifi**, **sf**, or **speculative fiction**—to stress its close kinship with fantasy and horror. Prominent conventions of scifi include aliens, apocalypses, robots, as well as travels to other times, planets, or universes. Examples range from *Metropolis* (1927), *King Kong* (1933), and *Star Wars* (1977) to *The Hunger Games* (2012), *Gravity* (2013), and *Robocop* (2014).

Subjective cameras provide viewers with the visual perspectives of leading characters. Instead of stitching together what a protagonist sees with sights of that figure acting and reacting, subjective cameras operate (for sustained shots) as though they were that character's own eyes. Thus they offer virtual experiences of a film's situations as a character sees them.

Subtexts are coherent sets of meanings implied by symbolism implicit in the literal details of a text, show, movie, drama, or the like. Authors might or might not intend them, and audiences might or might not discern them, but analysts do well to articulate them. An allegory has one strictly regimented subtext; but several—more ragged or complicated—subtexts might be available from a single novel, movie, or video game. *The Silence of the Lambs* (1991) offers a subtext about horrors of workplace sexism, yet it also provides an ample subtext about realist corruption of the institutions and virtues of republics.

Symbolical experiences are the senses we get of people, events, and settings through spreading activation of our cognitive and cultural networks of mythic associations among symbols. In turn, symbols are figures of speech, action, and perception that mean more—usually much more—than their literal referents or significations.

Thrillers are fast-paced movies in an action-adventure mode. Typically their heroes, heroines, and villains are clear-cut; their situations are extreme instances of well-known practices; their deeds and plots are melodramatic. Thrillers rely mainly on deceptions for mystery, cliff-hangers for suspense, and improvisations for success. Their subgenres stem mostly from their settings, giving us criminal, detective, finance, legal, medical, military, police, political, science, spy, and other species of thrillers. Examples are legion: the Bond and Bourne movies; the films based on bestsellers by Michael Crichton and John Grisham; and many of the diverse vehicles for Jason Statham, Denzel Washington, or Bruce Willis.

Vicarious experiences are the senses we get of people, events, and settings through observing another person's responses (in word or deed) to those people, events, and settings. In a way, this makes that other person—whether in factual or fictional terms—into the medium for our experiences of the otherwise inaccessible situation thus experienced vicariously.

Virtual experiences are the senses we get of people, events, and settings more or less as though we were in their situation. Virtual experiences are provided by devices of sight, sound, and sometimes other senses that simulate the otherwise inaccessible situation from the perspective of a person in that situation.

Voiceovers provide audible speech from characters not shown as they speak the words we hear. Often a voiceover narrates actions with the participants' voices muted or muffled, even when the source of the voiceover is one of the participants. At other times, a voiceover narrates links between major events in a movie, introduces its backgrounds, concludes with its lessons, or tells of its aftermath.

War movies focus on leaders, followers, friends, and enemies in military preparation, combat, or coping with the consequences. Notable cases of late include *Jarhead* (2005), *Inglourious Basterds* (2009), *War Horse* (2011), *Zero Dark Thirty* (2012), and *Lone Survivor* (2013).

Westerns feature figures prominent in our myths of the Wild West, the Old West, the Frontier West, or the American West in general. These include pioneers and scouts, cowboys and Indians, prospectors and saloon keepers, ranchers and rustlers, gunslingers and sheriffs, schoolmarms and railroad men, cavalries and cattle barons. Westerns come modern, set after the Second World War; but especially, they come classical, set in the aftermath of the American Civil War or similar cultural conditions elsewhere around the world. Yet also conventionally, if often subtly, westerns reconsider the virtues and vices of western civilization as a whole. Classical westerns span *Stagecoach* (1939), *The Searchers* (1956), *The Shootist* (1976), *Unforgiven* (1992), and *True Grit* (1969 and 2010). Modern westerns encompass *Hud* (1963), *The Last Picture Show* (1971), *Brokeback Mountain* (2005), and *No Country for Old Men* (2007).

NOTES

Chapter 1: Film Takes

1. Roger Ebert, "Movie Answer Man: Brief Critiques Actually Say a Lot," *Cedar Rapids—Iowa City Gazette*, March 15, 2003, 2D.

2. See Joseph Campbell, *Myths to Live By* (New York: Viking Press, 1972); George Lakoff and Mark Johnson, *Metaphors We Live By* (Chicago: University of Chicago Press, 1980). Also see Henry Tudor, *Political Myth* (New York: Praeger, 1972); H. Mark Roelofs, *Ideology and Myth in American Politics* (Boston: Little, Brown, 1976); Dan Nimmo and James E. Combs, *Subliminal Politics: Myths and Mythmakers in America* (Englewood Cliffs, NJ: Prentice-Hall, 1980); James Oliver Robertson, *American Myth, American Reality* (New York: Hill and Wang, 1980); Michael Parenti, *Land of Idols: Political Mythology in America* (New York: St. Martin's Press, 1994).

3. See Bill Nichols, *Ideology and the Image: Social Representation in the Cinema and Other Media* (Bloomington: Indiana University Press, 1981); Michael Ryan and Douglas Kellner, *Camera Politica: The Politics and Ideology of Contemporary Hollywood Film* (Bloomington: Indiana University Press, 1988); Mas'ud Zavarzadeh, *Seeing Films Politically* (Albany: State University of New York Press, 1991).

4. Murray Edelman, *From Art to Politics: How Artistic Creations Shape Political Conceptions* (Chicago: University of Chicago Press, 1995), 2.

5. Murray Edelman, *Constructing the Political Spectacle* (Chicago: University of Chicago Press), 6.

6. See Timothy W. Luke, *Screens of Power* (Urbana: University of Illinois Press, 1989).

7. See John S. Nelson: "Political Theory as Political Rhetoric," *What Should Political Theory Be Now?*, ed. Nelson (Albany: State University of New York Press, 1983), 169–240; "A Turn Toward Rhetoric," *North Dakota Quarterly*, 56, no. 3 (Summer 1988): 53–59.

8. See John S. Nelson: "Political Foundations for Rhetoric of Inquiry," *The Rhetorical Turn*, ed. Herbert W. Simons (Chicago: University of Chicago Press, 1990),

258–289; "Commerce among the Archipelagos: Rhetoric of Inquiry as a Practice of Coherent Education," *The Core and the Canon*, eds. L. Robert Stevens, G. L. Seligmann, and Julian Long (Denton, TX: University of North Texas Press, 1993), 78–100; "Prudence as Republican Politics in American Popular Culture," *Prudence*, ed. Robert Hariman (University Park: Pennsylvania State University Press, 2003), 229–257.

9. See Robert Hariman, "In Oratory as in Life: Civic Performance in Cicero's Republican Style," *Political Style: The Artistry of Power* (Chicago: University of Chicago Press, 1995), 94–140; Paul A. Rahe, *Republics Ancient and Modern: The Ancien Régime in Classical Greece* (Chapel Hill, NC: University of North Carolina Press, 1994).

10. See Marshall McLuhan: *The Gutenberg Galaxy* (Toronto: University of Toronto Press, 1962); *Understanding Media* (New York: McGraw-Hill, 1964). Also see Max Weber, "Bureaucracy," *From Max Weber*, eds. and trs. H. H. Gerth and C. Wright Mills (New York: Oxford University Press), 196–244; Hariman, "A Boarder in One's Own Home: Franz Kafka's Parables of the Bureaucratic Style," *Political Style*, 141–176.

11. See Garry Wills, *Lincoln at Gettysburg: The Words That Remade America* (New York: Simon and Schuster, 1992).

12. See Kathleen Hall Jamieson, "The Flame of Oratory, the Fireside Chat," *Eloquence in an Electronic Age* (New York: Oxford University Press, 1988), 43–66.

13. See Garry Wills, *Reagan's America* (New York: Penguin Books, 1987, second edition, 1988); Jamieson, "The 'Effeminate' Style," *Eloquence in an Electronic Age*, 67–89; John Hartley, *The Politics of Pictures: The Creation of the Public in the Age of Popular Media* (London: Routledge, 1992).

14. See Pippa Norris, *Digital Divide: Civic Engagement, Information Poverty, and the Internet Worldwide* (New York: Cambridge University Press, 2001); Cass R. Sunstein, *Republic.com* (Princeton, NJ: Princeton University Press, 2001). Also see Karen Mossberger, Caroline J. Tolbert, and Mary Stansbury, *Virtual Inequality: Beyond the Digital Divide* (Washington, DC: Georgetown University Press, 2003); Karen Mossberger, Caroline J. Tolbert, and Ramona S. McNeal, *Digital Citizenship: The Internet, Society, and Participation*, (Cambridge, MA: MIT Press, 2008); Karen Mossberger, Caroline J. Tolbert, and William W. Franko, *Digital Cities: The Internet and the Geography of Opportunity* (New York: Oxford University Press, 2013).

15. See Barry Brummett, *Rhetoric in Popular Culture* (Thousand Oaks, CA: Sage, second edition, 2006).

16. See Roland Barthes, *Mythologies*, trans. Annette Lavers (New York: Hill and Wang, 1972); *The Eiffel Tower, and Other Mythologies*, trans. Richard Howard (New York: Hill and Wang, 1972).

17. See Steven Johnson, *Everything Bad Is Good for You: How Today's Popular Culture Is Actually Making Us Smarter* (New York: Penguin Group, 2005).

18. See Harry M. Benshoff and Sean Griffin, *America on Film: Representing Race, Class, Gender, and Sexuality at the Movies* (Oxford: Blackwell, 2003, second edition, 2009); Johnson Cheu, ed., *Diversity in Disney Films: Critical Essays on Race, Ethnicity, Gender, Sexuality and Disability* (Jefferson, NC: McFarland, 2013).

19. See Fatimah Tobing Rony, *The Third Eye: Race, Cinema, and Ethnographic Spectacle* (Durham, NC: Duke University Press, 1996); Kevin J. Wetmore Jr., *The Empire*

Triumphant: Race, Religion and Rebellion in the Star Wars Films (Jefferson, NC: McFarland, 2005); Van Jaap Ginneken, *Screening Difference: How Hollywood's Blockbuster Films Imagine Race, Ethnicity, and Culture* (Lanham, MD: Rowman and Littlefield, 2007); Adillifu Nama, *Black Space: Imagining Race in Science Fiction Film* (Austin: University of Texas Press, 2008); Mary K. Bloodsworth-Lugo and Dan Flory, eds., *Race, Philosophy, and Film* (New York: Routledge, 2013).

20. See Sharon Willis, *High Contrast: Race and Gender in Contemporary Hollywood Films* (Durham, NC: Duke University Press, 1997); Gwendolyn Audrey Foster, *Class-Passing: Social Mobility in Film and Popular Culture* (Carbondale: Southern Illinois University Press, 2005); Keith Gandal, *Class Representation in Modern Fiction and Film* (New York: Palgrave Macmillan, 2007).

21. See E. Ann Kaplan, ed., *Women in Film Noir* (London: British Film Institute 1978, second edition, 1980); Teresa de Lauretis, *Alice Doesn't: Feminism, Semiotics, Cinema* (Bloomington: Indiana University Press, 1984); Teresa de Lauretis, *Technologies of Gender: Essays on Theory, Film and Fiction* (Bloomington, Indiana University Press, 1987); Mary Ann Doane, *Femmes Fatales: Feminism, Film Theory, Psychoanalysis* (New York, Routledge, 1991); Barry Keith Grant, *The Dread of Difference: Gender and the Horror Film* (Austin: University of Texas Press, 1996); Elizabeth Bell, Lynda Haas, and Laura Sells, eds., *From Mouse to Mermaid: The Politics of Film, Gender, and Culture* (Bloomington: Indiana University Press, 2008); Richard J. Gray II and Betty Kaklamanidou, eds., *The 21st Century Superhero: Essays on Gender, Genre and Globalization in Film* (Jefferson, NC: McFarland, 2011); Hilary Radner and Rebecca Stringer, eds., *Feminism at the Movies: Understanding Gender in Contemporary Popular Cinema* (New York: Routledge, 2011).

22. See John S. Nelson and G. R. Boynton: "Making Sound Arguments: Would a Claim by Any Other Sound Mean the Same or Argue So Sweet?" *Argument in a Time of Change*, ed. James F. Klumpp (Annandale, VA: National Communication Association, 1998), 12–17; "Arguing War: Global Television against American Cinema," *Arguing Communication and Culture*, ed. G. Thomas Goodnight (Annandale, VA: National Communication Association, 2002), 571–577. Also see John S. Nelson and Anna Lorien Nelson, "Story and More: Virtual Narratives for Electronic Times," *American Communication Journal*, 1, no. 2 (February 1998): http://americancomm.org/~aca/acj/acj.html.

23. See McLuhan, "Movies: The Reel World," *Understanding Media*, 284–296.

24. See Paul Virilio, *War and Cinema*, trans. Patrick Camiller (London: Verso, 1984), 1989.

25. See Mark Bowden, *Black Hawk Down* (New York: Atlantic Monthly Press, 1999).

26. See Anna Lorien Nelson and John S. Nelson, "Institutions in Feminist and Republican Science Fiction," *Legal Studies Forum*, 22, no 4 (1998): 641–653.

27. See Stanley Cavell, *The Claim of Reason: Wittgenstein, Skepticism, Morality, and Tragedy* (New York: Oxford University Press, 1979).

28. On the human sciences, see John S. Nelson, Allan Megill, and D. N. McCloskey, eds., *The Rhetoric of the Human Sciences: Language and Argument in Scholarship and*

Public Affairs (Madison: University of Wisconsin Press, 1987); Quentin Skinner, ed., *The Return of Grand Theory in the Human Sciences* (Cambridge: Cambridge University Press, 1985). On political theory, see John G. Gunnell, *Political Theory: Tradition and Interpretation* (Cambridge, MA: Winthrop, 1979); John S. Nelson, ed., *What Should Political Theory Be Now?* (Albany: State University of New York Press, 1983); John S. Nelson, ed., *Tradition, Interpretation, and Science: Political Theory in the American Academy* (Albany: State University of New York Press, 1986); John S. Nelson, *Tropes of Politics: Science, Theory, Rhetoric, Action* (Madison: University of Wisconsin Press, 1998), 72–98.

29. On political sciences, see John G. Gunnell, *Philosophy, Science, and Political Inquiry* (Morristown, NJ: General Learning Press, 1975); W. Phillips Shively, ed., *The Research Process in Political Science* (Itasca, IL: F. E. Peacock Publishers, 1984). Also see John S. Nelson: "Political Theory as Political Rhetoric," *What Should Political Theory Be Now?*, 169–240; "Stories of Science and Politics: Some Rhetorics of Political Research," *The Rhetoric of the Human Sciences*, 198–220; *Tropes of Politics*, 99–114.

30. See J. P. Telotte, *Science Fiction Film* (Cambridge: Cambridge University Press, 2001).

31. On politics in the conventions of scholarly argument, see Nelson, Megill, and McCloskey, eds., *The Rhetoric of the Human Sciences*; Nelson, *Tropes of Politics*, 3–71 and 99–114.

32. See Hannah Arendt, *The Human Condition* (Chicago: University of Chicago Press, 1958); Ferdinand Mount, *The Theatre of Politics* (New York: Schocken Books, 1972). Theorists of politics are likely to notice, though, that Hannah Arendt attended in detail to politics in some popular literature. Arendt's emphasis on action helps explain this departure.

33. See Irving Howe, ed.: *Orwell's Nineteen Eighty-Four* (New York: Harcourt Brace Jovanovich, 1963, second edition, 1982), 3–205; *1984 Revisited* (New York: Harper and Row, 1983).

34. See Mark R. Hillegas, *The Future as Nightmare* (New York: Oxford University Press, 1967); Raffaella Baccolini and Tom Moylan, *Dark Horizons: Science Fiction and the Dystopian Imagination* (New York, Routledge, 2003).

35. See Kim Stanley Robinson, *Three Californias* (New York, Tom Doherty Associates): *The Wild Shore* (1984); *The Gold Coast* (1988); *Pacific Edge* (1990). Also see Kim Stanley Robinson, *The Mars Trilogy* (New York, Bantam Books): *Red Mars* (1993); *Green Mars* (1994); *Blue Mars* (1996); *The Martians* (1999). And see Kim Stanley Robinson, *The Capital Trilogy*, (New York, Bantam Books): *Antarctica* (1998); *Forty Signs of Rain* (2004); *Fifty Degrees Below* (2005); *Sixty Days and Counting* (2007). Yes, I am listing four volumes for this last "trilogy." As you can tell from the titles, Robinson presents the last three novels as going together, but I've added *Antarctica* to the roster because it appeared first, shares characters and concerns with the others, hence lays the ground for the later novels.

36. See William Gibson: *Neuromancer* (New York, Ace Books, 1984); *Count Zero* (New York, Ace Books, 1986); *Mona Lisa Overdrive* (New York: Bantam Books, 1988); *Idoru*, (New York: Berkley Books, 1996). See William Gibson and Bruce Sterling, *The*

Difference Engine (New York: Bantam Books, 1991). See Bruce Sterling: *Islands in the Net* (New York: Ace Books, 1988); *The Caryatids* (New York: Del Rey, 2009). See Pat Cadigan: *Mindplayers* (New York: Bantam Books, 1987); *Synners* (New York: Bantam Books, 1991); *Fools* (New York: Bantam Books, 1992). See Rudy Rucker, *The Ware Tetralogy* (New York, Avon Books): *Software* (1982); *Wetware* (1988); *Freeware* (1998); *Realware* (2000).

37. See Bruce Sterling, *Distraction* (New York: Bantam Books, 1998); Neal Stephenson and J. Frederick George, *Interface* (New York: Bantam Books, 1994).

38. See David Brin (New York: Bantam Books): *The Postman* (1985); *Earth* (1990). Also see Marge Piercy (New York: Fawcett Crest): *Woman on the Edge of Time* (1976); *He, She and It* (1991). And see Sheri Tepper (New York: Bantam Books): *The Gate to Women's Country* (1988); *Sideshow* (1992).

39. Among his many instructive novels, see John le Carré: *The Spy Who Came in from the Cold* (New York: Bantam Books, 1963); *Tinker Tailor Soldier Spy* (New York: Bantam Books, 1974); *The Little Drummer Girl* (New York: Simon and Schuster, 1983); *A Perfect Spy* (New York: Simon and Schuster, 1986); *The Night Manager* (New York: Ballantine Books, 1988); *Our Game* (New York: Knopf, 1995); *The Tailor of Panama* (New York: Knopf, 1996); *The Constant Gardener* (New York: Scribner, 2001); *A Delicate Truth* (New York: Viking, 2013). Also see Myron J. Aronoff, *The Spy Novels of John le Carré: Balancing Ethics and Politics* (New York: St. Martin's Press, 1999); John S. Nelson, "John le Carré and the Postmodern Myth of the State," *Finnish Yearbook of Political Thought, 3: Conceptual Change and Contingency* (1999): 100–131. And see *The Spy Who Came in from the Cold* (1965), *The Little Drummer Girl* (1984), *The Tailor of Panama* (2001), *The Constant Gardener* (2005), and *Tinker Tailor Soldier Spy* (2011).

40. See Guy Debord, *Society of the Spectacle* (Detroit: Red and Black, 1967 and 1977); Jean Baudrillard, *Simulations*, trs. Paul Foss, Paul Patton, and Philip Beitchman (New York: Semiotext(e), 1983); Edelman, *Constructing the Political Spectacle*. Also see John S. Nelson, "All's Fair: Love, War, Politics, and Other Spectacles," *Poroi* 4, no. 2 (July, 2005): http://press.lib. uiowa.edu/poroi/papers/nelson050701.html.

41. See Mark Rose: ed., *Science Fiction: A Collection of Critical Essays* (Englewood Cliffs, NJ: Prentice-Hall, 1976); *Alien Encounters: Anatomy of Science Fiction* (Cambridge, MA: Harvard University Press, 1981). Also see Paul Kincaid, "On the Origins of Genre," *Extrapolation* 44, no. 4 (Winter 2003): 409–419.

42. See Vincent Di Fate, *Infinite Worlds: The Fantastic Visions of Science Fiction Art* (New York: Penguin Putnam, 1997).

43. See Carl Freedman, "Kubrick's *2001* and the Possibility of a Science-Fiction Cinema," *Science-Fiction Studies* 25, no. 2 (July, 1998): 300–318; Karl Wessel, "Alien Encounters: Science Fiction and the Mysterium: *2001, Solaris,* and *Contact,*" *The Science Fiction Film Reader,* ed. Gregg Rickman (New York: Limelight Editions, 2004), 181–209; Kevin L. Stoehr, "2001: A Philosophical Odyssey," *The Philosophy of Science Fiction Film,* ed. Steven M. Sanders (Lexington: University Press of Kentucky, 2008), 119–134.

44. See Yves Chevrier, "*Blade Runner*; or, The Sociology of Anticipation," ed. Robert M. Philmus, trans. Will Straw, *Science-Fiction Studies* 11, no. 1 (March, 1984): 50–60; Peter Fitting, "Futurecop: The Neutralization of Revolt in *Blade Runner,*"

Science-Fiction Studies 14, no. 3 (November, 1987): 340–354; Robin Wood, "*Blade Runner*," *The Science Fiction Film Reader*, 280–286.

45. See John Leonard with *Sunday Morning* for CBS on August 18, 2002.

46. See R. Barton Palmer, "Imagining the Future, Contemplating the Past: The Screen Versions of *1984*," *The Philosophy of Science Fiction Film*, 171–190.

47. See Yogi Berra and Tom Horton, *Yogi, It Ain't Over ...* (New York: Harper and Row, 1989).

48. See G. W. F. Hegel, *Philosophy of Right*, trans. T. M. Knox (Oxford: Oxford University Press, 1952).

49. See Keith Hamel, "Modernity and Mise-en-Scène: Terry Gilliam and *Brazil*," *The Science Fiction Film Reader*, 344–354.

50. See William Irwin, ed. (Chicago: Open Court): The Matrix *and Philosophy: Welcome to the Desert of the Real* (2002); *More* Matrix *and Philosophy: Revolutions and Reloaded Decoded* (2005). Also see Matt Lawrence, *Like a Splinter in Your Mind: The Philosophy behind the* Matrix *Trilogy* (Oxford: Blackwell, 2004); Christopher Grau, ed., *Philosophers Explore* The Matrix (Oxford: Oxford University Press, 2005).

51. As Americans know firsthand and Hollywood recognizes, 9/11 has even changed significantly our sense of that local airport unto spaceport just down the road: see Malcolm Gladwell, "Safety in the Skies: How Far Can Airline Security Go?" *New Yorker* 77, no. 29, (October 1, 2001): 50–53.

52. See Eduard Goldstücker, "Is There Any Future for Art?" *The Center Magazine* 5, no. 6 (November-December, 1972): 4–8; Lawrence L. Langer, *The Holocaust and the Literary Imaginatio/n* (New Haven: Yale University Press, 1975); Thomas Shevory, "From Censorship to Irony: Rhetorical Responses to 9/11," *Poroi* 2, no 1 (July, 2003): http://inpress.lib.uiowa.edu/poroi/papers/shevory030816.html.

53. See Nelson, *Tropes of Politics*, 150–179. Note that "eco-poesis" is a project of environmental politics.

Chapter 2: Politics in Conventions

1. Max Black, "More About Metaphor," *Metaphor and Thought*, ed. Anthony Ortony, (New York: Cambridge University Press, 1979), 19–43, on p. 31. With permission from Taylor and Francis, this chapter revises slightly my essay in *Political Communication* 20, no. 4 (October-December, 2003): 499–503.

2. See Rick Marin and T. Trent Gegax, "Conspiracy Mania Feeds Our Growing National Paranoia," *Newsweek* 128, no. 27 (December 30, 1996–January 6, 1997): 64–71.

3. Tamara Lipper and Howard Fineman, "W's Comfort Zone," *Newsweek* 141, no. 13 (March 31, 2003): 42.

4. See Dan Nimmo and James E. Combs, *Subliminal Politics: Myths and Mythmakers in America* (Englewood Cliffs, NJ: Prentice-Hall, 1980), 86–87 and 146; Ray Pratt, *Projecting Paranoia: Conspiratorial Visions in American Film* (Lawrence: University Press of Kansas, 2001).

5. Michael Ryan and Douglas Kellner, "Conspiracy Films," *Camera Politica: The Politics and Ideology of Contemporary Hollywood Film* (Bloomington: Indiana University Press, 1988), 95–105, on p. 99.

6. The main scholar in the social sciences whom I take to embrace conspiracy theories, treat conspiracy movies more or less literally, but still prize them for educating viewers is an instructive exception: In "Conspiracy and Intent," *Land of Idols: Political Mythology in America*, (New York: St. Martin's Press, 1994), 157–173, Michael Parenti defends conspiracy explanations of current social, economic, and political arrangements in Marxian terms, which are mostly structural and systemic.

7. Dan Nimmo and James E. Combs, "Devils and Demons: The Group Mediation of Conspiracy," *Mediated Political Realities* (New York, Longman, 1983, second edition, 1990) 203–222, on p. 204.

8. See Ted Remington, Conspiracy Theories as Socially Constructed Mythic Narratives (PhD diss., University of Iowa Department of Communication Studies, 2002).

9. One academic account does start to show how Hollywood makes conspiracy into a popularly accessible figure for the structures and politics of particular systems. "Totality as Conspiracy" in *The Geopolitical Aesthetic: Cinema and Space in the World System* (Bloomington: Indiana University Press, 1992), 7–84, is an argument in a Marxian vein by Fredric Jameson that "the older motif of conspiracy knows a fresh lease on life" in late-twentieth-century films which advance shadow conspiracies as allegories of "the world system" (p. 9). This recognizes conspiracy as a cinematic trope for system, but it globalizes and singularizes "system." Thus it misses how each film details its conspiracy to analyze the specific structures and functions of a particular system.

10. John S. Nelson, *Tropes of Politics: Science, Theory, Rhetoric, Action* (Madison: University of Wisconsin Press, 1998), 123–126.

11. Michel Foucault, *The Foucault Reader*, ed. Paul Rabinow (New York: Pantheon Books, 1984).

12. See Alan Moore and Eddie Campbell, *From Hell* (Paddington, Australia: Eddie Campbell Comics, 1989).

13. See Michel Foucault, *The History of Sexuality: An Introduction, Volume 1*, trans. Robert Hurley (New York, Vintage Books, 1978); Robert M. Pirsig, *Lila: An Inquiry into Morals* (New York: Bantam Books, 1991).

14. See David Edelstein, "One Film, Two Wars: *Three Kings*," *New York Times*, April 6, 2003: www.nytimes.com/2003/04/06/movies/06EDEL.html?ex=1050644 934&ei=1&en=f15345bed5f6d5f6; R. Delaney and J. Kenyon, "E. Iowans' Rental of War Movie Unprecedented," *The Cedar Rapids—Iowa City Gazette*, April 7, 2003: 2A.

Chapter 3: Politics in Subtexts

1. Terrence Rafferty, "Secret Sharers," *New Yorker* 64, no. 33 (October 3, 1988): 92–94, on p. 92. With permission from Taylor and Francis, this chapter revises slightly my essay in *Political Communication* 22, no. 3 (September, 2005): 381–386.

2. See Barbara J. Hill and John S. Nelson, "Facing the Holocaust: Robert Arneson's Ceramic Myth of Postmodern Catastrophe," *Human Rights / Human Wrongs: Art and Social Change*, eds. Robert Hobbs and Fredrick Woodard (Seattle: University of Washington Press, 1986), 189–209.

3. See Stephen King, *Danse Macabre* (New York: New American Library, 1981); Janice Hocker Rushing and Thomas S. Frentz, *Projecting the Shadow* (Chicago: University of Chicago Press, 1995).

4. See Jean Baudrillard: *In the Shadow of the Silent Majorities, or The End of the Social, and Other Essays*, trs. Paul Foss, John Johnston, and Paul Patton (New York: Semiotext(e), 1983); *The Evil Demon of Images* (Sydney: Power Institute of Fine Arts, 1987); *The Ecstasy of Communication*, ed. Sylèvre Lotringer, trs. Bernard and Caroline Schutze (New York: Semiotext(e), 1988); *Seduction*, trans. Brian Singer (New York: St. Martin's Press, (1979), 1990).

5. See Thomas Harris: *Red Dragon* (New York: Dell, 1981); *The Silence of the Lambs* (New York: St. Martin's Press, 1988); *Hannibal* (New York: Dell, 1999); *Hannibal Rising* (New York: Delacorte Press, 2006).

6. See Whitley Strieber, *The Wolfen* (New York: Avon Books, 1978).

7. See Stephen King, *The Shining* (New York: Penguin Books, 1977).

8. See Anne Rice (New York: Ballantine Books): *Interview with the Vampire* (1976); *The Vampire Lestat* (1985).

9. See Stephen King, *The Stand* (New York: Viking Press, 1978, unabridged edition, 1990). Also see John S. Nelson, "Stands in Politics," *Journal of Politics* 46, no. 1 (February, 1984): 106–131.

10. See Sigmund Freud, *The Interpretation of Dreams*, trans. James Strachey (New York: Basic Books, 1955).

11. See Dennis Etchison, *The Dark Country* (Santa Cruz, CA: Scream Press, 1982).

12. See Hannah Arendt, "What Is Existenz Philosophy?" *Partisan Review* 13, no. 1 (Winter 1946): 34–56. Also see Albert Camus (New York, Random House): *The Stranger*, trans. Stuart Gilbert (1946); *The Plague*, trans. Stuart Gilbert (1948); *The Rebel*, trans. Anthony Bower (1956). And see Jean-Paul Sartre: *Nausea*, trans. Lloyd Alexander (New York: New Directions, 1959); *Being and Nothingness*, trans. Hazel E. Barnes (New York, Philosophical Library, 1956).

13. See George Orwell, *Animal Farm* (New York: New American Library, 1946).

14. Tad Friend, "Remake Man," *New Yorker* 79, no. 14 (June 2, 2003): 40–47, on p. 41.

15. See G. W. S. Trow, *Within the Context of No-Context* (Boston: Little, Brown, 1978); Neil Postman, *Amusing Ourselves to Death* (New York: Viking Press, 1984); Joshua Meyrowitz, *No Sense of Place: The Impact of Electronic Media on Social Behavior* (New York: Oxford University Press, 1985); Raymond Williams, *Raymond Williams on Television*, ed. Alan O'Connor (London: Routledge, 1989); Raymond Williams, *Television* (Middletown, CT: Wesleyan University Press, 1974, second edition, 1992); Roderick Hart, *Seducing America: How Television Charms the Modern Voter* (New York: Oxford University Press, 1994). Also see Lance Bennett, *News* (New York: Longman, 1983, fifth edition, 2003); Murray Edelman, *Constructing the Political Spectacle* (Chicago:

University of Chicago Press, 1988); Murray Edelman, *The Politics of Misinformation* (Cambridge: Cambridge University Press, 2001); Robert M. Entman, *Democracy without Citizens* (New York: Oxford University Press, 1989); Doris A. Graber, *Processing Politics* (Chicago: University of Chicago Press, 2001); Kathleen Hall Jamieson, *Everything You Think You Know about Politics ... and Why You're Wrong* (New York: Basic Books, 2000); Kathleen Hall Jamieson and Paul Waldman, *The Press Effect* (New York: Oxford University Press, 2003); Thomas E. Patterson, *Out of Order* (New York: Knopf, 1993).

16.   See Rick Du Brow, "Fifteen Years Later, *Network* Prophecy Has Become Reality," *Des Moines Register* [*Los Angeles Times Service*], September 16, 1990, p. TV5.

17.   See Robert M. Entman, *Democracy without Citizens: Media and the Decay of American Politics* (New York: Oxford University Press, 1990); Thomas E. Patterson, *Out of Order* (New York: Knopf, 1993); David L. Paletz, *The Media in American Politics* (New York: Longman, 1999); W. Lance Bennett, *News: The Politics of Illusion.* 9th ed. (New York: Pearson, 2011).

18.   Ursula K. Le Guin, "It Was a Dark and Stormy Night; or, Why Are We Huddling about the Campfire?" *Critical Inquiry* 7, no. 1 (Autumn 1980): 191–199, on p. 199.

Chapter 4: Politics in Innovations

1.   Samuel Beckett, quoted from a conversation with John Driver in 1961 in Deirdre Bair, *Samuel Beckett: A Biography* (New York: Simon and Schuster, 1978, revised edition, 1990), ch. 21.

2.   A. O. Scott, "Emotion Needs No Translation," *New York Times*, October 27, 2006.

3.   See John S. Nelson, *Tropes of Politics: Science, Theory, Rhetoric, Action* (Madison: University of Wisconsin Press, 1998), 150–179.

4.   See Benjamin R. Barber, *Strong Democracy* (Berkeley: University of California Press, 1994); Adolf G. Gundersen, *The Environmental Promise of Democratic Deliberation* (Madison: University of Wisconsin Press, 1995); John S. Dryzek, *Deliberative Democracy and Beyond: Liberals, Critics, Contestations* (Oxford: Oxford University Press, 2000); Amy Gutmann and Dennis Thompson, *Why Deliberative Democracy?* (Princeton, NJ: Princeton University Press, 2004). Also see Nelson, *Tropes of Politics*, 180–204.

5.   See David Denby, "The New Disorder: Adventures in Film Narrative," *New Yorker* 83, no. 2 (March 5, 2007): 80–85; A. O. Scott, "Emotion Needs No Translation," *New York Times*, October 27, 2006; Anthony Lane, "Loves Lost," *New Yorker* 83, no. 5 (March 26, 2007): 94–95.

6.   See David Denby: "What If? Wishing Things Were Otherwise," *New Yorker* 82, no. 41 (December 11, 2006), 110–111.

7.   See Anthony Lane, "Lost," *New Yorker* 88, no. 34 (October 29 and November 5, 2012): 128–129.

8.   Denby, "The New Disorder," 85.

9.   Scott, "Emotion Needs No Translation." Also see David Ansen, "As the World Burns," *Newsweek* 148, no. 18 (October 30, 2006): 64.

10. Denby, "The New Disorder," p. 80. Also see David Denby, "Company Man," *New Yorker* 81, no. 39 (December 5, 2005): 109–111.

11. Thomas Cathcart and Daniel Klein, *Plato and a Platypus Walk into a Bar ... Understanding Philosophy through Jokes* (New York: Abrams Image, 2007), 68.

12. See Anthony Lane, "Road Trips: David Lynch and John Dahl Look Back," *New Yorker* 77, no. 30 (October 8, 2001): 88–89.

13. *Next* credits its inspiration to a great story by Philip K. Dick: "The Golden Man," *The Golden Man*, ed. Mark Hurst (New York: Berkley Books, 1980), 1–32. Yet the inferior film shares little with the story except the name for a lead character able to anticipate possible futures.

14. See James Gleick, *Chaos: Making a New Science* (New York: Viking Press, 1987); N. Katherine Hayles, ed., *Chaos and Order: Complex Dynamics in Literature and Science* (Chicago: University of Chicago Press, 1991).

15. See Rob Eyerman and Andrew Jamison, *Social Movements: A Cognitive Approach*, (University Park: Pennsylvania State University Press, 1991); Sidney Tarrow, *Power in Movement: Social Movements, Collective Action and Politics* (New York: Cambridge University Press, 1994); Doug McAdam, John D. McCarthy, and Mayer N. Zald, eds., *Comparative Perspectives on Social Movements: Political Opportunities, Mobilizing Structures, and Cultural Framings* (Cambridge: Cambridge University Press, 1966); Jeff Goodwin, James M. Jasper, and Francesca Polletta, eds., *Passionate Politics: Emotions and Social Movements* (Chicago: University of Chicago Press, 2001); Davis S. Meyer, Nancy Whittier, and Belinda Robnett, eds., *Social Movements: Identity, Culture, and the State* (Oxford: Oxford University Press, 2002); Mario Diani and Doug McAdam, eds., *Social Movements and Networks: Relational Approaches to Collective Action* (Oxford: Oxford University Press, 2003). Also see Carole Pateman, *The Disorder of Women: Democracy, Feminism, and Political Theory* (Stanford, CA: Stanford University Press, 1989); John S. Dryzek, David Downes, Christian Hunold, David Schlosberg, with Hans-Kristian Hernes, *Green States and Social Movements: Environmentalism in the United States, United Kingdom, Germany, and Norway* (Oxford: Oxford University Press, 2003).

16. See Robert Hariman, *Political Style: The Artistry of Power* (Chicago: University of Chicago Press, 1995).

17. See Daniel M. Shea, *Mass Politics: The Politics of Popular Culture* (New York: St. Martin's Press/Worth, 1999). Also see John S. Nelson and G. R. Boynton, *Video Rhetorics: Televised Advertising in American Politics* (Urbana: University of Illinois Press, 1997); Nelson, *Tropes of Politics*, 150–179.

18. See Aldo Leopold, *A Sand County Almanac, with Essays on Conservation from Round River* (New York, Ballantine Books, 1966); Wendell Berry, *Home Economics* (San Francisco, North Point Press, 1987); Michael Pollan, *Second Nature: A Gardener's Education* (New York: Dell, 1991); Andrew Szasz, *EcoPopulism: Toxic Waste and the Movement for Environmental Justice* (Minneapolis: University of Minnesota Press, 1994).

19. See Ray Pratt, *Projecting Paranoia: Conspiratorial Visions in American Film* (Lawrence: University Press of Kansas, 2001).

20. See Fredric Jameson, *Geopolitical Aesthetics* (Bloomington: Indiana University Press, 1992).

21. See Michel Foucault: *Discipline and Punish: The Birth of the Prison*, Alan Sherian, tr. (New York, Random House, 1977); *The History of Sexuality, Volume I: An Introduction*, trans. Robert Hurley (New York, Random House, 1978); *Language, Counter-Memory, Practice*, ed. Donald F. Bouchard, trans. Donald F. Bouchard and Sherry Simon (Ithaca, NY: Cornell University Press, 1977); *Power/Knowledge*, ed. Colin Gordon, trans. Colin Gordon and others (New York: Random House, 1980); *The Use of Pleasure: The History of Sexuality, Volume 2*, trans. Robert Hurley (New York: Random House, 1985). Also see Richard J. Bernstein, *Praxis and Action* (Philadelphia: University of Pennsylvania Press, 1971).

22. See Nelson, *Tropes of Politics*, 150–151.

23. See Malcolm Gladwell, *The Tipping Point: How Little Things Can Make a Big Difference* (Boston: Little, Brown, 2000, expanded edition, 2002). Gladwell works from epidemiology and geometric progressions by whole numbers rather than fractional dimensions, so that his implicit systems stay linear rather than chaotic in the mathematical sense. Nonlinear cusps and thresholds nonetheless can be treated as somewhat similar to Gladwell's tipping points.

24. See David Easton, *The Political System* (New York: Knopf, 1953, second edition, 1971); Morton A. Kaplan, "Systems Theory and Political Science," *Social Research* 35, no. 1 (Spring 1968): 30–47. Also see John S. Nelson, "Education for Politics: Rethinking Research on Political Socialization," *What Should Political Theory Be Now?* ed. Nelson (Albany: State University of New York Press, 1983), 413–478.

25. See David Denby, "Men Gone Wild," *New Yorker* 88, no. 6 (April 2, 2007): 88–89.

26. See Tracy B. Strong, *Friedrich Nietzsche and the Politics of Transformation* (Berkeley: University of California Press, 1975); Daniel Conway, *Nietzsche and the Political* (New York: Routledge, 1997).

27. On ethos as tone or atmosphere in cinema and post-modern forms generally, see John S. Nelson: *Tropes of Politics*, 38–139.

28. Denby, "The New Disorder," 85.

29. See Nicholas Christopher, *Somewhere in the Night: Film Noir and the American City* (New York: Henry Holt, 1997); Andrew Spicer, *Film Noir* (London: Pearson Education, 2002).

30. See John G. Gunnell, "In Search of the Political Object: Beyond Methodology and Transcendentalism," *What Should Political Theory Be Now?*, 25–52; John S. Nelson, "Political Theory as Political Rhetoric," *What Should Political Theory Be Now?*, 169–240.

31. See John S. Nelson, "Account and Acknowledge, or Represent and Control? On Postmodern Politics and Economics of Collective Responsibility," *Accounting, Organizations and Society* 18, no. 2–3 (February-April 1993): 207–229; John S. Nelson and Anna Lorien Nelson, "Story and More: Virtual Narratives for Electronic Times," *American Communication Journal* 1, no. 2 (February 1998): http://americancomm.org/~aca/acj/acj.html.

32. See Mark Rose, "Time," *Alien Encounters: Anatomy of Science Fiction* (Cambridge, MA: Harvard University Press, 1991), 96–138; Monte Cook, "Tips for Time Travel," *Philosophers Look at Science Fiction*, ed. Nicholas D. Smith (Chicago: Nelson-Hall, 1982), 47–55.

33. Thus the *Timecop* asymmetry between past and future or explanation and prediction that Roger Ebert ridicules in reviewing that film is a characteristic of nonlinear systems: see "Timecop," September 16, 1994, http://www.rogerebert.com/reviews/timecop-1994.

34. See Roger Ebert, "Frequency," April 28, 2000, http://www.rogerebert.com/reviews/frequency-2000.

35. See Michael Crichton, *Timeline* (New York: Ballantine Books, 1999).

36. Roger Ebert's appreciation in "The Lake House," June 15, 2006, http://www.rogerebert.com/reviews/the-lake-house-2006 is particularly telling: "*The Lake House* tells the story of a romance that spans years but involves only a few kisses. It succeeds despite being based on two paradoxes: time travel, and the ability of two people to have conversations that are, under the terms established by the film, impossible. Neither one of these problems bothered me in the slightest. Take time travel: I used to get distracted by its logical flaws and contradictory time lines. Now in my wisdom I have decided to simply accept it as a premise, no questions asked. A time travel story works on emotional, not temporal, logic."

37. Denby, "What If?" 111.

38. See Lane, "Loves Lost," 95.

39. In "Soldiers," *New Yorker* 83, no. 28 (September 24, 2007): 188–189, on p. 189, David Denby strangely writes, "I loved the heated, overflowing talk in *Crash*, most of which is wonderfully written, and I wasn't bothered by the movie's pileup of coincidences: *Crash* was a Los Angeles fable about twisted-metal automotive connection in a disconnected place—coincidence was not a mere device but what the movie was about." No, mere coincidence seems to fill the film only if we fail to see its take on racism as a nonlinear, turbulent, crash-inclined system.

40. The analogy is *not* to "mosaic novels," where different authors, with distinctive styles and preoccupations, contribute chapters meant to form a linear narrative. I know of no movies made fully in this way. A decent comparison would be to composite movies where different directors contribute free-standing mini-films that together tell no linear story but share a place, time, or other motif—after the fashion of many short-story anthologies. An example is *Paris, je t'aime* (2006). The literary form most similar to mosaic movies are the collections by a single author whose tales share a world and a set of characters without producing a linear narrative. Two examples from fantasy include the *Nevèrÿon* tales from Samuel R. Delany and the *Newford* stories by Charles de Lint.

41. See Sheldon S. Wolin, *Hobbes and the Epic Tradition of Political Theory* (Los Angeles: University of California Press, 1970); Dean A. Miller, *The Epic Hero* (Baltimore: Johns Hopkins University Press, 2000).

42. See Thomas Malory, *Le Morte D'Arthur*, ed. Norma Lorre Goodrich (New York: Washington Square Press, 1963); T. H. White, *The Once and Future King* (New York: Putnam, 1939).

43. Or if you do not like *Lions for Lambs*, you might say with Anthony Lane in "Hunting Grounds," *New Yorker* 83, no. 35 (November 12, 2007): 98–99, on p. 99: "Robert Redford's film, written by Matthew Michael Carnahan, is braided from three strands, like a rope. . . . The three stories are intercut throughout the film, to lend it at least the illusion of momentum."

44. See Mike Davis, *City of Quartz: Excavating the Future in Los Angeles* (New York: Random House, 1990).

45. See Gilles Deleuze and Félix Guattari, *A Thousand Plateaus: Capitalism and Schizophrenia*, trans. Brian Masumi (Minneapolis: University of Minnesota Press, 1987), 3–25 and 351–423.

46. Denby, "The New Disorder," 80.

47. See David Bordwell, *Narration in the Fiction Film* (Madison: University of Wisconsin Press, 1985); Michael Ryan and Douglas Kellner, *Camera Politica: The Politics and Ideology of Contemporary Hollywood Film* (Bloomington: Indiana University Press, 1988); Mas'ud Zavarzadeh, *Seeing Films Politically* (Albany: State University of New York Press, 1991); Michael Parenti, *Make-Believe Media: The Politics of Entertainment* (New York: St. Martin's Press, 1992).

48. See David Mitchell, *Cloud Atlas* (New York: Random House, 2004); Aleksandar Hemon, "Beyond the Matrix: The Wachowskis Travel to Even More Mind-Bending Realms," *New Yorker* 88, no. 27 (September 10, 2012): 66–75.

49. As an exception to prove the earlier rule, *Grindhouse* can even be viewed as a "mosaic movie" in much the same (family-resemblance) sense as a "mosaic novel," since the film's different *auteurs* create successive episodes unto chapters for a fractal narrative overall that is much more than a mere sum of its parts. Edgar Wright directed the pseudopreview for "Don't," and Rob Zombie directed the fake preview for "Werewolf Women of the S. S." Robert Rodriguez directed the mock preview for "Machete" as well as the feature-length contribution of "Planet Terror." Eli Roth directed the spoof preview for "Thanksgiving." And Quentin Tarantino directed the feature-length segment called "Death Proof."

50. See Paul Auster (New York: Penguin Books): *The Country of Last Things* (1987); *The Music of Chance* (1990). Also see John Straley (New York: Bantam Books): *The Woman Who Married a Bear* (1992); *The Curious Eat Themselves* (1993); *The Music of What Happens* (1996); *Death and the Language of Happiness* (1997); *The Angels Will Not Care* (1998); *Cold Water Burning* (2001).

51. In the social sciences, at least, statistics of linear regression are used to distinguish Humean causal correlations from mere coincidences. In practice, however, these statistics clarify in tropal, nonlinear, systemic terms more plausibly than they do in literal, linear, mechanical modes: see Nelson, *Tropes of Politics*, 99–114.

52. See Samuel A. Chambers, *Untimely Politics* (New York: New York University Press, 2003).

53. Neither a mosaic movie nor a neo noir, Baz Luhrmann's version of *The Great Gatsby* (2013) shares some of these aesthetics of late films by Tony Scott, including experiments with words on the screen. And it spurs a similar distaste in some quarters: see David Denby, "All That Jazz: *The Great Gatsby*," *New Yorker* 89, no. 13 (May 13, 2013): 78–79.

54. There is a similar musical moment at the end of Thomas Mann's great novel *Doctor Faustus*, trans. H. T. Lowe-Porter (New York: Random House, 1948). See John S. Nelson, "Toltechs, Aztechs, and the Art of the Possible: Parenthetic Comments on the Political Through Language and Aesthetics," *Polity* 8, no. 1 (Fall 1975): 80–116.

Chapter 5: Emotion and Empathy

1. Roger Ebert, "Powerful Tale of *Passion* Soaked in Extreme Violence," *Cedar Rapids—Iowa City Gazette*, February 26, 2004, 4W.

2. David Denby, "Nailed: Mel Gibson's *The Passion of the Christ*," *New Yorker* 80, no. 2 (March 1, 2004): 84–86, on p. 86.

3. See Sean Smith, "Will Oscar Listen?" *Newsweek* 144, no. 17 (October 25, 2004): 98–99.

4. See "The Passion of the Arab World," *Atlantic Monthly* 294, no. 1 (July–August 2004): 62; from Aluma Dankowitz, "Reactions in the Arab Media to *The Passion of the Christ*," Middle East Research Institute, April 21, 2004, http:// www. memri.de/ uebersetzungen_ analysen/themen/liberal_voices/ges_passion_christ_21_04_04. html.

5. See Sean Smith, "Who'll Buy Mel's Movie?" *Newsweek* 142, no. 15 (October 13, 2004): 72; Sean Smith, "Passion Play," *Newsweek* 142, no. 18 (November 3, 2003: 12; Jon Meacham, "Who Killed Jesus?" *Newsweek* 143, no. 7 (February 16, 2004): 44–53; David Ansen, "So What's the Good News? The Debate Over *The Passion* May Be Less Harsh than the Film," *Newsweek* 143, no. 9 (March 1, 2004): 60; David Gates, "Jesus Christ Movie Star," *Newsweek* 143, no. 10 (March 8, 2004): 50–52; Anna Quindlen, "At the Left Hand of God," *Newsweek* 143, no. 10 (March 8, 2004): 64.

6. See David Denby, "The Quick and the Dead: *Bon Voyage* and *Dogville*," *New Yorker* 80, no. 6 (March 29, 2004) 103–105, on p. 103; Denby, "Nailed."

7. Through its first June, four months after its initial release, *The Passion* had grossed over $370 million in the United States alone. By the September release of the DVD, the worldwide gross had reached $600 million. Reportedly it cost Gibson $30 million to make, and he is said to have reaped most of the profit.

8. See Amy Sullivan, "Jesus Christ, Superstar: When Hollywood Stopped Making Bible Movies, Right-Wing Christians Took Over," *Washington Monthly* 36, no. 6 (June 2004): 48–51.

9. Ansen, "So What's the Good News?," 60.

10. Ebert, "Powerful Tale of *Passion* Soaked in Extreme Violence."

11. Keith E. Gottschalk, "*Passion* Offers Brutal but Honest Portrayal," *Cedar Rapids—Iowa City Gazette*, February 26, 2004, 4W.

12. See Mark Rahner, "Second Thoughts as Gibson's *Passion* Hits DVD," *Seattle Times* reprinted in the *Cedar Rapids—Iowa City Gazette*, September 6, 2004, 2W.

13. See Denby, "Nailed," 84.

14. Denby, "Nailed," 84.

15. See Peter J. Boyer, "The Jesus War: Mel Gibson's Obsession," *New Yorker* 79, no. 26, September 15, 2003, 58–71.

16. See Stephen A. Tyler, *The Unspeakable: Discourse, Dialogue, and Rhetoric in the Postmodern World*, 1987.

17. See David Depew, "Empathy, Psychology, and Aesthetics: Reflections on a Repair Concept," *Poroi* 4, no. 1 (March 2005): http://inpress.lib.uiowa.edu/poroi/ papers/depew050301.html; Russell Valentino, "The Oxymoron of Empathic Criticism: Readerly Empathy, Critical Explication, and the Translator's Creative Understand-

ing," *Poroi* 4, no. 1 (March, 2005): http://inpress.lib.uiowa.edu/poroi/papers/valentino050301.html.

18. Denby, "The Quick and the Dead," 103.

19. Denby, "The Quick and the Dead," 103.

20. See Robert Hariman, "No One Is In Charge Here: Ryszard Kapucinski's Anatomy of the Courtly Style," *Political Style: The Artistry of Power* (Chicago: University of Chicago Press, 1995), 51–94.

21. On apathy, see Daniel M. Gross, *The Secret History of Emotion: From Aristotle's Rhetoric* to Modern Brain Science (Chicago: University of Chicago Press, 2006), 51–111.

22. On the pathetic strategy, see John S. Nelson, *Tropes of Politics* (Madison: University of Wisconsin Press, 1998), 141–143.

23. See Elaine Scarry: *The Body in Pain: The Making and the Unmaking of the World* (New York: Oxford University Press, 1985); "Obdurate Sensation: Pain," *Resisting Representation* (New York: Oxford University Press, 1994), 13–48. Also see Bruce B. Lawrence and Aisha Karim, eds., "The Representation of Violence," *On Violence: A Reader* (Durham, NC: Duke University Press, 2007), 491–553.

24. See Barbara Maria Stafford, *Good Looking: Essays on the Virtue of Images* (Cambridge, MA: MIT Press, 1996), 129–199.

25. See Robert Jay Lifton: *Death in Life: Survivors of Hiroshima* (New York: Random House, 1967); *Home from the War; Vietnam Veterans: Neither Victims nor Executioners* (New York: Simon and Schuster, 1973).

26. See Lois Parkinson Zamora and Wendy B. Faris, eds., *Magical Realism: Theory, History, Community* (Durham, NC: Duke University Press, 1995); Maggie Ann Bowers, *Magic(al) Realism: The New Critical Idiom* (New York: Routledge, 2004); Wendy B. Faris, *Ordinary Enchantments: Magical Realism and the Remystification of Narrative* (Nashville: Vanderbilt University Press, 2004).

27. On gross-out horror, see Stephen King, *Danse Macabre* (New York: Berkley Books, 1981), 4 and 23–28.

28. See Edmund Burke, *A Philosophical Enquiry into the Origin of Our Ideas of the Sublime and Beautiful*, ed. James T. Boulton (Notre Dame, IN: University of Notre Dame Press, (1757), 1958). Also see Richard Kuhns, "The Beautiful and the Sublime," *New Literary History*, 13, no. 2 (Winter 1982), 287–307; Suzanne Guerlac, "Delights of Grotesque and Sublime," *Diacritics* 15, no. 3 (Fall 1985), 47–54; Ralph Cohen, ed., "The Sublime and the Beautiful: Reconsiderations," special issue of *New Literary History* 16, no. 2 (Winter 1985): 213–437; François Lyotard, ed., *Of the Sublime: Presence in Question*, trans. Jeffrey S. Librett (Albany: State University of New York Press, (1988), 1993).

29. Ansen, "So What's the Good News?"

30. On moving beyond communication and resisting representation, see Scarry, *Resisting Representation*; John Durham Peters, *Speaking into the Air* (Chicago: University of Chicago Press, 1999); Laurence A. Rickels, *The Vampire Lectures* (Minneapolis: University of Minnesota Press, 1999).

31. On hyperreality in politics, see Murray Edelman, *Constructing the Political Spectacle* (Chicago: University of Chicago Press, 1988); John S. Nelson, "All's Fair:

Love, War, Politics, and Other Spectacles," *Poroi* 4, no. 2 (July 2005): http://inpress. lib.uiowa.edu/poroi/papers/nelson050701.html.

32. Ansen, "So What's the Good News?," 60.

33. The survey was released by the *Washington Post* and ABC News at the end of May, 2004. See *Houston Chronicle*, http://www.chron.com/cs/CDA/ssistory.mpl/ nation/2597834.

34. See Robert C. Solomon: *The Passions: Emotions and the Meaning of Life* (India-napolis: Hackett, 1993); *Not Passion's Slave: Emotions and Choice* (New York: Oxford University Press, 2003); ed., *Thinking about Feeling: Contemporary Philosophers on Emotions* (New York: Oxford University Press, 2004); *True to Our Feelings: What Our Emotions Are Really Telling Us* (New York: Oxford University Press, 2007). Also see Antonio R. Damasio: *Descartes' Error: Emotion, Reason, and the Human Brain* (New York: Putnam, 1994); *The Feeling of What Happens: Body and Emotion in the Making of Consciousness* (New York: Harcourt Brace, 1999). And see George Lakoff and Mark Johnson, *Philosophy in the Flesh: The Embodied Mind and Its Challenge to Western Thought* (New York: Basic Books, 1999).

35. See Stanley Cavell, "Opera and the Lease of Voice," *A Pitch of Philosophy* (Cambridge, MA: Harvard University Press, 1994), 129–169.

36. See David Hume, *A Treatise of Human Nature*, ed. L. A. Selby-Bigge (Oxford: Oxford University Press, (1739), 1888); Adam Smith, *The Theory of Moral Sentiments* (Indianapolis: Liberty Fund, (1853), 1969). Also see George Lakoff and Mark Turner, *More than Cool Reason: A Field Guide to Poetic Metaphor* (Chicago: University of Chi-cago Press, 1989); John S. Nelson, "Voice and Music in Political Telespots: Emotions as Reasons in Public Arguments," *Critical Problems in Argumentation*, ed. Charles Arthur Willard (Washington, DC: National Communication Association, 2005), 230–237.

37. On dread, see Søren Kierkegaard, *The Concept of Dread*, trans. Walter Lowrie (Princeton, NJ: Princeton University Press, 1944). On facing, see Barbara J. Hill and John S. Nelson, "Facing the Holocaust: Robert Arneson's Ceramic Myth of Postmodern Catastrophe," *Human Rights / Human Wrongs: Art and Social Change*, eds. Robert Hobbs and Fredrick Woodard (Seattle: University of Washington Press, 1986), 189–209.

38. See Aristotle, *Nicomachean Ethics*, trans. Robert C. Bartlett and Susan D. Collins (Chicago: University of Chicago Press, 2011).

39. On persuasion by these three modes of experience, see John S. Nelson and G. R. Boynton, *Video Rhetorics: Televised Advertising in American Politics* (Urbana: University of Illinois Press, 1997), 204–232.

40. Anthony Burgess: *A Clockwork Orange* (New York: Ballantine Books, 1962), 71. See Anthony Burgess, "The Clockwork Condition: The Author Comments on His Most Famous Book, in 1973," *New Yorker* 88, no. 16 (June 4 and 11, 2012): 69–76.

41. See Christopher Sharrett, ed., *Mythologies of Violence in Postmodern Media* (Detroit: Wayne State University Press, 1999); Stephen Prince, ed., *Screening Violence* (New Brunswick, NJ: Rutgers University Press, 2000); J. David Slocum, ed., *Violence and American Cinema* (New York: Routledge, 2001); Eric Lichtenfeld, *Action Speaks Louder: Violence, Spectacle, and the American Action Movie* (Middletown, CT: Wesleyan University Press, 2004, expanded edition, 2007).

42. See Richard E. Nisbett and Dov Cohen, *Culture of Honor: The Psychology of Violence in the South* (Boulder, CO: Westview Press, 1996); Alex Alvarez and Ronet Bachman, *Violence: The Enduring Problem* (Thousand Oaks, CA: Sage, 2008); Randall Collins, *Violence: A Micro-sociological Theory* (Princeton, NJ: Princeton University Press, 2008); Slavoj Žižek, *Violence: Six Sideways Reflections* (New York: Picador, 2008); Douglass C. North, John Joseph Wallis, and Barry R. Weingast, *Violence and Social Orders: A Conceptual Framework for Interpreting Recorded Human History* (Cambridge: Cambridge University Press, 2009).

Chapter 6: Character and Community

1. Glenn Tinder, "Freedom of Expression, The Strange Imperative," *Yale Review* 49, no. 2 (Winter 1980): 161–176, on p. 173. With permission from the Finnish Political Science Association, this chapter revises my article from *Politiikka* 4 (1998), 286–296.

2. See John S. Nelson, Allan Megill, and D. N. McCloskey, eds., *The Rhetoric of the Human Sciences: Language and Argument in Scholarship and Public Affairs* (Madison: University of Wisconsin Press, 1987).

3. See Hannah Arendt, "What Is Existenz Philosophy?" *Partisan Review* 13 (Winter 1946): 34–56.

4. See John S. Nelson, "Commerce among the Archipelagos: Rhetoric of Inquiry as a Practice of Coherent Education," eds. L. Robert Stevens, G. L. Seligmann, and Julian Long, *The Core and the Canon* (Denton, TX: University of North Texas Press, 1993), 78–100.

5. See Hannah Arendt, *The Human Condition* (Chicago: University of Chicago Press, 1958).

6. See Hannah Arendt, *Between Past and Future* (New York: Viking Penguin, 1963, extended edition, 1968), 227–264.

7. See Hannah Arendt, *Crises of the Republic* (New York: Harcourt Brace, 1972), 103–198.

8. See Arendt, *Crises of the Republic*, 1–47.

9. See Hannah Arendt, "Home to Roost: A Bicentennial Address," *New York Review of Books* 22, no. 11 (June 26, 1975): 3–6.

10. See Hannah Arendt: *The Origins of Totalitarianism*, 4th ed. (New York: Harcourt Brace Jovanovich, 1973); "Home to Roost."

11. See John S. Nelson "Politics and Truth: Arendt's Problematic," *American Journal of Political Science* 22, no. 2 (May 1978): 270–301.

12. See Friedrich Nietzsche, "On Truth and Falsity in Their Extramoral Sense," ed. Warren Shibles, *Essays on Metaphor* (Whitewater, WI: Language Press, 1972), 1–13.

13. See John S. Nelson, *Tropes of Politics: Science, Theory, Rhetoric, Action* (Madison: University of Wisconsin Press, 1998).

14. See Michael Pollan, *Second Nature* (New York: Dell, 1991), 178–208.

15. See Arendt, *The Human Condition*.

16. See Hannah Arendt, *The Life of the Mind*, in 2 vols. (New York: Harcourt Brace Jovanovich, 1978).

17. See Arendt, *Between Past and Future*.

18. See Judith N. Shklar, "Rethinking the Past," *Social Research* 44, no. 1 (Spring 1977), 80–90.

19. See Friedrich Nietzsche, *On the Advantage and Disadvantage of History for Life*, trans. Peter Preuss (Indianapolis: Hackett, 1982).

20. See Arendt, *The Origins of Totalitarianism*; John S. Nelson, "Orwell's Political Myths and Ours," eds. Robert L. Savage, James E. Combs, and Dan D. Nimmo, *The Orwellian Moment* (Fayetteville: University of Arkansas Press, 1989), 11–44. On Orwell's sense of truth in relation to politics, see David Dwan, "Truth and Freedom in Orwell's *Nineteen Eighty-Four*," *Philosophy and Literature* 34, no. 2 (October 2010), 381–393.

21. See Thomas Hobbes, *Leviathan*, ed. C. B. Macpherson (New York: Penguin Books, (1651), 1968).

22. See Nelson, *Tropes of Politics*, 124–126.

23. See Nelson, *Tropes of Politics*, 123–124.

24. See John Durham Peters, *Speaking into the Air: A History of the Idea of Communication* (Chicago: University of Chicago Press, 1999); Nelson, *Tropes of Poltiics*, 99–204.

25. See Christopher Matthews, *Hardball* (New York: HarperCollins, 1988), 107–116.

26. See Arendt, *Between Past and Future*, 143–171.

27. See Arendt, *The Origins of Totalitarianism*, 212–219; Roger W. Smith, "Redemption and Politics," *Political Science Quarterly* 86, no. 2 (June 1971), 205–231; Kurt Wolff, "On the Significance of Hannah Arendt's *Human Condition* for Sociology," *Inquiry* 4, no. 2 (1961), 67–106.

28. See Hannah Arendt, *On Revolution* (New York: Viking Penguin, 1963).

29. See Bonnie Honig, "Declarations of Independence: Arendt and Derrida on the Problem of Founding a Republic," eds. Frederick M. Dolan and Thomas L. Dumm, *Rhetorical Republic* (Amherst: University of Massachusetts Press, 1993), 201–225.

30. See John S. Nelson, "Political Foundations for Rhetoric of Inquiry," Herbert W. Simons, ed., *The Rhetorical Turn* (Chicago: University of Chicago Press, 1990), 258–289.

31. See Bruno Bettelheim, "The Art of Moving Pictures: Man, Superman, and Myth," *Harper's Magazine* 263, no. 1577 (October 1981): 80–83.

32. See Octavio Paz, "Poetry in Motion: The Video Muse," trans. Eliot Weinberger, *New York Times Book Review* 91, no. 6 (February 6, 1986): 1 and 30–31.

33. See Carl Sagan, *Contact* (New York: Pocket, 1985).

34. Anthony Lane, "Spaced Out," *New Yorker* 73, no. 20 (July 21, 1997): 81–82, on p. 82.

35. Lane, "Spaced Out," 82.

36. See Tom Wolfe, *The Right Stuff* (New York: Bantam, 1979).

37. Lane, "Spaced Out," 82.

38. See Harold Bloom, *Shakespeare: The Invention of the Human* (New York: Penguin Putnam, 1998).

39. See Hannah Arendt, *The Human Condition*; *On Revolution*; *Between Past*

and Future. Also see Ferdinand Mount, *The Theatre of Politics* (New York: Schocken Books, 1972); Michael Ende, *Momo*, trans. J. Maxwell Brownjohn (Garden City, NY: Doubleday, (1974) 1985); Sue-Ellen Case and Janelle Reinelt, eds., *The Performance of Power: Theatrical Discourse and Politics* (Iowa City: University of Iowa Press, 1991).

40. See Howard Rheingold: *Virtual Reality* (New York: Simon and Schuster, 1991); *The Virtual Community* (Reading, MA: Addison-Wesley, 1993).

41. See John S. Nelson and G. R. Boynton, *Video Rhetorics: Televised Advertising in American Politics* (Urbana: University of Illinois Press, 1997), 135–149.

42. See Rachel O. Moore, *Savage Theory: Cinema as Modern Magic* (Durham, NC: Duke University Press, 2000), 48–72.

43. A complementary argument appears in Jill Lepore, "The Prism: Privacy in an Age of Publicity," *New Yorker* 89, no. 18 (June 24, 2013): 32–36.

Chapter 7: Atmosphere and Argument

1. Gore Vidal, "Reel History," *New Yorker* 73, no. 34 (November 10, 1997): 112–120, on p. 115.

2. See John S. Nelson and Anna Lorien Nelson, "Story and More: Virtual Narratives for Electronic Times," *American Communication Journal* 1, no. 2 (February): http://americancomm.org/~aca/acj/acj.html.

3. See William J. Palmer, *The Films of the Eighties: A Social History* (Carbondale: Southern Illinois University Press, 1993), 16–113.

4. See Ernest R. May, *"Lessons" of the Past: The Use and Misuse of History in American Foreign Policy* (New York: Oxford University Press, 1975); Richard E. Neustadt and Ernest R. May, *Thinking in Time: The Uses of History for Decision-Makers* (New York: Free Press, 1986).

5. Judith N. Shklar, "Rethinking the Past," *Social Research* 44, no. 1 (Spring 1997), 80–90.

6. See John S. Nelson, *Tropes of Politics: Science, Theory, Rhetoric, Action* (Madison: University of Wisconsin Press, 1998), 138–139.

7. See Stephen E. Toulmin, *The Uses of Argument* (Cambridge: Cambridge University Press, 1964).

8. See Garry Wills, *John Wayne's America: The Politics of Celebrity* (New York: Simon and Schuster, 1997), 82–83.

9. The much later sequels are somewhat similar: see *The Dirty Dozen: Next Mission* (1985) and *The Dirty Dozen: The Fatal Mission* (1988).

10. See Plato, "The Three Parts of the Soul," *Republic*, Francis MacDonald Cornford, trans. (New York: Oxford University Press, 1945), Chapter XIII, 129–138.

11. See Mark Rose, *Alien Encounters* (Cambridge, MA: Harvard University Press, 1981).

12. See Stanislaw Lem, *Solaris*, trans. Joanna Kilmartin and Steve Cox (New York: Berkley Books, 1970). Also see Herbert, Frank (New York: Berkley Books): *Dune* (1965); *Dune Messiah* (1969); *Children of Dune* (1976). And see Kim Stanley Robinson (New

York: Bantam Books): *Red Mars* (1993); *Green Mars* (1994); *Blue Mars* (1996); *The Martians* (1999).

13. See James Fallows, *National Defense* (New York: Random House, 1981).

14. David Ansen, "Heartstops and Heartbreak," *Newsweek* 123, no. 5 (January 31, 1994): 58.

15. See John S. Nelson and G. R. Boynton, *Video Rhetorics: Televised Advertising in American Politics* (Urbana: University of Illinois Press, 1997), 100–118.

16. See Stanley Cavell, "Identifying Praise: At Moments in Henry James and in Fred Astaire," Foundations of Political Theory Plenary Address (Washington, DC: 1997). A different version of this essay appears in print as Stanley Cavell, "Something Out of the Ordinary," *Cavell on Film*, ed. William Rothman (Albany: State University of New York Press, 2005), 223–240.

17. See G. R. Boynton and John S. Nelson, *Hot Spots: Multimedia Analyses of Political Ads* (Urbana: University of Illinois Press, 1997, videocassette); Nelson and Boynton, *Video Rhetorics.*

18. See Vivian Sobchak: *The Address of the Eye: A Phenomenology of Film Experience* (Princeton, NJ: Princeton University Press, 1992); *Carnal Thoughts: Embodiment and Moving Image Culture* (Berkeley: University of California Press, 2004).

19. See Howard Rheingold: *Virtual Reality* (New York: Simon and Schuster, 1991); *The Virtual Community* (Reading, MA: Addison-Wesley, 1993). Also see Timothy Druckrey, ed., *Electronic Culture: Technology and Visual Representation* (Denville, NJ: Aperture Foundation, 1996).

20. See D. N. Rodowick, *Reading the Figural: Or, Philosophy after the New Media* (Durham, NC: Duke University Press, 2001).

21. See Janet Maslin, "Beauty and Destruction in Pacific Battle," *New York Times*, December 23, 1998, http://www.nytimes.com/1998/12/23/movies/film-review-beauty-and-destruction-in-pacific-battle.html; Roger Ebert, *"The Thin Red Line,"* January 8, 1999, http://www.rogerebert.com/reviews/the-thin-red-line-1999.

22. See Janet Maslin, *"Saving Private Ryan*: A Soberly Magnificent New War Film," *New York Times*, July 24, 1998, http://partners.nytimes.com/library/film/072498ryan-film-review.html.

23. On environmentalism, see Andrew Szasz, *Ecopopulism: Toxic Waste and the Movement for Environmental Justice* (Minneapolis: University of Minnesota Press, 1994); Kevin Michael DeLuca, *Image Politics: The New Rhetoric of Environmental Activism* (New York: The Guilford Press, 1999). On feminism, see Tania Modleski, ed., *Studies in Entertainment* (Bloomington: Indiana University Press, 1986); Lilly J. Goren, *You've Come a Long Way, Baby: Women, Politics, and Popular Culture* (Lexington: University Press of Kentucky, 2009).

24. Steven Spielberg, quoted in Hendrik Hertzberg, "Theatre of War," *New Yorker* 74, no. 21 (July 27, 1998): 30–33, on p. 31.

25. See Nelson and Boynton, *Video Rhetorics*, 195–232.

26. See J. P. Telotte, *Voices in the Dark: The Narrative Patterns of Film Noir* (Urbana: University of Illinois Press, 1989). Also see Michel Chion, *The Voice in Cinema*, Claudia Gorbman, trans. (New York: Columbia University Press, (1982), 1999).

27. See John S. Nelson and G. R. Boynton, "Making Sound Arguments: Would a Claim by Any Other Sound Mean the Same or Argue So Sweet?" *Argument in a Time of Change*, ed. James F. Klumpp (Annandale, VA: National Communication Association, 1998), 12–17.

28. See Kenneth Turan, "*Saving Private Ryan*: Soldiers of Misfortune," *Los Angeles Times*, July 23, 1998, http://web.archive.org/web/20070929134652; http://www. calendarlive. com/movies/reviews/cl-movie980723-5,0,6595970.story.

29. See Jeanine Basinger "Translating War: The Combat Film Genre and *Saving Private Ryan*," *Perspectives* 36 (October, 1998): 1 and 43–47; Phil Landon, "Realism, Genre, and Saving Private Ryan," *Film and History* 28, no. 3–4 (1998): 58–63.

30. See Roger Ebert, "*Saving Private Ryan*," July 24, 1998, http://www.rogerebert. com/reviews/saving-private-ryan-1998.

31. See John Bodnar, "*Saving Private Ryan* and Postwar Memory in America," *American Historical Review* 106, no. 3 (June 2001): 805–817.

32. See Francis A. Beer and Robert Hariman, ed., *Post-Realism: The Rhetorical Turn in International Relations* (East Lansing: Michigan State University Press, 1996).

Chapter 8: Movies Prefigure Politics

1. Kenneth Tynan, "The Third Act: Entries from Kenneth Tynan's Journals, 1975–78," *New Yorker* 76, no. 23 (August 14, 2000): 60–71, on p. 64.

2. See Murray Edelman, *From Art to Politics: How Artistic Creations Shape Political Conceptions* (Chicago: University of Chicago Press, 1995), 7.

3. See Doris A. Graber: *Processing the News* (New York: Longman, 1984, second edition, 1988); *Processing Politics* (Chicago: University of Chicago Press, 2001).

4. See John S. Nelson and G. R. Boynton, *Video Rhetorics: Televised Advertising in American Politics* (Urbana: University of Illinois Press, 1997), 27–86.

5. See Timothy Corrigan, *A Short Guide to Writing about Film*, 3rd ed. (New York: St. Martin's Press, 1998); Rick Altman, *Film/Genre* (London: British Film Institute, 1999).

6. On this kind of information, more full-bodied and active than cybernetic and realist modes of information as mere data, see John S. Nelson, *Tropes of Politics: Science, Theory, Rhetoric Action* (Madison: University of Wisconsin Press, 1998), 124–126.

7. See Hayden White: *Metahistory* (Baltimore: Johns Hopkins University Press, 1973); *Tropics of Discourse* (Baltimore: Johns Hopkins University Press, 1978). Also see John S. Nelson: "Review Essay [on *Metahistory* by Hayden White]," *History and Theory* 14, no. 1 (1975): 74–91; "Tropal History and the Social Sciences," *History and Theory* 19, no. 4 (1980), 80–101.

8. See Maurice Merleau-Ponty: *Phenomenology of Perception*, trans. Colin Smith, (New York: Humanities Press, 1962); *The Primacy of Perception*, ed. James M. Edie (Evanston, IL: Northwestern University Press, 1964); *Sense and Non-Sense*, trans. Hubert L. Dreyfus and Patricia A. Dreyfus (Evanston, IL: Northwestern University Press, 1964). Also see Susan T. Fiske and Shelley E. Taylor, *Social Cognition* (New York: McGraw-Hill, 1984, second edition, 1991).

9. See Vivian Sobchak: *The Address of the Eye: A Phenomenology of Film Experience* (Princeton, NJ: Princeton University Press, 1992); *Carnal Thoughts: Embodiment and Moving Image Culture* (Berkeley: University of California Press, 2004).

10. See Nelson, *Tropes of Politics*, especially xvi and 99–114.

11. See G. R. Boynton and John S. Nelson, "Paradigms of Politics," *Hot Spots: Multimedia Analyses of Political Ads* (Urbana: University of Illinois Press, 1997), first video.

12. See Johann Wolfgang von Goethe, *Elective Affinities*, trans. Elizabeth Mayer and Louise Brogan (Chicago: Henry Regnery, 1963).

13. See Boynton and Nelson, "Orchestrating Politics," *Hot Spots*, third video.

14. See Pippa Norris, Montague Kern, and Marion Just, eds., *Framing Terrorism: The News Media, the Government, and the Public* (New York: Routledge, 2003).

15. On the CIA meeting with Hollywood screenwriters about terrorist scenarios after 9/11, see Nikki Finke, "Does America Owe Hollywood Its Gratitude?" *Deadline*, May 4, 2011, http://www.deadline.com/2011/05/does-america-owe-hollywood-its-gratitutde. On the Bush Administration and the Pentagon getting advice from Hollywood screenwriters on plausible kinds of terrorist plots in the aftermath of 9/11, see *ABC World News*, October 21, 2004.

16. See Nelson and Boynton, *Video Rhetorics*, 195–232.

17. See William J. Palmer, *The Films of the Eighties: A Social History* (Carbondale: Southern Illinois University Press, 1993), 114–178.

18. See Bethami A. Dobkin (Westport, CT: Praeger): *Tales of Terror: Television News and the Construction of the Terrorist Threat* (1992); *Framing the Enemy: The Construction and Use of Terrorism in Public Discourse* (1993). Also see Nicholas Lemann, "The Next World Order: The Bush Administration May Have a Brand-New Doctrine of Power," *New Yorker* 78, no. 6 (April 1, 2002): 42–48, especially 44–46.

19. Television treatments of political terrorism mostly came after 2001: see *Stacy Takacs, Terrorism TV: Popular Entertainment Post-9/11 America* (Lawrence: University Press of Kansas, 2012).

20. See Thomas E. Patterson, *Out of Order* (New York: Knopf, 1993), 53–133; Doris A. Graber, *Processing Politics: Learning from Television in the Internet Age* (Chicago: University of Chicago Press, 2001).

21. Compare *Casino Royale* (2006) and *Quantum of Solace* (2008) to *Skyfall* (2012).

22. At least that held until *The Dark Knight Trilogy* from Christopher Nolan: see *Batman Begins* (2005), *The Dark Knight* (2008), and *The Dark Knight Rises* (2012).

23. For a figural inventory of such modern ideologies, see Nelson, *Tropes of Politics*, 161; and for more on liberalisms in particular, see 147–149. Also see George Lakoff: *Moral Politics: How Liberals and Conservative Think* (Chicago: University of Chicago Press, 1996, second edition, 2002); *The Political Mind: Why You Can't Understand 21st-Century Politics with an 18th-Century Brain* (New York, Viking, 2008).

24. On nonideological forms of postmodern politics, see Nelson, *Tropes of Politics*, 205–230.

25. See J. G. A. Pocock, *The Machiavellian Moment* (Princeton, NJ: Princeton University Press, 1975); Jack P. Geise, "Republican Ideals and Contemporary Realities," *Review of Politics*, 46, no. 1 (January 1984): 23–44; Anne Norton, *Republic of Signs*

(Chicago: University of Chicago Press, 1993); Robert Hariman, "In Oratory as in Life: Civic Performance in Cicero's Republican Style," *Political Style: The Artistry of Power* (Chicago: University of Chicago Press, 1995), 95–140; John S. Nelson, "Prudence as Republican Politics in American Popular Culture," *Prudence*, ed. Robert Hariman (University Park: Pennsylvania State University Press, 2003), 229–257.

26. See Kelefeh Sanneh, "Paint Bombs: David Graeber's *The Democracy Project* and the Anarchist Revival," *New Yorker* 89, no. 13 (May 13, 2013): 72–76.

27. See Boynton and Nelson, *Hot Spots*.

28. On style in politics, see Robert Hariman, "Introduction," *Political Style*, 1–12; Andrew Benjamin, *Style and Time: Essays on the Politics of Appearance* (Evanston, IL: Northwestern University Press, 2006).

29. See John S. Nelson: "Political Foundations for Rhetoric of Inquiry," *The Rhetorical Turn*, Herbert W. Simons, ed. (Chicago: University of Chicago Press, 1990), 258–289; "Commerce among the Archipelagos: Rhetoric of Inquiry as a Practice of Coherent Education," *The Core and the Canon*, L. Robert Stevens, G. L. Seligmann, and Julian Long, eds. (Denton, TX: University of North Texas Press, 1993), 78–100.

30. See Garry Wills, *A Necessary Evil: A History of American Distrust of Government* (New York: Simon and Schuster, 1999).

31. See James C. Scott, *Two Cheers for Anarchism* (Princeton, NJ: Princeton University Press, 2012); David Graeber, *The Democracy Project: A History, a Crisis, a Movement* (New York: Spiegel and Grau, 2013), Also see Kelefa Sanneh, "Paint Bombs: David Graeber's *The Democracy Project* and the Anarchist Revival," *New Yorker* 89, no. 13 (May 13, 2013): 72–76.

32. See John S. Nelson, "Stands in Politics," *Journal of Politics* 46, no. 1 (February, 1984): 106–131.

33. See Friedrich Nietzsche, *On the Advantage and Disadvantage of History for Life*, Peter Preuss, trans. (Indianapolis: Hackett, 1982).

34. See Edelman, "The Construction and Uses of Social Problems," *Constructing the Political Spectacle*, 12–36. Also see Kenneth R. Minogue, *The Liberal Mind* (New York: Random House, 1963); Roberto Mangabeira Unger, *Knowledge and Politics* (New York: Free Press, 1975); Terence Ball and Richard Dagger, "Liberalism," *Political Ideologies and the Democratic Ideal* (New York: HarperCollins, 1991), 49–90; Andrew Heywood, "Liberalism," *Political Ideologies* (New York: Palgrave Macmillan, 2012), 24–64.

35. See Hannah Arendt, "Action," *The Human Condition* (Chicago: University of Chicago Press, 1958), 175–247; Paul A. Rahe, *Republics Ancient and Modern, Volume 1: The Ancien Régime in Classical Greece* (Chapel Hill, NC, University of North Carolina Press, 1994), 14–65.

36. See Edmund Burke, *Reflections on the Revolution in France* (Garden City, NY: Doubleday, 1961). Also see Kenneth R. Minogue, *Conservative Realism* (New York: HarperCollins, 1966); Ball and Dagger, "Conservatism," *Political Ideologies and the Democratic Ideal*, 91–117; Heywood, "Conservatism," *Political Ideologies*, 65–96.

37. See Robert Paul Wolff, *In Defense of Anarchism* (New York: Harper and Row, 1970); Murray Bookchin, *Post-Scarcity Anarchism* (Berkeley: The Ramparts Press, 1971); Heywood, "Anarchism," *Political Ideologies*, 140–167.

38. See Albert Camus, *The Rebel*, trans. Anthony Bower (New York: Random House, (1951), 1956). Also see Nelson, *Tropes of Politics*, 205–230.

39. See Friedrich Nietzsche: *The Portable Nietzsche*, ed. and trans. Walter Kaufmann (New York: Viking Press, 1954); *The Birth of Tragedy* and *The Genealogy of Morals*, Francis Golffing, trans. (Garden City, NY: Doubleday, 1956); trans. *Twilight of the Idols* and *The Anti-Christ*, R. J. Hollingdale (Baltimore: Penguin Books, (1889 and 1885), 1968); *The Will to Power*, ed. Walter Kaufmann, trans. Walter Kaufmann and R. J. Hollingdale (New York: Random House, 1967). Also see Robert Goldman and Stephen Papson, *Nike Culture: The Sign of the Swoosh* (Thousand Oaks, CA: Sage, 1998). For a more Aristotelian take on perfectionism, see Thomas Hurka, *Perfectionism* (Oxford: Oxford University Press, 1993).

40. This is evident also in the inspiriting novel of the same name: Chuck Palahniuk, *Fight Club* (New York: Henry Holt and Company, 1996).

41. See Raymond Chandler, *The Simple Art of Murder* (New York: Random House, 1939); ed. John Ball, *The Mystery Story* (New York: Penguin Books, 1980); ed. Robin W. Winks, *Colloquium on Crime* (New York: Scribner, 1986); Tony Hilfer, *The Crime Novel: A Deviant Genre* (Austin: University of Texas Press, 1990); Maxim Jakubowski, ed., *100 Great Detectives* (New York: Carroll and Graf, 1991).

42. Ernest Mandel, *Delightful Murder: A Social History of the Crime Story* (Minneapolis: University of Minnesota Press, 1984).

43. See Steve Coll, "The Unthinkable: Can the United States Be Made Safe from Nuclear Terrorism?" *New Yorker* 83, no. 3 (March 12, 2007): 48–57. This is the title of a post-9/11 movie on nuclear terrorism directed by Gregor Jordan and starring Samuel L. Jackson, Carrie-Anne Moss, and Michael Sheen: see *Unthinkable* (2010).

44. See White, *Metahistory*, 29–31. Also see Karl Mannheim, *From Karl Mannheim*, Kurt H. Wolff, ed. (New York: Oxford University Press, 1971).

45. See Philip Pettit, *Republicanism* (Oxford: Oxford University Press, 1997); Quentin Skinner, *Liberty Before Liberalism* (Cambridge: Cambridge University Press, 1998).

46. See Merleau-Ponty, *Sense and Non-Sense*, 187.

47. See Henry Fairlie, "Too Rich for Heroes," *Harper's Magazine* 257, no. 1542, (November 1978): 33–43 and 87–88.

48. See Nelson DeMille, "Author's Foreword: *The General's Daughter*, the Book and the Movie," *The General's Daughter* (New York: Warner Books, 1999), xi–xxiv.

49. See William Ker Muir Jr., *Police: Streetcorner Politicians* (Chicago: University of Chicago Press, 1977).

50. See John S. Nelson, "Account and Acknowledge, or Represent and Control? On Postmodern Politics and Economics of Collective Responsibility," *Accounting, Organizations and Society* 18, no. 2–3 (February–April 1993): 207–229.

51. See Anna Lorien Nelson and John S. Nelson, "Institutions in Feminist and Republican Science Fiction," *Legal Studies Forum* 22, no. 4 (1998): 641–653.

52. See Nelson, *Tropes of Politics*, 205–230.

53. See Louis Menand, "The Iron Law of Stardom: What It Means for Cruise, Camus—and You," *New Yorker* 73, no. 5 (March 24, 1997): 36–39. *Swordfish* features John Travolta as its charismatic figure, meshing well with Menand's arguments.

54. See Carr, *The Lessons of Terror*; Mark Juergensmeyer, *Terror in the Mind of God* (Berkeley: University of California Press, 2000, second edition, 2001); George Packer, "Knowing the Enemy: Can Social Scientists Redefine the 'War on Terror?'" *New Yorker* 82, no. 42 (December 18, 2006): 60–69.

55. See Gabriel Weimann and Conrad Winn, *The Theater of Terror: Mass Media and International Terrorism* (New York: Longman, 1994). Also see John le Carré, *The Little Drummer Girl* (New York: Bantam Books, 1983).

56. Terrence Rafferty, "Lost at Sea," *New Yorker* 71, no. 23 (August 7, 1995): 83–85, on p. 84.

57. See Carr, *The Lessons of Terror*; Juergensmeyer, *Terror in the Mind of God*.

58. See Carr, *The Lessons of Terror*; Nicholas Lemann, "What Terrorists Want: Is There a Better Way to Defeat Al Qaeda?" *New Yorker* 77, no. 33 (October, 29, 2001): 36–41.

59. On the need and difficulty of stopping to think before acting in these and related situations, see Hannah Arendt, "Thinking and Moral Considerations," *Social Research* 38, no. 3 (Autumn 1971): 417–446.

60. See Carr, *The Lessons of Terror*.

61. On vicarious and virtual experiences, see Nelson and Boynton, *Video Rhetorics*, 195–232.

62. See Richard A. Clarke: *Against All Enemies: Inside America's War on Terror* (New York: Free Press, 2004); *Your Government Failed You: Breaking the Cycle of National Security Disasters* (New York: HarperCollins, 2008).

63. See Anthony Lane, "This Is Not a Movie: Same Scenes, Different Story," *New Yorker* 77, no. 28 (September 24, 2001): 79–80.

64. See Nicholas Lemann, "Terrorism Studies: Social Scientists Do Counterinsurgency," *New Yorker* 86, no. 10 (April 26, 2010): 73–77.

65. See David Frum, *The Right Man: An Inside Account of the Bush White House* (New York: Random House, 2003, second edition, 2005), 224–245.

66. See Nicholas Lemann, "What Terrorists Want: Is There a Better Way to Defeat al Qaeda?" *New Yorker* 77, no. 33 (October 29, 2001): 36–41; Nichole Argo, "The Role of Social Context in Terrorist Attacks," *Chronicle of Higher Education* 52, no. 22 (February 3, 2006), B15.

67. See Nicholas Lemann, "The War on What? The White House and the Debate about Whom to Fight Next," *New Yorker* 78, no. 27 (September 16, 2002): 36–44; George Packer, "A Democratic World: Can Liberal take Foreign Policy Back from the Republicans?" *New Yorker* 80, no. 1 (February 16 and 23, 2004): 100–108, especially 105–108.

68. See Malcolm Gladwell, "Safety in the Skies: How Far can Airline Security Go?" *New Yorker* 77, no 29 (October 1, 2001): 50–53.

69. See Barack Obama, speech transcript on terrorism, National Defense University, *New York Times*, May 23, 2013, http://www.nytimes.com/2013/05/24/us/politics/transcript-of-obamas-speech-on-drone-policy.html?pagewanted=all&_r=0.

70. See Edward Rothstein, "Seeing Terrorism as Drama with Sequels and Prequels," *New York Times*, December 26, 2005, http://www.nytimes.com/2005/12/26/arts/26conn.html?pagewanted=all&_r=0.

Chapter 9: Movies Disfigure Politics

1. George W. Bush, Quoted in "Perspectives," *Newsweek*, 142, no. 2 (July 14, 2003): 23.

2. See H. Mark Roelofs, *Ideology and Myth in American Politics* (Boston: Little, Brown, 1976); James Oliver Robertson, *American Myth, American Reality* (New York: Hill and Wang, 1980); Bruce Miroff, *Icons of Democracy* (New York: Basic Books, 1993).

3. See Susan Sontag: *Against Interpretation* (New York: Farrar, Straus and Giroux, 1966); *Illness as Metaphor* (New York: Farrar, Straus and Giroux, 1978); *AIDS and Its Metaphors* (New York: Farrar, Straus and Giroux, 1989).

4. See Henry Tudor, *Political Myth* (New York: Praeger, 1972). Also see John S. Nelson: "Orwell's Political Myths and Ours," *The Orwellian Moment*, eds. Robert L. Savage, James E. Combs, and Dan D. Nimmo (Fayetteville: University of Arkansas Press, 1989), 11–44; *Tropes of Politics: Science, Theory, Rhetoric, Action* (Madison:University of Wisconsin Press, 1998), 99–204.

5. See John S. Nelson and G. R. Boynton, *Video Rhetorics: Televised Advertising in American Politics* (Urbana: University of Illinois Press, 1997), 195–232.

6. See Roland Barthes, "Soap-powers and Detergents," *Mythologies*, Annette Lavers, trans. (New York: Hill and Wang, (1957), 1972), 36–38. Also see Anne Norton, "The President as Sign," *Republic of Signs* (Chicago: University of Chicago Press, 1993), 87–121, on 113–119.

7. See Bram Stoker, *Dracula* (New York: Penguin Books, (1897), 1992).

8. Played by Hugh Jackman, the title figure of *Van Helsing* (2004) is more recent but much less memorable. In part, this is because his movie is the sort of fractured fairy tale turned thriller that seems jaunty or silly rather than intense or potent. Other cases include *The League of Distinguished Gentlemen* (2003) and *Hansel & Gretel: Witch Hunters* (2013).

9. See Seth Grahamé-Smith, *Abraham Lincoln: Vampire Hunter* (New York: Grand Central Publishing, 2010).

10. Evan Thomas, "The Twelve-Year Itch," *Newsweek*, 141, no. 13 (March 31, 2003): 54–65, on p. 56.

11. The plain speech of cowboys comes from Indians: see Robert M. Pirsig, *Lila* (New York: Bantam Books, 1991), 30–48.

12. Thomas, "The Twelve-Year Itch," 56.

13. But for me, at least, an imaginary audition of Bush for Johnny Depp's role in the latest film version of *The Lone Ranger* (2013) is somewhere between amusing and disturbing.

14. Stephen King emphasizes this for his mythic gunslinger Roland in *The Dark Tower*, 7 vols. (New York: Scribner, 1982, 1987, 1991, 1997, 2003, 2004, 2004). Also see Stephen King, *The Wind Through the Keyhole* (New York: Simon and Schuster, 2012).

15. Thomas, "The Twelve-Year Itch," 55–56.

16. Thomas, "The Twelve-Year Itch," 56.

17. See Lisa Jane Disch, "The Critique of Power as Leverage," *Hannah Arendt and the Limits of Philosophy*, Ithaca, Cornell University Press, 1994), 20–67.

18. See Thomas Hobbes, *Leviathan*, ed. Michael Oakeshott (New York: Collier Books, 1962).

19. See John S. Nelson, "John le Carré and the Postmodern Myth of the State," *Finnish Yearbook of Political Thought* 3 (1999): 100–131.

20. See Thomas, "The Twelve-Year Itch," 55.

21. Thomas, "The Twelve-Year Itch," 55.

22. Thomas, "The Twelve-Year Itch," 56.

23. See Stephen Kinzer, *All the Shah's Men: An American Coup and the Roots of Middle East Terror* (New York: Wiley, 2003).

24. See Jonathan Alter, "'Let Them Eat Cake' Economics," *Newsweek* 142, no. 4 (July 28, 2003): 36: "Bush is a regular guy who doesn't care a whole lot about regular people."

25. See *Captain America: The First Avenger* (2011) and *The Avengers* (2012).

26. Thomas, "The Twelve-Year Itch," 56.

27. See Paul Oppenheimer, *Evil and the Demonic* (New York: New York University Press, 1996).

28. An instructive symbol from a different vampire movie is the degenerate Vampire Theatre—where vamps perform ritual murders of humans for human audiences in France early in the twentieth century—as evoked by *Interview with the Vampire* (1994).

29. On dandies, see Susan Sontag, "Writing Itself: On Roland Barthes," *New Yorker* 58, no. 10 (April 26, 1982): 122–141; John Lahr, "King Cole: The Not So Merry Soul of Cole Porter," *New Yorker* 80, no. 19 (July 12 and 19, 2004): 100–104.

Chapter 10: Movies Configure Politics

1. Caleb Carr, *The Lessons of Terror* (New York: Random House, 2002), 11.

2. Carr's terror-tory includes novels of crime, detection, and political prophecy in the guise of a techno-thriller: *The Alienist* (New York: Bantam Books, 1994); *The Angel of Darkness* (New York: Ballantine Books, 1997); *Killing Time* (New York: Warner Books, 2000).

3. See Nicholas Lemann, "What Terrorists Want: Is There a Better Way to Defeat Al Qaeda?" *New Yorker* 77, no. 33 (October, 29, 2001), 36–41.

4. See Michael Walzer, "On 'Failed Totalitarianism'," *1984 Revisited: Totalitarianism in Our Century*, ed. Irving Howe (New York: Harper and Row, 1983), 103–121; Anne Applebaum, *Iron Curtain: The Crushing of Eastern Europe, 1944–956* (Garden City, NY: Doubleday, 2012).

5. See Søren Kierkegaard, *The Concept of Dread*, Walter Lowrie, trans. (Princeton, NJ: Princeton University Press, 1944).

6. Hannah Arendt observed a comparable dynamic in the wake of totalitarian regimes: "The Aftermath of Nazi Rule," *Commentary* 10, no. 4 (October 1950): 342–353.

7. See Gabriel Weimann and Conrad Winn, *The Theater of Terror* (New York: Longman, 1994); Ferdinand Mount, *The Theatre of Politics* (New York: Schocken Books, 1972). Also see Robert Hariman, *Political Style: The Artistry of Power* (Chicago:

University of Chicago Press, 1995); John S. Nelson, *Tropes of Politics: Science, Theory, Rhetoric, Action* (Madison:University of Wisconsin Press, 1998).

8. See Richard A. Clarke, *Against All Enemies: Inside America's War on Terror* (New York: Free Press, 2004); *Your Government Failed You: Breaking the Cycle of National Security Disasters* (New York: Harper Perennial, 2009).

9. See Spencer R. Weart, *Nuclear Fear: A History of Images* (Cambridge, MA: Harvard University Press, 1988); William J. Palmer, *The Films of the Eighties: A Social History* (Carbondale: Southern Illinois University Press, 1993), 179–205. Also see Gunther Anders, "Reflections on the H-Bomb," trans. Norbert Guterman, *Dissent* 3, no. 2 (Spring 1956): 146–155; Ron Rosenbaum, "The Subterranean World of the Bomb," *Harper's Magazine* 256, no. 1534 (March 1978): 85–105.

10. See Hayden White: *Metahistory* (Baltimore: Johns Hopkins University Press, 1973); *Tropics of Discourse* (Baltimore: Johns Hopkins University Press, 1978). Also see John S. Nelson: "Review Essay [on *Metahistory* by Hayden White]," *History and Theory* 14, no. 1 (1975): 74–91; "Tropal History and the Social Sciences," *History and Theory* 19, no. 4 (1980): 80–101.

11. See Alain Silver and James Ursini, eds., *Film Noir Reader* (New York: Limelight Editions, 1996).

12. See Nelson, *Tropes of Politics*, 142.

13. See *Insomnia* (2002), directed by Christopher Nolan, and its inspiriting film from Sweden with the same title (1997).

14. On this kind of information rather than mere data, see Nelson, *Tropes of Politics*, 124–126.

15. See John S. Nelson and G. R. Boynton, "Arguing War: Global Television against American Cinema," *Arguing Communication and Culture*, ed. G. Thomas Goodnight (Washington, DC: National Communication Association, 2002), 571–577.

16. See Nadezhda Mandelstam, trans. Max Hayward, (New York: Atheneum): *Hope Against Hope* (1970); *Hope Abandoned* (1974).

17. See Stephen King, *Danse Macabre* (New York: Berkley Books, 1981); *Bare Bones*, eds. Tim Underwood and Chuck Miller (New York: McGraw-Hill, 1988). Also see Ron Rosenbaum, "Gooseflesh: The Strange Turn Toward Horror," *Harper's Magazine* 259, no. 1552 (September 1979): 86–92.

18. See Julia Kristeva, *Powers of Horror*, trans. Leon S. Roudiez (New York: Columbia University Press, 1982).

19. Dennis Etchison, quoted in Douglas E. Winter, *Faces of Fear* (New York: Berkley Books, 1985), 62.

20. See King, *Danse Macabre*, 144–153.

21. See Stephen King, *The Dead Zone* (New York: New American Library, 1979).

22. Other horror westerns I know—like *Cowboys and Vampires* (2010), *Cowboys & Aliens* (2011), or *Cole Younger and the Black Train* (2012)—do not feature political terrorism.

23. See J. R. R. Tolkien, *The Lord of the Rings*, 3 vols. (Boston: Houghton Mifflin, 1954, 1955, 1956). Of course, the films from Peter Jackson came later: 2001, 2002, 2003.

24. See Peter A. French, *The Virtues of Vengeance* (Lawrence: University Press of Kansas, 2001).

25. See Norman Spinrad, *Agent of Chaos* (New York: Popular Library, 1967). Also see Cormac McCarthy, *No Country for Old Men* (New York: Random House, 2005).

26. See Arendt, "The Aftermath of Nazi Rule."

27. George Orwell, "1984," *Orwell's Nineteen Eighty-Four*, Irving Howe, ed. (New York: Harcourt Brace Jovanovich, 1963, second edition, 1982), 3–205, on p. 178.

28. See Nadia Khouri, "Reaction and Nihilism: The Political Genealogy of Orwell's 1984," *Science-Fiction Studies* 12, no. 2 (July 1985): 136–147.

29. See John S. Nelson, "Orwell's Political Myths and Ours," *The Orwellian Moment*, eds. Robert L. Savage, James E. Combs, and Dan D. Nimmo (Fayetteville: University of Arkansas Press, 1989), 11–44.

30. See John S. Nelson and G. R. Boynton, *Video Rhetorics: Televised Advertising in American Politics* (Urbana: University of Illinois Press, 1997), 221–230.

31. See King, *Danse Macabre*, 263–294.

32. See Rick Marin and T. Trent Gegax, "Conspiracy Mania Feeds Our Growing National Paranoia," *Newsweek* 128, no. 27, (December 30, 1996–January 6, 1997): 64–71.

33. For a better effort, see Dan Nimmo and James E. Combs, "Devils and Demons: The Group Mediation of Conspiracy," *Mediated Political Realities* (New York: Longman, 1983, second edition, 1990), 203–222.

34. See Carr, *The Lessons of Terror*; Brent L. Smith, *Terrorism in America* (Albany: State University of New York Press, 1994).

35. See Orwell, "1984"; Hannah Arendt, *Eichmann in Jerusalem* (New York: Viking Press, 1963, enlarged edition, 1964).

36. It is not hard, however, to see the martyr videos, recruitment movies, and training films from terrorist organizations as possible steps toward a counter-cinema.

37. See Walter Laquer, *The Age of Terrorism* (Boston: Little, Brown, 1987), 202.

38. See Mark Juergensmeyer, *Terror in the Mind of God* (Berkeley: University of California Press, 2000, second edition, 2001); Daniel Levitas, *The Terrorist Next Door* (New York: St. Martin's Press, 2002).

39. See Nelson, *Tropes of Politics*, 205–230.

40. See Benjamin R. Barber, *Jihad vs. McWorld: How Globalism and Tribalism Are Reshaping the World* (New York: Ballantine Books, 1995); Thomas L. Friedman, *The Lexus and the Olive Tree: Understanding Globalization* (New York: Random House, 1999, second edition, 2000).

41. See Stanley Cavell, *Pursuits of Happiness: The Hollywood Comedy of Remarriage* (Cambridge, MA: Harvard University Press, 1981).

42. On the increasingly conservative politics of this initially liberal "task," see Michael J. Shapiro, "The Rhetoric of Social Science: The Political Responsibilities of the Scholar," *The Rhetoric of the Human Sciences: Language and Argument in Scholarship and Public Affairs*, John S. Nelson, Allan Megill, and D. N. McCloskey, eds. (Madison: University of Wisconsin Press, 1987), 363–380, especially 370–375.

43. See Edward Rothstein, "Seeing Terrorism as Drama with Sequels and Prequels," *New York Times*, December 26, 2005, http://www.nytimes.com/2005/12/26/arts/26conn.html?pagewanted=all&_r=0.

44. See R. Barton Palmer, *Hollywood's Dark Cinema: The American Film Noir*

(New York: Twayne, 1994); Alain Silver and James Ursini, *The Noir Style* (Woodstock, NY: Overlook Press, 1999). Also see Gyan Prakash, *Noir Urbanisms: Dystopic Images of the Modern City* (Princeton, NJ: Princeton University Press, 2010).

45. On recently resurgent noir, often called neo noir, see Foster Hirsch, *Detours and Lost Highways: A Map of Neo-Noir* (New York: Limelight Editions, 1999); Ronald Schwartz, *Neo-Noir* (Lanham, MD: Rowman and Littlefield, 2005); Mark T. Conrad, ed., *The Philosophy of Neo-Noir* (Lexington: University Press of Kentucky, 2007); Mark Bould, Kathrina Gilitre, and Greg Tuck, eds., *Neo-Noir* (New York: Columbia University Press, 2009).

46. On the classical period of noir and its inspirations, see J. P. Telotte, *Voices in the Dark: The Narrative Patterns of Film Noir* (Urbana: University of Illinois Press, 1989); Joan Copjec, ed., *Shades of Noir* (London: Verso, 1993); Paul Duncan, *Film Noir: Films of Trust and Betrayal* (Harpenden, UK: Pocket Essentials, 2000); Mark T. Conrad, ed., *The Philosophy of Film Noir* (Lexington: University Press of Kentucky, 2006).

47. Maureen Dowd, "Touch of Evil," *New York Times*, October 7, 2001, http://www.nytimes.com/2001/10/07/opinion/07DOWD.html?ex=1003468906&ei=1&en=d7d1a5eda5168771.

48. See Guy Debord, *Society of the Spectacle* (Detroit: Black and Red, (1967), 1977); Murray Edelman, *Constructing the Political Spectacle* (Chicago: University of Chicago Press, 1988).

49. Weimann and Winn, *The Theater of Terror*, 4.

50. See Jean Baudrillard, *The Evil Demon of Images* (Sydney: Power Institute of Fine Arts, 1987); Larry Beinhart, *American Hero* (New York: Ballantine Books, 1993).

51. See Giambattista Vico, *The New Science*, trans. Thomas Goddard Bergin and Max Harold Fisch (Ithaca, NY: Cornell University Press, (abridged from the third edition, 1744; 1948), 1961), 1106, 381–382.

52. See William Marling, *The American Roman Noir: Hammett, Cain, and Chandler* (Athens, University of Georgia Press, 1995); John T. Irwin, *Unless the Threat of Death Is Behind Them: Hard-Boiled Fiction and Film Noir* (Baltimore: Johns Hopkins University Press, 2006).

53. See Nicholas Christopher, *Somewhere in the Night: Film Noir and the American City* (New York: Henry Holt, 1997).

54. See Mike Davis, *City of Quartz: Excavating the Future in Los Angeles* (New York: Random House, 1990).

55. See Andrew Spicer, *Film Noir* (London: Pearson Education, 2002).

56. Susan Zickmund and Merrie Snell, organizers, "Infinite Respect, Enduring Dignity: Voices and Visions on the September Attacks," sponsored by the Project on Rhetoric of Inquiry, University of Iowa (Iowa City: IA, January 25–26, 2002).

Chapter 11: Conclusion

1. Anthony Lane, "Star Bores," *New Yorker* 75, no. 12 (May 24, 1999): 80–84, on p. 83.

2. Connie Willis, *Remake* (New York: Bantam Books, 1995), 48.

3. See Hannah Arendt, *The Human Condition* (Chicago: University of Chicago Press, 1958).

4. Kenneth Tynan, "The Third Act: Entries from Kenneth Tynan's Journals, 1975–78," *New Yorker* 76, no. 23 (August 14, 2000): 60–71, on p. 64–65.

5. See Steven Johnson, *Mind Wide Open: Your Brain and the Neuroscience of Everyday Life* (New York: Scribner, 2004). Also see Milton Lodge and Kathleen McGraw, eds., *Political Judgment* (Ann Arbor, University of Michigan Press, 1995).

6. See Doris A. Graber: *Processing the News* (New York: Longman, 1984, second edition, 1988); *Processing Politics* (Chicago: University of Chicago Press, 2001). Also see David L. Paletz, *The Media in American Politics* (New York: Longman, 1999), 103–116.

7. See Michael Paul Rogin, *Ronald Reagan, the Movie* (Berkeley: University of California Press, 1987); "Perspectives," *Newsweek* 142, no. 2 (July 14, 2003), 23; Garry Wills, *Reagan's America: Innocents at Home* (New York: Penguin Books, 1987, second edition, 1988). Also see Michael Ryan and Douglas Kellner, *Camera Politica* (Bloomington: Indiana University Press, 1988); Michael Parenti, *Make-Believe Media* (New York: St. Martin's Press, 1992); Michael Parenti, *Land of Idols* (New York: St. Martin's Press, 1994).

8. See John S. Nelson, *Tropes of Politics* (Madison: University of Wisconsin Press, 1998), 138–143.

9. See Nelson, *Tropes of Politics*, 143–147.

10. See John Fiske and John Hartley, *Reading Television* (London: Routledge, 1978); Dan Nimmo and James E. Combs, *Subliminal Politics* (Englewood Cliffs, NJ: Prentice-Hall, 1980); Dan Nimmo and James E. Combs, *Mediated Political Realities* (New York: Longman, 1983, second edition, 1990); Tania Modleski, ed., *Studies in Entertainment* (Bloomington: Indiana University Press, 1986); Todd Gitlin, ed., *Watching Television* (New York: Random House, 1986); Cynthia Schneider and Brian Wallis, ed., *Global Television* (Cambridge, MA: MIT Press, 1988); Patricia Mellencamp, ed., *Logics of Television: Essays in Cultural Criticism* (Bloomington: Indiana University Press, 1990); John Hartley, *Tele-ology: Studies in Television* (London: Routledge, 1992). Also see Guy Cook, *The Discourse of Advertising* (New York: Routledge, 1992); Mady Schutzman, *The Real Thing: Performance, Hysteria, and Advertising* (Hanover, NH: Wesleyan University Press, 1999). And see Bruce E. Gronbeck, "Mythic Portraiture in the 1988 Iowa Presidential Caucus Bio-Ads," *American Behavioral Scientist* 32, no. 4 (March–April 1989): 351–364; G. R. Boynton *The Art of Campaign Advertising* (Chatham, NJ: Chatham House, on *cd-rom*, 1996); G. R. Boynton and John S. Nelson, *Hot Spots: Multimedia Analyses of Political Ads* (Urbana: University of Illinois Press, 1997, videotape with five chapters); John S. Nelson and G. R. Boynton, *Video Rhetorics: Televised Advertising in American Politics* (Urbana: University of Illinois Press, 1997).

11. See Nelson, *Tropes of Politics*, 150–204; Ron Burnett, *How Images Think* (Cambridge, MA: MIT. Press, 2004). Also see Paul De Man, *Allegories of Reading* (New Haven: Yale University Press, 1979); D. N. Rodowick, *Reading the Figural, or, Philosophy after the New Media* (Durham, NC: Duke University Press, 2001).

12. See Paul Ricouer: *The Rule of Metaphor*, trans. Robert Czerny (Toronto: University of Toronto Press, (1975), 1977); *Interpretation Theory* (Fort Worth: Texas

Christian University Press, 1976); *Time and Narrative, Volume I*, trans. Kathleen McLaughlin and David Pellauer (Chicago: University of Chicago Press, (1983), 1984). Also see Jacques Derrida: *Of Grammatology*, trans. Gayatri Chakravorty Spivak (Baltimore: Johns Hopkins University Press, (1967), 1974); *Writing and Difference*, trans. Alan Bass (Chicago: University of Chicago Press, (1967), 1978); *Dissemination*, trans. Barbara Johnson (Chicago: University of Chicago Press, (1972), 1981).

13. See Thomas S. Kuhn, *The Structure of Scientific Revolutions* (Chicago: University of Chicago Press, (1962), 1970); eds. Imre Lakatos and Alan Musgrave, *Criticism and the Growth of Knowledge* (Cambridge: Cambridge University Press, 1970); Paul K. Feyerabend, *Against Method* (Atlantic Highlands: Humanities Press, 1975). Also see John S. Nelson, "Once More on Kuhn," *Political Methodology* 1, no. 2 (Spring 1974): 73–104.

14. *The Spirit* (2008) makes wonderful fun of this game, making sure it extends into absurdity.

15. See S. S. Prawer, *Caligari's Children: The Film as Tale of Terror* (Oxford: Oxford University Press, 1980); Barry Keith Grant, ed., *Planks of Reason: Essays on the Horror Film* (Metuchen, NJ: Scarecrow Press, 1984); Gregory A. Waller, ed., *American Horrors: Essays on the Modern American Horror Film* (Urbana: University of Illinois Press, 1987); Vera Dika, *Games of Terror: Halloween, Friday the 13th, and the Films of the Stalker Cycle* (Rutherford: Farleigh Dickinson University Press, 1990); Laurence A. Rickels, *The Vampire Lectures* (Minneapolis: University of Minnesota Press, 1999); Darryl Jones, *Horror: A Thematic History in Fiction and Film* (London: Arnold, 2002); Stephen Prince, ed., *The Horror Film* (New Brunswick, NJ: Rutgers University Press, 2004).

16. See Michel Foucault: *Discipline and Punish*, trans. Alan Sheridan (New York: Random House, (1975), 1977); *Language, Counter-Memory, Practice: Selected Essays and Interviews*, ed. Donald F. Bouchard, trans. Donald F. Bouchard and Sherry Simon (Ithaca, NY: Cornell University Press, 1977); *Power / Knowledge: Selected Interviews and Other Writing, 1972–1977*, ed. Colin Gordon, trans. Colin Gordon, Leo Marshall, John Mepham, and Kate Soper (New York: Pantheon Books, 1980). Also see Nelson, *Tropes of Politics*, 205–230.

17. See Jane Tompkins, *West of Everything* (New York: Oxford University Press, 1992); Richard Slotkin, *Gunfighter Nation: The Myth of the Frontier in Twentieth-Century America* (New York: Atheneum, 1992); Lee Clark Mitchell, *Westerns: Making the Man in Fiction and Film* (Chicago: University of Chicago Press, 1996); Peter A. French, *Cowboy Metaphysics: Ethics and Death in Westerns* (Lanham, MD: Rowman and Littlefield, 1997); Peter A. French, *The Virtues of Vengeance* (Lawrence: University Press of Kansas, 2001); Stanley Corkin, *Cowboys as Cold Warriors: The Western and U.S. History* (Philadelphia: Temple University Press, 2004); Robert B. Pippin, *Hollywood Westerns and American Myth: The Importance of Howard Hawks and John Ford for Political Philosophy* (New Haven: Yale University Press, 2010).

18. See Will Wright, *The Wild West: The Mythical Cowboy and Social Theory* (Thousand Oaks, CA: Sage, 2001). Also see David Lavery, ed., *Reading Deadwood: A Western to Swear By* (New York: I. B. Tauris, 2006).

19. See Judith N. Shklar, "Rethinking the Past," *Social Research* 44, no. 1 (Spring

1977), 80–90; Anne Norton, *Republic of Signs: Liberal Theory and American Popular Culture* (Chicago: University of Chicago Press, 1993); Frederick M. Dolan and Thomas L. Dumm, eds., *Rhetorical Republic: Governing Representations in American Politics* (Amherst: University of Massachusetts Press, 1993). Also see John S. Nelson, "Prudence as Republican Politics in American Popular Culture," *Prudence: Classical Virtue, Postmodern Practice*, ed. Robert Hariman (University Park: Pennsylvania State University Press, 2003), 229–257.

20. See Robert Hariman, "In Oratory as in Life: Civic Performance in Cicero's Republican Style," *Political Style: The Artistry of Power* (Chicago: University of Chicago Press, 1995), 95–140. Also see Ferdinand Mount, *The Theatre of Politics* (New York: Schocken Books, 1972); Sue-Ellen Case and Janelle Reinelt, eds., *The Performance of Power: Theatrical Discourse and Politics* (Iowa City: University of Iowa Press, 1991).

21. See Andrew Benjamin, *Style and Time: Essays on the Politics of Appearance* (Evanston, IL: Northwestern University Press, 2006).

22. See Stuart Ewen, *All Consuming Images: The Politics of Style in Contemporary Culture* (New York: Basic Books, 1988); Robert Hariman, *Political Style: The Artistry of Power* (Chicago: University of Chicago Press, 1995); Barry Brummett, *A Rhetoric of Style* (Carbondale: Southern Illinois University Press, 2008).

23. Edmund Burke, *A Philosophical Inquiry into the Origin of Our Ideas of the Sublime and the Beautiful* (Oxford: Basil Blackwell, 1987). Also see Steffen H. Hantke, "The Function of the Sublime in Contemporary Horror: From Edmund Burke to Michael Blumlein," *Foundation*, 71 (Autumn 1997): 45–62.

24. See Nelson Goodman, *Ways of Worldmaking* (Indianapolis: Hackett, 1978), 23–40; Dick Hebdige, *Subculture: The Meaning of Style* (London: Routledge, 1979).

25. See Hariman, *Political Style*. Also see Francis A. Beer and Robert Hariman, ed., *Post-Realism: The Rhetorical Turn in International Relations* (East Lansing: Michigan State University Press, 1996).

26. See Mark Rose, *Alien Encounters: An Anatomy of Science Fiction* (Cambridge, MA: Harvard University Press, 1981), 24–32.

27. See Friedrich Nietzsche: "On Truth and Falsity in Their Extramoral Sense," *Essays on Metaphor*, ed. Warren Shibles (Whitewater, WI: Language Press, 1972), 1–13; *Twilight of the Idols* and *The Antichrist*, trans. R. J. Hollingdale (New York: Penguin Books, (1889 and 1885), 1968); *Human All Too Human*, trans. Gary Handwerk (Stanford, CA: Stanford University Press, 1995). Also see Daniel Conway, *Nietzsche and the Political* (New York: Routledge, 1997), 130–138; Steven D. Hales and Rex Welshon, *Nietzsche's Perspectivism* (Urbana: University of Illinois Press, 2000). And see Tracy B. Strong, *Friedrich Nietzsche and the Politics of Transformation* (Berkeley: University of California Press, 1975); Mark E. Warren, *Nietzsche and Political Thought* (Cambridge, MA: MIT Press, 1988).

28. As a genre, science fiction mostly embraces "the republic of science." See Michael Polanyi, "The Republic of Science," *Minerva* 1, no. 1 (Autumn 1962): 54–73. Also see Kim Stanley Robinson, *The Mars Trilogy* (New York: Bantam Books): *Red Mars* (1993); *Green Mars* (1994); *Blue Mars* (1996); *The Martians* (1999).

29. See Frederik Pohl, *Syzygy* (New York: Bantam Books, 1981).

30. See Jill Lepore, *The Whites of Their Eyes: The Tea Party's Revolution and the Battle over American History* (Princeton, NJ: Princeton University Press, 2010); Scott Rasmussen and Douglas Schoen, *Mad as Hell: How the Tea Party Movement Is Fundamentally Remaking Our Two-Party System* (New York: HarperCollins, 2010); Sean Wilentz, "Confounding Fathers: The Tea Party's Cold War Forebears," *New Yorker* 86, no. 32 (October 18, 2010): 32–39; Kate Zernicke, *Boiling Mad: Inside Tea Party America* (New York: Henry Holt, 2010); Paul Street and Anthony DiMaggio, *Crashing the Tea Party: Mass Media and the Campaign to Remake American Politics* (Boulder, CO: Paradigm Publishers, 2011); Theda Skocpol and Vanessa Williamson, *The Tea Party and the Remaking of Republican Conservatism* (New York: Oxford University Press, 2012). Also see Sarah van Gelder, ed., *This Changes Everything: Occupy Wall Street and the 99% Movement* (San Francisco: Barrett-Koehler, 2011); Todd Gitlin, *Occupy Nation: The Roots, the Spirit, and the Promise of Occupy Wall Street* (New York: HarperCollins, 2012); W. J. T. Mitchell, Bernard E. Harcourt, and Michael Taussig, *Occupy: Three Inquiries in Disobedience* (Chicago: University of Chicago Press, 2013). And see Thomas Frank, *What's the Matter with Kansas? How Conservatives Won the Heart of America* (New York: Henry Holt, 2004); Thomas Frank, *Pity the Billionaire: The Hard-Times Swindle and the Unlikely Comeback of the Right* (New York: Henry Holt, 2012); Chrystia Freeland, *Plutocrats: The Rise of the New Global Super-Rich and the Fall of Everyone Else* (New York: Penguin Press, 2012).

31. See Margaret Canovan, *Populism* (New York: Harcourt Brace Jovanovich, 1981); Michael Kazin, *The Populist Persuasion: An American History* (Ithaca, NY: Cornell University Press, 1995, revised edition, 1998); Paul Taggart, *Populism* (Philadelphia: Open University Press, 2000); John Lukacs, *Democracy and Populism: Fear and Hatred* (New Haven: Yale University Press, 2005).

32. See Susan Sontag, "The Imagination of Disaster," *Science Fiction: A Collection of Critical Essays*, ed. Mark Rose (Englewood Cliffs, NJ: Prentice-Hall, 1976), 116–131. Also see Rose, *Alien Encounters*, 176–195.

33. TriStar Pictures, "Plot Summary for *Elysium*," *Internet Movie Database*, July 18, 2013.

34. See Rose, *Alien Encounters*, 139–175.

35. See Donna J. Haraway, "A Cyborg Manifesto: Science, Technology, and Socialist-Feminism in the Late Twentieth Century," *Simians, Cyborgs, and Women: The Reinvention of Nature* (New York: Routledge, 1991), 149–181.

36. See Joe Klein, *Politics Lost: How American Democracy Was Trivialized by People Who Think You're Stupid* (New York: Doubleday, 2006). Also see Sam Tanenhaus, "North Star: Populism, Politics, and the Power of Sarah Palin," *New Yorker* 85, no. 40 (December 7, 2009): 84–89. *O Brother, Where Art Thou?* (2000) is a terrific treatment of populist "re-form" in the American South: even better than *All the King's Men* (1949, 2006).

37. See Rose, *Alien Encounters*, 96–138.

38. See Rose, *Alien Encounters*, 50–95.

39. See Suzanne Collins, *The Hunger Games* (New York: Scholastic Press): *The Hunger Games* (2008); *Catching Fire* (2009); *Mockingjay* (2010).

40. See L. Frank Baum, *The Wizard of Oz* (New York: HarperCollins, (1899), 1999). Also see Henry M. Littlefield, "*The Wizard of Oz*: A Parable on Populism," http://www. amphigory.com/oz.htm.

41. There are at least two other postapocalypse films among the 2010–13 scifi films, but they are not particularly populist: *The Book of Eli* (2009) and *Priest* (2011).

42. See Garry Wills, *Cincinnatus: George Washington and the Enlightenment* (Garden City, NY: Doubleday, 1984); Walter Isaacson, *Benjamin Franklin: An American Life* (New York: Simon and Schuster, 2003).

43. See Linda Beail and Rhonda Kinney Longworth, *Framing Sarah Palin: Pit Bulls, Puritans, and Politics* (New York: Routledge, 2013).

INDEX

Concepts, Genres, and Politics

Directors, Showrunners, Politicians, and Theorists

ABOUT THE AUTHOR

John S. Nelson does political theory and communication at the University of Iowa, where he has directed the Project on Rhetoric of Inquiry, the Bridging Project, and the Honors Program. He has edited *Poroi,* an electronic journal, plus university-press series from Chicago and Wisconsin. His books include *Video Rhetorics* (Illinois) and *Tropes of Politics* (Wisconsin).